Roots of
Modern Mormonism

Roots of
Modern Mormonism

Mark P. Leone

HARVARD UNIVERSITY PRESS
Cambridge, Massachusetts,
and London, England
1979

L90⁄1427

Library of Congress Cataloging in Publication Data
LEONE, MARK P
Roots of modern Mormonism.

Bibliography: p.
Includes index.
1. Mormons and Mormonism. I. Title.
BX8611.L46   301.5'8   78-25965
ISBN 0-674-77970-3

Preface

In this study of the long-term shaping and reshaping of Mormonism I have relied on historical materials and ethnographic observations to show how a religious minority is created, maintained, and changed. I have attempted to preserve the integrity of Mormonism and its institutions by exploring how Mormons think and the material reasons for their symbolic inclinations.

My approach owes much to the work of others. Robert N. Bellah and Thomas Luckmann in their studies of modern religions anticipated my views. Roy A. Rappaport's ideas about the ritual regulation of subsistence activities contributed to my understanding of the role of religion in cultural evolution. Materialist theory proved especially useful for dealing with a consciously materialist religion. Louis Althusser, Janet Dolgin, David Kemnitzer, David Schneider, and Robert F. Murphy, all of whom employ Marxist analyses, provided a key to Mormonism's complexity.

A major changing relationship traced here is between different parts of Mormonism itself. I have assumed that Mormonism's internal structure is best understood in Mormon terms, not as viewed from the East Coast or from orthodox Christianity. Accordingly, the book underplays the role of the federal government at the turn of the century in transforming Mormonism. Even though the United States government crushed the Mormon kingdom for reasons similar to those that caused it to defeat the South in the Civil War, Mormons were a subject minority before as well as after the

United States intervention. They are still one. In my judgment it is more important to see how a minority keeps itself
in that status than how that status was imposed externally.
The aim of the book is not to show Mormonism as an isolate
but rather to show how islands of minorities maintain
themselves.

The nineteenth century regarded Mormonism as the perfect American religion and a microcosm of America, from
which lessons could be learned about America's future. Pre-
dictably, these views projected many things onto Mormonism and derived many predictions, whose accuracy has
never been checked. My own analysis reveals Mormons and
Mormonism as a special kind of minority in a particular kind
of society. Mormonism is a way of thinking used by increasingly powerless people in modern society. Thus it is not a
microcosm of the present or a vision of the future; it is a religion for subordinates which serves to maintain their condition intact.

Mormons' subordination has never been noted before.
Normally Mormonism presents itself to non-Mormons as an
intensely authoritarian religion, sure of its beliefs. This view
has been expressed best by Thomas F. O'Dea and Sterling
McMurrin. My aim is to show that the conceptual looseness
both hidden beneath and supported by authoritarianism is
one of Mormonism's central qualities. The looseness was expressed in early Mormonism through its powerful critique
of industrial society, which assumed that change was reality
and that knowledge would increase as reality changed. Mormonism was not supposed to be a creed but a method for
perceiving human purpose; it was conscious in the sense that
it repeatedly examined itself and the outside world, then
acted on what it saw. Mormonism assumed change and
changed accordingly. This practice made Mormons self-
conscious, flexible, and disciplined.

The assumption that everything changes is still alive
among Mormons, not as a conscious idea but as a way of
thinking and acting. Yet this part of the religion has not been
noticed by students or the faithful. Students of the religion
note its directionlessness while the faithful believe in its fix-

ity, but the two have not been combined to reveal what the religion of Joseph Smith has become: one in which conceptual looseness works with authoritarianism to create subordination.

My introduction to Mormonism came through people in east central Arizona along the Little Colorado River. To these people I owe my initial and best insights. They represent what is most attractive about Mormonism. I want to thank Ken DeWitt, Jack McLaws, Judge Melvin Shelley, Drew Shumway, Gilbert Sullivan, Judge and Mrs. Don Udall, and Bishop Maynard Zufelt. Lafe S. Hatch asked the Golden Question and gave the friendship that made the answer worth finding. Al Levine provided friendship, guidance, and initial contacts, as well as my first understanding that Mormons had written down their entire past. I am grateful for the support and warmth of the Mormons in Holbrook, Snowflake, and Vernon, Arizona, in the Eighteenth Ward in Salt Lake City, and in the Princeton Ward in New Jersey. The members of the Snowflake Stake Genealogical Society, Virginia Probst of the Holbrook Public Library, and Leona Downing of the Clerk of the Court's Office in Holbrook guided me through important records.

Mormon scholars have been unendingly generous, so much so that they shaped this book in more ways than I can say. I hope they find some satisfaction in it. A reading by John Sorensen, who has the happy facility of finding more in people's work than they do themselves, had an important impact on this book. Charles Peterson and Melvin Smith never tired of explaining aspects of Mormonism which I did not understand. They shared their Mormonism with me, for which I am in their debt. George S. Tanner benefited me not only by all his data but mostly by his greatness and liberality. Leonard Arrington, who read the manuscript, has been unfailingly generous and courteous to this gentile anthropologist. Sterling McMurrin, Davis Bitten, Earl Olson, and Gary Forebush listened, reacted, and made a difference in my understanding. Alfred Bush helped me to move anthropology closer to his culture.

My anthropological friends and colleagues helped in endless ways. The late Paul Martin sponsored my initial venture into ethnography while I was connected with the Field Museum's Southwest Archaeological Expedition. Thomas Kirsch, Martin Silverman, Janet Dolgin, Richard Parmentier, Jean-Paul Dumont, Frederick D'Agostino, and Ingrid Olsen-Tjensvold encouraged my study of religion while I was teaching in the Department of Anthropology at Princeton University. For the faculty and, especially, the graduate students of that department I have warm feelings for what they taught me. I am also grateful for the help of the undergraduates in the Department of Anthropology at the University of Maryland, College Park.

This book was read and generously encouraged by Robert N. Bellah and Roy A. Rappaport. Similarly, I owe a debt to John Bennett. Irving Zaretsky painted the whole picture of marginal churches, of which Mormonism was one. Robert Schuyler identified the colonial process of which nineteenth century Mormonism was an instance. For help on specific points and for supportive encouragement I counted on Carmel Schrire, Iles Minoff, Yehudi Cohen, Ezra Zubrow, and David Crabb. Donald MacNeil, Douglas Miller, Michael Merle, Joel Klein, and Robert Gutierrez contributed technical skill in data collection and analysis. Michael Corbett prefaced my analysis of eccelesiastical courts with his own analysis of Presbyterian courts. R. C. Johnson, Robert Rockwell, and Russell Handsman were good audiences and helped to form my thoughts.

Nan Wells made a big difference. To Jeanette Mirsky I would answer: yes, your work made a substantial contribution. Emmett Wilson, Jr., showed me how my book is a mirror for me as Mormonism is for America. For their sustaining friendship and thoughtful reactions to my work I thank Barbara Shimshak, Elizabeth Beatson, Norman and Leanore Itzkowitz, Lewis Bateman, Thomas Stapp, Christian and Freda Murck, and Michael and Mary Ellen Capek. For my family: my thanks for doing all that families do.

Initial support for the research effort was provided by a National Institutes of Mental Health Small Grant. Early support also came through funds from a National Science

Foundation Institutional Grant to Princeton University. Princeton subsequently awarded several grants from its Grants Committee and Committee on Research in the Humanities and Social Sciences. The groundwork was turned into a book with the help of a National Endowment for the Humanities Fellowship for Independent Study and Research in 1976. Virtually none of this work could have been done without these generous sources of aid.

Permission to quote has been kindly granted by Annual Reviews, Inc., Palo Alto, for "The Sacred in Human Evolution" by Roy A. Rappaport in *Annual Review of Ecology and Systematics*, vol. 2, 1971; by the University of Arizona Press, Tucson, for *Take Up Your Mission* by Charles S. Peterson (copyright 1973); by Bookcraft, Salt Lake City, for *Mormon Doctrine* by Bruce R. McConkie (copyright 1966); and by the Historical Department of the Church of Jesus Christ of Latter-day Saints for "History and Settlement of the Snowflake Area, 1870–1912," "Historical Record, Snowflake Stake, 1890–1892," "St. Johns Stake Historical Record, 1887–1915," "High Priests Quorum Minute Book, Snowflake Stake, 1886–1892," "Record of Stake Funds, Snowflake Stake, 1882–1901," and letters from Wilford Woodruff to Lot Smith, John Taylor to Lot Smith, and Lot Smith to John Taylor.

Tables

Map

Roots of
Modern Mormonism

Modern Mormon Towns on the Little Colorado River

1

Religion for Unstable Conditions

Of all the utopias founded in the United States during the nineteenth century, Mormonism was the most successful. It was also the only American utopia able to turn itself into a national and even international church during the twentieth century. This outstanding record over two centuries raises the question of how a harassed religion of farmers, founded by one of them, became a successful religion of white-collar workers run by businessmen. Mormonism, originating in 1830 with a dozen members, now has almost four million. Half its annual growth is provided by converts. It has members around the world and is growing fast on the East Coast as well as in Europe, the Pacific, Japan, and Latin America. Mormonism is in fact growing so fast in Latin America that church leaders think that in ten years half of all Mormons will be Latin American. No longer a Utah church, Mormonism boasts half a million members in California, has its biggest Temple in Washington, D.C., owns a forty-story headquarters in Manhattan and sends out 28,000 missionaries annually all over the world. It is middle-class, business oriented, and urban, having given up its agrarian orientation.

Yet this fast-growing and nationally known church started as a utopian experiment in direct opposition to the United States. During much of the nineteenth century its goals were common ownership of property and classlessness, both of which were based on an outspoken criticism of industrial capitalism as it then existed in Europe and the

United States. At one point, from 1847 to 1890, Mormonism functioned as a territorially separate religious commonwealth. During this period a little empire was founded in the Great Basin, blossomed, struggled with the Union, and remerged with it. Thereafter as Mormonism spread across the globe, it developed a close association with many of the American ideals it had previously criticized. This surprising transformation from isolated utopia to international church merits explanation. Why did Mormonism survive when all other American utopias died? And how are its survival and spread tied to its changed character?

A partial answer to these questions is provided by nineteenth century Mormonism when looked at in terms of cultural ecology, that is, by examining the articulation between the culture and its natural environment. Ecological explanations have usually focused on a culture's economy and demography, although sometimes on its social organization as well. Until recently cultural ecology has never included religion, let alone how religion might be tied to matters of earning a living. Most cultural ecologists have been materialists, claiming that the links between the economy and the environment are the key to all other aspects of a culture and that social organization and religion are in no way primary to it. Yet there is a material connection between what people believe and how they behave. It is this tie that Mormonism illustrates. The religion and practical reality so coincide that each makes the other possible. Mormonism shows the workings of a religion that is truly responsible for the economic success of its people, manifesting a real tie between subsistence and the supernatural.

Roy A. Rappaport (1968) was the first to show how major portions of the economy of stone-age farmers in New Guinea were kept regulated through arcane religious rituals, which had no obvious tie to the economy. In general, religion had been given credit for accomplishing everything except the material well-being of society. In materialist circles the very hypothesis that believers held to be true, namely that material well-being was derived from forces beyond a person's grasp, was unacceptable. What Rappaport, a materialist, showed was not that the supernatural existed but that acting as though it did was the key to making a whole economy work. He discovered that New Guinean rituals triggered war, alliances, animal slaughter, planting, and similar events that were essential for survival. The rituals did not act merely to legitimize decisions already consciously made in other contexts; they formed the mechanism by which those events were begun. Religion was the only regulating authority available to the society, and in the absence of any other source of power, power derived from the supernatural was used to govern economic and political processes.

It is one thing to find that paganism affects the economy of a distant and simple group of stone-age agriculturists, but quite another to suppose that similar intimacies exist between religion and daily subsistence activities in a Christian community. Church rituals are known to have regulated the economies of communities in the Italian peninsula during the fifth and sixth centuries A.D. after the decline of Roman power. It is also likely that in early seventeenth-century New England major regulatory power was derived from religion, since no individual or group had sufficient coercive power to govern. But these examples provide little information about the actual working of the system.

Nineteenth century Mormonism is a recent Christian community with complete records of how religious rituals regulated the whole of daily life. Though without real power, Mormonism made a desert productive and filled it with tens of thousands of settlers, all by using the supernatural as the chief organizing power for every major activity and rituals as the chief instruments for securing material success. Starting off as a religious utopia, Mormonism grew into a genuine theocracy, governed by priests whose authority was derived not from police, armies, surpluses, and plutocratic, aristocratic, or democratic election—none of which existed at the time in Utah—but mainly from the fact that everybody believed in the same version of the supernatural. There are quantities of diaries, letters, local histories, minutes of religious meetings, and recorded testimony, all showing in intimate, intricate detail how religion governed the rest of society.

Mormondom in Utah was more or less autonomous from the United States during the period 1847–1890, and as a new state emerging on the edge of an older one, it revealed something about the role of religion in developing states. In this sense it was comparable to the city-states in ancient southern Mesopotamia, which were both newly formed and run by a religious hierarchy (Adams 1966). Mormondom was a theocracy for forty years; the Mesopotamian states had theocratic phases lasting for several centuries. The ancient city-states were the first of their kind but poorly documented, whereas the Mormon state was derivative but fully documented. Together they inform about the role of religion in states founded in unstable conditions.

The Mesopotamian city-states, founded along the Tigris and Euphrates rivers in the late fourth millennium B.C., were small, the population of each numbering in the low thousands. They nevertheless had a different form of social and political life from any that had yet existed. They were economically heterogeneous, bringing together from nearby areas a variety of people, including farmers, fishermen, herders, and traders, who exchanged their surpluses for necessities. These earliest centers of exchange grew up around religious shrines, or temples, whose priestly caretakers administered the markets. Since material affairs were entirely regulated by temple personnel, the city-states are also called temple-communities.

These communities made the first attempt in history to farm a desert. In all likelihood the original population of the area came from the hills, where ample rainfall allowed for dry farming. The new settlers had to fit their experience to farming a semiarid area, which meant that they must learn how to control the river water, putting it onto the land and draining it off as needed. They must also learn to experiment with crops that could be successfully grown under the new conditions. The whole complex process of settling into the region was an experimental, risk-running venture, initially providing very little control over the environment. Under such tenuous, ecologically frail circumstances, without adequate knowledge of land, water, climate, and crops, and consequently without wealth, the chief power to govern was derived from the supernatural.

Victorian Utah reveals a similar situation: it too was a new state in a semidesert occupied by a diverse population inexperienced in irrigated farming, whose ability to organize for survival derived from mutual agreement on the existence of the supernatural. The Mormon records shed clear light on how a religious state was set up, operated at the peak of success, began an internal transformation away from sacred authority after acquiring wealth and power, and finally became secularized after being absorbed by a bigger civil state. Fifty years of the rituals' minutes show how the supernatural was used to govern people, an aspect of religious rule not available from Mesopotamia. The half-century of Mormon records also shows how religious regulation operated over time and changed under stress, information not available on economic regulation by rituals in New Guinea. The Mormon case thus complements the New Guinean and Mesopotamian cases by providing new knowledge on how religion generates material success in ecologically fragile conditions.

These fifty years also revealed that, in a state backed by power derived from a source whose existence could be rationally doubted, reliance on such power declined in direct proportion to the advent of material success and the real power it generated. The unempirical was replaced by a more tangible source of power in Utah by 1890. With this development the era of Mormon independence and material success generated by religion came to an end. The "Americanization" of Utah, as the next period has been called, began with the forceful intervention of the United States in the late 1880s and ended with the complete absorption of Mormon economic and political institutions. Once the Mormon state had been absorbed by the federal Union, it became, not a partner, but a colony. Whereas nineteenth century Mormonism showed the operation of a theocratic state, twentieth century Mormonism shows the operation of a colonial religion. Even though Mormondom disappeared, having been replaced by United States rule and economic control, Mormonism itself did not disappear but changed, trying to help its people make the best of being owned and governed by distant powers. In consequence of serving a subordinate population, Mormonism began to reflect its members' subordination and in time came to foster that condition.

The pivotal era when Mormonism became such a religion was fully documented on both the American and the Mormon sides. There were illuminating debates among Mormons over possible responses to the anticipated reabsorption by the United States. Some Mormons made efforts to hold onto theocracy, while others tried to accommodate to the change. The reorganization of the economic, political, and social worlds that took place in this era became the foundation for modern Mormonism, determining the present shape of America's biggest home-grown church and one of its most powerful religious minorities. The era thus shows what happened to the religion of a small, weak state when taken over by the industrialized Western world. It illustrates the conversion of a religion founded in unstable ecological circumstances to one existing in colonial circumstances, which are also by definition unstable.

Subjection to instability marks much of modern life and consequently influences much of modern religion. According to Robert Bellah (1970), despite a nearly universal belief in God, many people both inside and outside today's churches work out the answers to questions of ultimate concern on their own, unaided and unchecked by external authority. These people build and revise paradigms of meaning which have in them a degree of flexibility, personal idiosyncracy, and changeability unprecedented in the history of religion. Such an approach is endorsed by a large group of nontraditional churches, whose members exhibit a conceptual diffuseness that permits continual self-transformation and redefinition. Of this institutional network that supports paradigms for individual belief and behavior, Mormonism is one.

When the Mormon state became the Mormon church, political and economic centralization disappeared, but even though a visibly centralized church remained, modern Mormonism cannot be understood in terms of the same institution that made so much sense for the nineteenth century. A switch was made from theocracy to the individual, from state to believer, not from state to church. At present Mormons possess a do-it-yourself system of personal interpretation which envelops their church's theology, philosophy, and history and which works within the framework of an institution known for its hierarchical organization and authoritarian stance. But neither hierarchy nor authoritarianism, typical of the nineteenth century church-state, is the clue to understanding Mormon success today. Each in fact hides the endless conceptual and psychological revision taking place in the individual, whose habits of thought have replaced institutional structure as the way of comprehending Mormonism in the twentieth century.

Elaborating on the nature of modern religion, Thomas Luckmann (1967) argued that when society had an official religion, in which all people participated to some degree while growing up, the dynamics between the two—official religion and the individual—produced variations in belief that were regarded as normal. But in the modern industrialized world, where churches and similar institutions now offer only a fragment of the official world view, their restriction to a specialized domain has resulted in the creation of a private sphere in which individuals are free to act and believe more or less autonomously. The subjectivism of modern religiosity produces flexibility, but it also creates inconsistency. Thus, as an individual's personal paradigm changes and rearranges, its positive side appears as flexibility, and its negative side as uncertainty.

Such duality characterizes Mormonism. It is hierarchical, authoritarian, and fundamentalist, but it is also individualistic, democratic, and loose-constructionist. Mormonism exhibits the first characteristics openly; the last are concealed. Yet it is the hidden traits that are responsible for Mormonism's current success.

Mormonism's two-sided nature developed after the granting of statehood in 1896. The church, which had been founded explicitly to improve the lot of the economically deprived, recognized that in order to fulfill this role, it could operate only under conditions that were the antithesis of its original aim, because economic integration with the United States had also brought subordination. Under these circumstances Mormonism became a colonial religion whose major task was to give individuals leading a precarious life some way of achieving success by utilizing that very condition of uncertainty. Since the changeable and unpredictable world to which Mormons had to adapt had passed beyond their control, they built on Joseph Smith's injunctions to develop personal understandings of a dynamic world in order to create syntheses of belief that were idiosyncratic and thus diffuse. They came to hold a wide range of interpretations, which neither they nor their observers tended to notice because of the social discipline that is the most visible aspect of the church.

Mormonism as a colonial religion fitted its adherents to economic conditions beyond their control by giving them freedom to interpret their religion. Under colonial conditions, land and industry are owned by others, the price of goods is subject to rises and declines beyond local control, and employment changes, requiring frequent job shifts, moves, and marked fluctuations in income. Mormons accommodate themselves to external control and rapid, unpredictable change through a religion which encourages them to understand all events as part of God's plan. Because each Mormon may search his or her life for illustrations of divine intention, the meanings given to the religion are flexible and varied. Because personal experience is the main source of meaning in the religion, it has become a reflection of everyday life and is thus ill-defined and vague because life is so changeable. Thus Mormonism has lost all consistency because everyone can define it and because personal meanings change as life does. In this sense it is the modern religion outlined by Bellah and Luckmann because it changes as fast as the everyday world and places responsibility for making sense of those changes with the individual.

Mormonism is colonial in another way because it has eliminated the usual way people make contrasts. It has reorganized the distinctions between past, present, and future so that these are no longer separate from each other but are considered equally understandable because they are equally accessible. As a result, the normal way of giving meaning to the present, by comparing it with a time assumed to be different, is gone. To a novel degree Mormonism made all events equally understandable and thus the same. Mormonism did so by holding that life has neither beginning nor end but is a continuous existence which always was and ever will be. This continuum, which embraces the whole of time, is known as salvation history. The past represents attempts to found and refound God's Kingdom on earth. The future contains the millennium and then existence, not in heaven, but in worlds governed by processes like those we know now. Because Mormons understand the meaning of history, the meaning of all past times is available to them; they also have foreknowledge of heaven through the joys of life here. Nothing at another time is beyond understanding just because it is past or future; nothing in life is beyond comprehension, because there is only one plan, which each Mormon has the ability and right to know and interpret.

Mormons have made all the experiences of life equivalencies. Anything from history, any prediction about the future, any event in a person's life can be understood through Mormonism. The effect is to elide events in the past, present, and future, eliminating the differences between them. The present absorbs both past and future, collapsing contrasts; in so doing, it extinguishes the ability to see present conditions as any different from those that have been or might be. Once all contrast with the past or future is lost, Mormons' subordinate, colonial status cannot be seen, and thus their religion acts to fix them more firmly in the condition it was founded to eliminate.

Because Mormonism has eliminated a comparative point of view, its people describe the many changes they live with in everyday life as order, not chaos, as expected change, not arbitrariness. Nothing is ever seen as profoundly new, different, or incomprehensible. When the elimination of contrasts is combined with the Mormons' obligation to give meaning to their religion, they blind themselves to the colonial condition they serve. Mormons thus illustrate the two chief traits of modern religion among the economically subordinate: they think alone and are excluded from the collective memory of all who went before.

intended a husband to have more than a single wife and family.

Although this practice became public and well-developed only after the move to Utah, some of Smith's closest followers were taught the doctrine, took plural wives, and established separate families. This reorganization of traditional family life, though the most famous of all the Mormon social experiments, was in fact only one part of the complete reorganization of society that Smith finished in Nauvoo.

While there, the core of Mormon doctrine took final shape. Smith understood that he had been appointed to build a society, not just a church, that it would inevitably conflict with the society from which it sprang, and that at some point the task must pass from his hands if it were to come to fruition. Mormon uniqueness and peculiarity took on a new fixity; compromise was less possible or desirable. The Mormons began to develop a culture and way of life from their ideology. Mormonism was no longer just another revival movement, socialist utopia, or brand of renovated Calvinism; it was a profoundly different version of Christianity.

Largely because of the changes in certain Mormon practices that accompanied this development, Smith fought with his fellow Saints, and the Saints fought with the surrounding communities of non-Mormons. After 1844, when Smith was shot in jail in a town near Nauvoo while awaiting trial for alleged criminal acts, the course of Mormonism in Illinois was a tragic replay of the scene in Missouri: neighbors became frightened of Mormon peculiarities and success and started to pillage and murder, a timid state government did little to stop the violence, and Mormons faced expulsion once more.

By now Mormons had established a cyclical pattern. They had been forced to experiment to survive, and each time they experimented more radically because of the conditions demanded for survival. The greater their success with their more radical solutions, the more they were hounded, and so the circle of mutual cause and effect—a radical society and a radicalizing response—continued.

In general, most of the people attracted to Smith had their roots in poverty, whether economic or spiritual. Forced off lands that had become too expensive for family agriculture, many had migrated to the newly developing industrial areas. There, unskilled, badly paid, and poorly housed, with their traditional fabric of social relations destroyed, they became part of a huge labor force whose plight was responded to by social innovators like the Shakers, Owenites, and Fourierists, and by ideological critics like Joseph Smith and Karl Marx. In America the response to these conditions was religious, which in combination with an open frontier, where farming was the accepted mode of life, produced a communism of the kind instituted by Smith. His experiments between 1830 and 1844 are critical to understanding both Mormonism and society's responses to it, because both Smith and his parent society were experiencing the Industrial Revolution and forming opposite reactions to it.

As the Mormons moved from place to place in a general westward pattern, there was a dynamic at work between Mormonism and its parent society. The economic and missionary success that followed Mormon social and ideological innovation at every stage of its development brought inevitable pressure from the outside community, which in turn pushed Mormons into increasingly marginal areas. Each new area permitted and required progressively more dramatic innovations, many of which led to even greater economic growth. This in turn provoked suspicion, which again resulted in expulsion and movement further West, where experimentation and growth were once more both required for survival and permitted by the increasing closeness of the frontier with its absence of developed institutions. The final move, to Utah, passed beyond the frontier into an institutional vacuum, where a totally new social order had to be established for survival, but where it could at the same time enjoy uninhibited growth.

With the prophet's death in 1844, the Mormon adventure was in jeopardy. For almost any other community, such an event would have meant the end; extinction would have followed in a few decades. The Mormons in Nauvoo faced a double crisis, founded on the absence of a leader with the same aura of authority as Smith's, since no chain of succession had been established, and on the hostile movements in the surrounding area. Before Smith's assassination, he had considered plans to move his people into some part of the unsettled West outside the federal Union, and two years after his death hostilities in Illinois had grown so serious that removal westward was no longer a choice but an inevitability.

During those years there was a struggle for church leadership, which culminated in splits in the church. Brigham Young emerged as organizer of the westward movement, for which most of the Saints opted. Some immediate members of Smith's family led another, smaller group that moved back to Missouri. This group became the Reorganized Church of Jesus Christ of Latter-day Saints, which is presently centered in Independence. Several even smaller groups were also formed, which in time disappeared.

The westward trek under Young began in 1847. The bulk of the Saints walked fifteen hundred miles to the basin of the Great Salt Lake outside United States territory. Young, who had organized the orderly departure from Nauvoo while it was effectively under seige, led the successful crossing of more than ten thousand people into the wastes of the Great Basin. Afterward he was invested with Smith's prerogatives as prophet, seer, and revelator—titles that he had earned as no succeeding church president would have to.

The Mormon exodus from Nauvoo paralleled earlier ones, though it was bigger, harder and better organized, having been prepared for some time before it actually took place. Like most such unifying events, it created bonds that would last a generation, as well as a history that would serve as a mirror to ennoble and justify future events. It was an instant epic.

Much of western North America is a semiarid desert running along the western flank of the Rocky Mountains from the Canadian border well into northern Mexico. The desert region stops at the edge of the Rockies, whose western

edge is irregular, spreading in southern California almost to
the sea. The Mormons found this whole area largely empty
when they entered it in 1847. There was a well-adapted but
necessarily thin aboriginal population, which had been there
for at least 12,000 years. A Mexican population had lived in
the southern section since early in the seventeenth century,
but it too was thin, being numerous only in western New
Mexico and California. There were, in addition, traders and
various Anglo settlers who had come to ranch and, where
possible, to farm.

Once in the Great Basin, the Mormons faced the
opportunity for which they had implicitly been preparing
ever since leaving Palmyra: to turn a church and its
associated practices into a nation with a distinct culture. The
founding of the Mormon state occupied the period from
1847 to 1890. In the Salt Lake area, which still belonged to
Mexico when the Mormons arrived and only became United
States territory in 1849 after the Mexican War, the religious
community blossomed into a full-blown religious state.
Between 1847 and the late 1880s Utah Territory, though
legally part of the United States, was in fact more independent from the United States than the South was
before and during the Civil War.

The Mormons colonized this area with close supervision,
setting up planned towns all over the desert. They tied
the whole of the kingdom together in a well-designed
administrative structure in which all functions were filled by
churchmen and all churchmen had to be either farmers or
workers. In the trackless Great Basin, Mormons established
an entire social environment, complete with schools, courts,
irrigation systems, exchange networks, price controls,
systems of weights and measures, a monetary system
including specie, a network of roads, maps, an exploration
plan, land, timber and water rights management, and
printing facilities. Everything from the founding of basic
agrarian industries to the invention of a new alphabet sprang
into existence as much from necessity as from conscious
forethought, and it all spread quickly over the vast territory which was to become Mormondom or the Mormon
theocratic state.

Young worked for thirty years to build a domain in the western United States that would offer the Mormons protection from their earlier difficulties and establish them as an entity to be reckoned with. The present boundaries of the state of Utah, which date from the 1880s, represent only a partial reflection of the Mormon ambition. Young wanted to acquire, besides Utah, a western seaport at San Bernardino, the area that is now Sonora and Chihuahua, Mexico, and much of Arizona, Nevada, and Idaho. But the reasons he wanted this large area went beyond mere acquisitiveness.

Within a decade or two after the Mormon arrival in 1847, the valleys of central Utah were overpopulated, and families had been sent out in groups to preselected areas to the west, north, and south of Salt Lake City to found new communities that would extend the borders of the kingdom. During this time, tens of thousands of Mormons arrived from the East and Europe and spread into southern Idaho, much of Nevada, all the rest of Utah, southwestern Colorado, northwestern New Mexico, much of northern and central Arizona, northern Sonora and Chihuahua, and southern California as far as San Bernardino. Given the fairly primitive technology brought to the Great Basin, the near impossibility of dry farming in most of it, and the increasing number of people arriving through the late 1880s, the Mormons needed a larger territory, and Young's plans matched the needs. Orderly, often free passage was provided for immigrants from Europe to Utah, and people so transported not only reinforced the kingdom but provided the crucial dynamic that forced territorial expansion and the Mormonizing of large unclaimed areas. This process went on through the nineteenth century: the church, head-quartered in Salt Lake City, acted as a pump to draw off the economic and spiritual wreckage of the rural and industrial East, regenerated it through Mormonism, and spread it across the agrarian desert West in an ever-expanding flood of people and towns.

In Utah and much of the Western desert, the Mormon utopia of the early days in Ohio, Missouri, and Illinois was transformed into the Mormon religious state. To accomplish this monumental achievement in a land that had been rejected by all those who crossed it to get to California, the Mormons perfected a number of institutions. Some were the direct heritage of Smith, like centralized church control of government and finances; others, like irrigation systems, agricultural and industrial experimentation, immigration management and church courts, had only the merest of antecedents before Utah.

Although the role of the church in the successful adaptation was primary, there were several other essential components. Since the Salt Lake valley had quickly filled up, newcomers were sent out to towns in less densely populated valleys. As Salt Lake City developed, it could absorb many who came trained as craftsmen and laborers, but it could not absorb the farmers. The areas where these were sent had already been explored by parties sent out for that purpose by Young, a policy he had begun shortly after his arrival. Exploration parties selected sites that would be successful for agriculture in advance, to save the settlers from disastrous failures. It was just such a party that had located the Salt Lake valley well before the Mormon arrival.

After an area had been explored and the decision for settlement made, population was funneled into it. The leaders of the new towns were usually selected by Young himself and then "called" to the undertaking. "Calls" were direct and personal: Brigham either took a man aside or rose in the Tabernacle and announced publicly that Brothers X, Y, and Z were requested to sell their holdings and take their families to the new area as directed by the will of God. And sell and go they usually did—some several times. The men chosen to lead in establishing a new town were given access to capital, expressed in terms of cattle and stored surplus food. Often, too, these men could ask church leaders to call specific individuals with needed skills or, if the initial population in a town needed reinforcement, to issue a general call in Salt Lake City for new settlers.

The initial founders of a new town or group of towns were often selected so as to include the appropriate complement of agrarian skills. This was especially true in areas requiring water control. The enormous distances separating the parts of the kingdom—necessitating a month, for example, to cover the 700 miles from Salt Lake City to eastern Arizona by wagon—made it essential for both survival and self-sufficiency that the right set of skills and tools be available to complement farming. A miller, carpenter, brickmaker, blacksmith, tanner, surveyor, and dam or canal builder were usually enlisted, and they were equipped with appropriate machines and tools.

This complement of people was invariably set down in a town rather than scattered over the region. Each town was laid out in a grid, called the Plat of Zion originally drawn up by Joseph Smith. Rectangles were marked out as soon as the settlers had arrived, and all were given free pieces of land of equal quality in the town and equivalent pieces of farm or range land outside the town. The two significant features of the settlement pattern were the placement of all residents in a town, as opposed to scattering them over the countryside, and the equal distribution of arable land. This pattern preserved the Mormon community and guaranteed initial economic equality and cooperation.

Almost all Mormon towns held water and timber resources in common. Access to both was guaranteed to all and limited alike for all. Beyond this egalitarianism, however, irrigation demanded dams, canals, and systematic, controlled access to water. The paramount necessity for irrigation intensified the type of hierarchical control that had characterized Mormonism from its start. Balanced against equal access to resources was therefore the hierarchy necessary to ensure continued equality.

Mormondom was unified from Idaho to Sonora and from Nevada to western New Mexico by a single faith coupled with a uniform mode of settlement, uniform mode of local government, and uniform direction emanating from Salt Lake City. The whole Mormon area had many microdifferences of a cultural sort, and many of an ecological sort. But even though the Mormon population, neighboring American Indian tribes, rainfall, temperature, and topography varied throughout this vast region, each area within it was about equally diversified, all facing the same combination of problems. The whole area is semiarid, with frosts in the late spring and early fall, difficult-to-harness rivers, and mountainous terrain. Consequently, Mormon settlement at any one location and one time exhibited similarities to all other settlements. Techniques and policies, though varying to a degree over time, did not change much at any one time.

When planning the development of the southern part of the kingdom, including Arizona, Brigham Young had in mind a chain of settlements that would lead into Mexico and thus would ultimately include Mormon communities under another flag, for the church wanted an area of refuge in case of attack by the United States. To accomplish this goal, northern Arizona was scouted and colonized in the late 1870s and 1880s. Settlement, which was at first to include only the huge area along the Little Colorado River in east-central Arizona, was extended during these years into western New Mexico and then into central and southern Arizona to Phoenix. By the mid-1880s two dozen towns and three thousand people were established along the Little Colorado, forming part of the Mormon corridor into Sonora and Chihuahua.

A special purpose was added to the Little Colorado settlements because they were near the major Hopi, Navajo, and Western Apache populations. Mormons regarded it as their duty, expressed in the *Book of Mormon,* to convert the Indians, a duty that in the nineteenth century applied especially to the sedentary Pueblo as opposed to the more mobile Navajo and Apache. Young told the Arizona Saints several times by letter that every help possible was to be extended to Indians. Arizona Mormons fed both Hopi and Navajo at times of need.

The towns along the Little Colorado River provide a full complement of records concerning their founding, development, maturity, and in this century, their transformation after being integrated into the state of Arizona. Every important decision made there or in Salt Lake City was recorded and has survived. Beyond a complete social and statistical history, the diaries, journals, personal letters, and oral traditions preserve the texture of life, allowing a clear view of the intangibles behind founding towns, walking 700 miles, living in isolation, and lasting through the growth and change of a sacred kingdom into a secular society.

Coincidental with the colonization of Arizona in the 1870s and 1880s was Young's rising interest in Smith's revelation concerning the United Order of Enoch. It had early been revealed to Smith that the perfect way to live was cooperatively, with the central management of all property and the communal sharing of all goods beyond basic necessities. Young not only founded the United Order of Enoch on this idea but. also established the first Little Colorado towns on this basis. Cooperative economics proved successful from the church's point of view, because once communal towns had been set up, they supported all later settlement efforts in central Arizona. The Arizona settlements also offered church leadership a chance to reestablish a revealed way of life.

In the early and mid-1880s a dozen other Mormon towns not operating on the United Order principle were founded along the Little Colorado and its tributaries. These communities housed the bulk of the Mormon population and, like the United Order communities, were based on irrigated farming and supposed to be self-sufficient. They were in fact closely protected during their maturation by the church leadership in Salt Lake City. The land for all the Arizona towns, which had been purchased either by wealthy Mormons or directly by the church, was initially divided into equal parcels based on size and quality and distributed free to settlers, who drew their parcels by lot. The pieces of land were numbered, slips of paper were put into a hat, and a drawing was held by family heads, entitled to one farm each. In this way all families started off with equal access to resources. New settlers were given unclaimed land or took up abandoned plots. A few wealthy Mormons could buy extra range land around a town, but this practice was not thought to contravene equal economic opportunity for the average Mormon since the local economy was cooperative, not competitive.

Cooperative economic policy required that every family head tithe 10 percent of his family's annual increase, usually paid in kind. This produce was stored centrally in the town and formed a communal store against any want or crisis experienced by either a local family or any other Mormon town. The entire community produced only for itself and not for an outside market. Through a complex network of exchange with other Mormon towns, each town was self-sustaining, with the result that the towns were largely free of market forces beyond the Mormon world.

During the whole Utah period, including the time when colonies were set up in Arizona, Mormon communities had a mixed economy. Although it was cooperative, people could retain private wealth either earned through their judicious efforts or acquired prior to their conversion to the church. While there were no really poor or really rich compared to the rest of the contemporary United States, such classes did exist, and they were sanctioned by the church after the failure of complete communalism in Kirtland. Uneven wealth and therefore uneven property, as expressed in land and cattle, existed, as did private business. There was also some selling of produce on the open market for profit and some wage labor. Nonetheless, 10 to 15 percent of the surplus was socialized, and leadership was not based on access to private wealth.

By coupling cooperative economics and hierarchical leadership, the Mormons were able to build and maintain a complex irrigation network involving fickle streams, frail dams, easily washed-out canals, periodic floods, and the huge labor force needed to operate the whole system successfully. In addition, the exchange system, roads, public buildings, schools, and hundreds of other operations needed to ensure subsistence success were maintained by means of cooperative labor and funds. Volunteer labor led by the priestly hierarchy built the towns with shared resources of food and money, derived at first from tithing funds in Salt Lake City and later from local surpluses. The whole edifice was orchestrated by a single hierarchy having the highest authority in religious and political terms.

During the second half of the nineteenth century Mormons defined, more or less on their own terms, the relationship that they would have with the rest of the world, principally the United States. These years saw Mormonism become a working society, growing to maturity through its capacity to handle a harsh environment. With a fully operating government and a dynamic economy centrally managed along socialist lines, Mormonism strove to create internal self-sufficiency, and to a remarkable degree it succeeded. These years were in many ways Mormonism's finest. The church ran itself according to its own lights and, in so doing, became the only American utopia ever to turn itself into a state.

The data on the Mormon towns of eastern Arizona, covering roughly a century, are selected not to provide in any sense a complete history of Mormon society but rather to highlight particular aspects of it. For the nineteenth century, the areas treated are tithing, irrigation, and the judicial system, because these reveal critical aspects of how the Mormon adaptive strategy worked. The data for the twentieth century involve Mormon rituals and Mormon methods of constructing history, because these show how local, Arizona Mormonism is similar to Mormonism everywhere.

The particular character of Mormonism in nineteenth century Arizona resembles contemporary Mormonism in that it took people who had never been prosperous or enjoyed a stable economy and created habits of thinking and modes of organizing which built stability out of instability, not by denying it, but by maximizing it. Today many converts are attracted to Mormonism because of dissatisfaction with the conditions of their own existence, conditions not very different from those in the desert West under which Mormonism developed. While economic situations may have improved for Mormons in Salt Lake City, California, or on the East Coast, the religion in which they all participate emerged and was perfected under adverse economic conditions which, by and large, still prevail.

Today the Little Colorado River towns are still basically Mormon, although each also has a population of non-Mormons. Mormons still control most of the power, hold most of the elected political positions, and own most of the local small businesses. But the economy of the area is essentially a function of major Arizona businesses centered in Phoenix and of the federal bureaucracies which manage the area's vast Indian reservations, oversee its national parks (the Petrified Forest and Painted Desert), and lease out its national forests. These agencies provide important sources of employment. Their local employees in turn form a well-paid market. Cattle and timber or pulp-paper companies with headquarters outside the area form the other major segment of the economy and, like the local branches of Arizona banks, function to siphon off wealth, not to create capital that would promote self-sufficiency. The subordinate position that now characterizes the area, which is quite different from the nineteenth century era of independence, began to take shape with the eclipse of the Mormon state in the late 1880s.

The federal government which had long wanted to move forcefully to remove the church from political and economic affairs in Utah, finally did so during the 1880s by dismembering the church's apparatus for unifying and regulating the vital affairs of the kingdom. The destruction of Mormondom was inevitable as soon as the Civil War was over. In their 1856 party platform the Republicans had denounced both slavery and polygamy as "twin relics of barbarism." Under this double banner the Union attacked the only two regions that had achieved a degree of political and economic autonomy beyond that thought compatible with a strong federal government. After a number of ineffectual attempts to control Utah by legislating against polygamy and the church, the federal government moved in 1886 to jail over 1200 Mormon leaders on polygamy charges, to disincorporate the church by removing over a million dollars of its property, to saddle the government of the territory with a complex carpetbag administration, and to deprive Mormons in Idaho of their right to vote and achieve nearly the same in

Utah—all this in the name of a nationwide campaign against the alleged evils of plural marriage. Under this barrage the church capitulated, abandoning plural marriage in 1890, dissolving its own political party in 1896, and divesting itself of all industrial property by 1907.

By the time Utah was allowed into the Union as a state in 1896, Mormondom was dead as an effective, independent entity in the desert West. After 1890 Mormonism turned from a state into a church, and as it became less critical of its parent society, it became more openly American. During the next forty years the great American industries peculiar to the desert West—mining, cattle and sheep-raising, timber-cutting, and railroads—dominated Utah's economy. From 1890 the history of Utah and the rest of Mormondom was largely a history of economies that were subordinated to and politicians who were dominated by Eastern interests. Through this period the church played less and less of a role in the economic affairs of its people and lost its dominance both in the public eye and in fact.

By statehood, the church was deeply in debt. Having been hounded to the edge of existence as an institution, it had to realize, as it never had to before, that it could not be American on its own terms, but only on America's. With this concrete defeat, coupled with the impossibility of further westward removal, Mormonism began a transformation from a nineteenth century socialist commonwealth predicated on a radical critique of the American economy and class structure to a twentieth century church endorsing an ideology of acceptance of American society.

From 1930 to the present, Mormonism again changed drastically. Since the Great Depression, when its population suffered enormous privation, the church has become respectable and respected, moving into the circles of power, public responsibility, and international success. During this period the conservatism that first appeared within the church during the 1880s and 1890s has become a part of America's new stereotype of Mormonism, replacing the earlier hate-filled caricature of Mormons as sexual libertines who confused political and religious loyalties.

Since the 1930s, and especially since World War II, the Mormon population outside Utah has also grown enormously. The church has become internationalized, its leaders now maintaining that Zion is not solely in Utah but wherever there are Mormons. In addition, the church has achieved a degree of economic success that makes it one of the richest churches in the United States. Through the capital provided by tithing, conservative politics, and the reorientation of its attitude to the United States, the bankruptcy and dissolution of the turn of the century have been left far behind. What has not been left behind, however, are the attitudes fostered by the earlier difficulties.

Today the peculiarities of Mormon theology are almost never highlighted. Rather, "America first" is the attitude most people see when looking at Mormonism. It is a church of middle class, hard-working, honest, and reliable people, associated with business, Republicanism, missionary activity, and institutional wealth. The church is once again a powerful institution, having made a spectacular comeback, both economically and demographically, to play a dominant role in the economy of its home territory and a noticeable role in national politics.

The business and social practices of the modern church—the use of tithing as investment capital, the presence of church officials on boards of large corporations, opposition to labor, church patronage of favored businesses, an extensive welfare system that has virtually eliminated poverty, and church reinvestment in large enterprises like sugar refining—have combined with other practices to regenerate its wealth and sustain its growth. Less tangible but more important is the conceptual system of Mormonism, which has reoriented and reestablished the institution as a power in America. It is not that Mormons have thought their way back to success but that their way of thinking is an important part of their reemergence.

This, then, is the skeletal history of Mormonism: from self-exclusion and expulsion, to independent statehood, to subordination in the Union, to full and powerful membership in the United States. The history contains a major metamorphosis: the death of a socialist society and the rise of a church which fully supports the free enterprise capitalism that it earlier condemned.

It is paradoxical that Mormons are widely known for the efficiency of their church organization and for the peculiarities of their history, but not so well known for what is most spectacular, even unique, about Mormonism: its theology. This extraordinary set of conceptions was "a real religious creation, one intended to be to Christianity as Christianity was to Judaism: that is, a reform and a consummation" (Brodie 1963:viii). Mormonism was not just another Christian sect seeking to cast out a few faulty additives to Christianity; it was meant to cut through centuries of accumulated error and misinterpretation.

Coming long after the struggle of the Reformation, Smith did not have to fight the same battle for independence and distinctiveness based on rejection and hatred of the older tradition. He was remarkably unpolemical in his treatment of the existing Christian churches. Instead, between the 1820s and his death in 1844 he gave himself free rein to create a completely new system. This system creates for both the individual and the church a seamless web of existence and an easily understood purpose that do not terminate in historical time. Ultimately, there was no creation, for God and a part of everyone's personal being always existed and will continue to exist into the infinite future. After life, people will not become mere souls but will continue as sentient, creative beings whose final goal is to become gods.

Mormons believe that the gospel, the teachings of Jesus as recorded in the New Testament, contain the essence of Christianity. In this they are no different from any other Christian group. But they believe that the church which Jesus set up to teach and propagate his truths began to be misdirected and prostituted soon after its founding and that God eventually decided to reestablish his true church, using Joseph Smith as his agent. At the time of this decision God also decided to add to the corpus of his revelations to mankind, using Smith as his prophet.

There is an inevitable dilemma in the founding of any

new religion: if God endorsed it, why did he wait so long? To resolve the paradox of the time of his own election as prophet, Smith said that God had established his anointed priesthood many times in the course of history, all of which are recorded in the Old Testament, and that God was doing so one last time in the person of Smith before assuming personal rule of the world, thereby ending the need for further intercessions. In this sense Smith was creating a historical continuity, not just with the early Christian church that the sixteenth century reformers had taken as their touchstone, but with everything that passed as a revealed institution in the Bible as a whole. Smith was not interested in taking metaphors from the Old Testament; he was interested in representing his part in man's history as no different from any ancient prophet's. He, however, was to be the last of a line begun with Adam, God's first priest, and would himself be quickly followed by God's direct and personal rule. Smith was the latest prophet and the last.

Since Smith was the most recent of God's special messengers, it followed that he should receive messages about God's intentions. The general import of these messages was twofold. They were to improve mankind's understanding of God and to provide new solutions to old problems. The American Indians posed one of the most obvious problems for nineteenth century America, because of their conflict with Christianity and opposition to European settlement. The *Book of Mormon* addressed the problem by recording a visit of Christ to the New World to preach the same messages as he had already preached in the Old, a visit that gave the pre-Columbian world a plausible history, linked the American Indian to the Hebrew heritage, and charted a joint future for the Indian and European inhabitants of the hemisphere. This account turned the Indian from a savage to be exterminated into a fallen brother to be reconverted.

Beyond addressing specific problems, Smith proposed a new doctrine about creation and humanity's relation to it. It maintains that there are three constituents of being: God, intelligence, and a primal element of which the visible world is made. All three components are uncreated, timeless, and separate though interacting. God is not the transcendent, omnipotent figure of traditional Christianity but is "a temporal being with a past, present and future, a being genuinely involved in the processes of the world" (McMurrin 1965:13). Since God did not create the world from nothing but organized it out of intelligence and the primal element, he is subject to the constraints of using pre-existing materials.

Intelligence is roughly the capacity for truth, and God has the greatest intelligence. In the beginning God organized the undifferentiated mass called intelligence into discrete units by taking a wife and having spirit children. Each spirit child, embodying a bit of intelligence, is God's literal child, existing in his image. Each will eventually become a member of mankind and have an earthly life in order to experience free will.

Both God and man are subject to the natural processes of the universe, and both cooperate, under these constraints, to improve man's estate. This cooperative process is called the Plan of Salvation. According to the plan, God gave mankind life with rules to live by (the gospel), a redeemer to atone for their sins (Christ), and an opportunity to achieve God's glory. The ultimate goal of salvation is not to unite with God in the usual Christian sense but to become godlike.

Corporeal existence is included in the Plan of Salvation as a time for exercising intelligence, gaining knowledge, and giving full reign to one's freedom. It is also a time of joy rather than sorrow or punishment for original sin. And it is a time for progression along a path outlined by God and previously followed by God, because "As God once was so we are now, and as God now is so we shall become."

Since God is subject to the same laws governing existence, mankind and all of human history take on a degree of mutability and freedom unimagined in traditional Christian thinking. Progressive change governs God, man, history, and the conditions of existence. Everything is amenable to positive modification, and to aid in this progressive betterment, God cooperates with man. To achieve so free and optimistic a view, Mormonism turns God into man's helper and defines

God almost exclusively in terms of man. At the same time, man alone is responsible for evil. Thus, while Mormonism severely compromises the absoluteness of God, it mitigates that presumption by lifting all responsibility for evil from God's shoulders—something that a Christianity insisting on an omnipotent creator could never do.

All these factors of Mormon theology—a limited deity, a humanity capable of becoming just like God, an external world having an existence of its own, and an infinity of orderly change—are linked by the Law of Eternal Progression. This law specifies that just as God organized and populated this world, the most select of his children will create and people other worlds. Progression, for the Mormon, is thus a grand scheme which includes a democratization of the powers of divinity to the point that each individual has the capacity to achieve godlike status.

The Mormon exegesis on the meaning of Christianity tries to resolve certain inconsistencies in the traditional Christian theology, including the relationship between spirit and matter, the responsibility for evil, free will, and the nature of God's humanity and man's divinity. In the resolution Mormonism reveals a degree of polytheism only vaguely visible in traditional Christianity. God has become mankind's real father, and in producing children, he has given birth to all mankind, not just to Christ. Christ was God's most intelligent child, having the greatest truth; and Adam, the founder of the race of men, was God's second most intelligent child. All others are related to them in a way that gives a literalness or simplicity to kinship terms used in the Bible that is absent from the rest of Christian theology. All humans are siblings, differentiated only in terms of degree of intelligence and role in God's plan, but nonetheless undergoing the same progressive development to more godlike status. In this sense, then, there are a multitude of children of God who grow up to be neither servants nor worshipers but, like their Father, gods.

A group usually acts out its essential beliefs in rituals, and Mormonism's rituals are the theater for many of its crucial tenets. Excluding public or secular ceremonials, such as holiday celebrations, Mormons have two sets of rituals: those that occur in a temple and those that take place in a local chapel. There are eighteen Mormon temples scattered around the world and thousands of chapels, usually one in each Mormon community. Mormon rituals are differentiated not just by place of occurrence but also by function and by frequency. Some rituals recur, such as Sacrament Meetings, and others occur only once, such as marriages. But to distinguish between uniqueness and recurrence obscures the fact that almost any ritual is experienced many times in life although only once for oneself.

Temple rituals are private and may be attended only by properly certified Mormons. A Mormon may go to the temple as little as once a year, and there is no rule or expected average for attendance. Many Mormons go more frequently and others much less so, but a person must go sometime. Chapel rituals, which occur far more often, center on the Sacrament Meeting but also include Sunday School classes for all ages and meetings of the orders of priesthood. These rituals are like the Sunday services of traditional churches, while the temple rituals have no parallel in Christianity.

Although the temple rituals are secret, their general outline is known. Through a long, involved series of ceremonies, Mormons witness the key sacred events of world history, learning from them the meaning of life and death and the way to lead this life in order to guarantee enjoyment of the one coming after death. The ceremonies may be performed for either the living or the dead. In Mormon belief the afterlife consists of a series of three kingdoms that encompass all of mankind except those few people who are damned. The kingdoms are telestial, terrestrial, and celestial, differentiated by degree of personal glory that one merits. God dwells only in the last kingdom, and it is for this one that Mormons prepare. It can be entered only by obedience to the gospel and by receiving God's spiritual blessings, called endowments, which are administered in the temple ceremonies. If people have led a decent life, an assumption that Mormonism makes about most of mankind, then regardless of their acceptance of the Christian gospel in any of its forms, they will merit a degree of eternal glory. The degree received will be limited, and they will have to serve those enjoying higher degrees, but they will nevertheless be optimally fulfilled.

It is in the temple that Mormons learn how to lead lives that will merit future godlike status. Here the reasons for existence are explained and a person is enabled to participate in the Plan of Salvation. Mormons believe that they have led a long pre-existence where they received instruction as God's spirit children. Their present corporeal existence contains further instruction which will be useful in a future state. Entrance to the highest degree of the afterlife depends upon the quality of one's life here and of the rules and blessings taught and received in the temple. One temple ceremony is Celestial Marriage, which is for a Mormon the key to achieving "eternal progression." Celestial marriage binds a couple together "for time and eternity," which means both here on earth and in the next life. The ceremony permits a couple to procreate in the next life and bring forth spirit children in the event that the couple attains the ultimate level of celestial being. Sometimes parents can have their children "sealed" to them so that they may live as a family unit in the hereafter. Men also receive various aspects of the priesthood in the temple.

Temple rites were referred to in the Old Testament and also in the early Christian church. Their existence is based on man's inability to attain God's purpose without his revealed help. From time to time through history, God has given such help and is doing so again today, in "the greatest and grandest era in human history" (McConkie 1966:227). The modern era is also the last one, which will see the end of history as it is currently known.

Any branch of Christianity also faces the problem of saving those who lived before the gospel was announced. For Mormons this problem is solved by taking one's dead kinsmen through the temple rites by proxy, so that if the deceased individuals choose to hear and to elect the true church they will be equipped to enter into the highest form of the afterlife. Many millions of dead relatives have been taken vicariously through the temple rites, which include baptism, ordination to the priesthood in the case of men, and marriage. Work for the dead is by far the most frequent temple activity.

While the temple rituals are the most significant ones for Mormons, they are relatively infrequent as compared to the chapel services where Mormons come together weekly and sometimes even daily. The Sacrament Meeting, which is the central spiritual event of a Mormon's week, takes place each Sunday in the chapel and lasts about an hour and a half. It is composed of talks, which are analogous to sermons, hymn-singing, and the administration of the sacrament. Mormons of every age are also expected to attend Sunday School each week, and men must go to priesthood meetings each Sunday. As a result, a Mormon man may spend most of Sunday at the chapel. Both the Sunday School and priesthood meetings have manuals of instruction, prepared at church headquarters in Salt Lake City, which provide an outline for the class or meeting but do not govern the content, which is expected to be extemporaneous.

Every fourth week is Fast and Testimony Sunday. For a day before it Mormons observe a complete fast, and during the regular Sunday Sacrament Meeting they offer their testimony. Starting with small children but centering on adults, those in the congregation who feel so moved may reaffirm their belief in the gospel and the church. Often citing a solved problem or crisis lived through, they tell how their belief aided them in the moment of trial. The intention of these personal, sometimes moving episodes is to fortify belief.

In addition to these rituals, there are conferences. The most important are the semiannual conferences of the whole church held in April and October, usually in Salt Lake City. Presided over by the church hierarchy, these meetings often serve to address key issues.

Since Mormonism has no professional clergy, services at all levels are led by laymen. Any one service is directed by many people, depending on the purpose of each segment. For the weekly Sacrament Meeting, members of the congregation form the choir, lead the singing, do the talking, and distribute the sacrament. The service is flexible, composed of an easy blend of extemporaneous content in fixed categories like announcements, testimonials, and the administration of the sacrament. For all the informality of its content, the service has a predictable sequence and a few formulas, like the short blessing of the sacrament and the frequently repeated testimony about the truth of the gospel and of Smith's prophetic calling.

Since rituals are affirmations of ideology, the two major Mormon rituals—chapel and temple—affirm two critical beliefs. The Sacrament Meeting celebrates the truth of the gospel, whose central message is Christ's atonement. The sacrament symbolizes the atonement by recalling Christ's sacrifice and offering the symbols of it for each person to consume. The Sacrament Meeting thereby reifies the central act of the gospel, the core of historic Christianity, for its participants, and also celebrates the community of all Mormons through the act performed by Christ on behalf of each.

The second principle common to all Mormons, the truth of Joseph Smith's church, is celebrated in the other important Mormon ritual, the temple rite. In this ritual, where an individual stands before God, the believer gains admission to the celestial kingdom. It therefore reaffirms the church's uniqueness and truth, showing the path to ultimate glory.

Even though the events of the church's history have been varied, with the church sometimes benefiting from circumstances and sometimes not, its contacts both with the external world and within itself have been entirely channeled through a firmly established social organization. From the bottom up, the church has dozens of organizations of varying degrees of specialization. The whole church is organized into wards (parishes), which are presided over by a bishop (pastor) and two councilors (assistants). Wards average about seven hundred people but can be smaller or larger. New wards are created through the subdivision of old ones grown too large for their organization to handle; a thousand members pushes the limit. In areas where the church is new and members are few, branches are set up instead of wards.

The bishops are appointed at Salt Lake City headquarters but with much local input in the decision-making process. Choosing a bishop is certainly not a democratic process, but neither is it as hierarchical as sometimes portrayed.

Wards are collected into larger administrative divisions or dioceses, called Stakes of Zion, which contain ten wards more or less. Each is headed by a stake president who also has two councilors. Stakes are the major link between the local areas and Salt Lake City. Today the church leadership usually knows stake presidents personally but is much less likely to know bishops. Within the last few years stakes have been gathered into regions for ease of administration. The region has not yet become a major organizational link in the church, nor is its function manifest to most Mormons.

The stake has regular meetings of all its members. Stakes now hold conferences twice a year on Sunday, when they replace the usual Sacrament Meeting. But in the nineteenth century stake conferences met four times a year, brought together all the people in an area, and served as both major social events and key economic regulators. Their functions, other than preaching, are now much curtailed: whereas in the last century they lasted two and a half days, today they take a morning or afternoon. Despite the changes, church organization seems to be little different from what it was in the nineteenth century. Although many new functions have been added and others lost, none of the names of the organizations have changed, and to the Mormon the history of the church organization is one of historical continuity, not change.

Above the stake and regional level is the highest level of church leadership. These General Authorities consist of the president with his two councilors, the Quorum of the Twelve Apostles with their assistants, the church patriarch, the presiding bishop, and a few other officers. These men actually run the church. They make the decisions, handle the power, money, and human resources, and lead the chief rituals. They are the public as well as the private leadership.

The president, who has often been a descendent of the Smith family, inherits Joseph Smith's mantle as prophet.

The apostle with greatest seniority becomes president on the death of a president. The Quorum of the Twelve was set up by Smith originally as missionaries; however, since the early days in Utah they have become the real managing group in the church. Today many people are called as apostles after becoming successful in business. These men often sit on the boards of directors of companies which have large holdings in Utah or in which the church itself has a major interest. The assistants to the apostles do much of the traveling to local congregations that is required of church leaders. The presiding bishop heads a large organization within the church devoted to handling its fiscal needs.

The entire organization from top to bottom is composed of laymen. Only the men at the top are permanent employees receiving living allowances that amount to salaries. In this sense, the church is developing a class of official functionaries or ecclesiastical bureaucrats, who might be called a clergy. This is not true at any other level in the church, since all other leadership posts revolve and are unsalaried.

The major public function of the highest level of church leaders is visiting wards and stakes throughout the church. Since the early days, apostles have visited Mormon groups. Once settlers began to spread out through the Western desert, the periodic visits of these high and powerful men guaranteed the links necessary to preserve unity. Such visits maintained, as they still do, a clear line between church decisions and policies, on the one hand, and aid of all sorts to local groups on the other. For the towns spread out in central Arizona, visits by one, two, and even three apostles occurred every year, especially during the early years of settlement.

The church runs a massive bureaucracy in Salt Lake City, employing thousands of people to handle its domain. There are well-staffed offices to run all publications, public relations, genealogical research, architectural planning of church buildings, welfare, tithing, record-keeping, and the huge library of original documents. Each of these offices is tied to an apostle who links it to the Quorum of the Twelve.

As a result of its layman status, the church leadership has

a special quality. There is no school for leadership in the church, no seminary in the usual Christian sense. Both in the nineteenth century and today, apostles and other high leaders rose to their positions through demonstrating ability in their regular employment and in their work for the church. Most church leaders in the nineteenth century were competent as farmers, managers, organizers, or financiers, often more so than many others in the same fields. Consequently, in times of crisis anywhere in the church, the leader who visited the afflicted Saints could pitch in, give advice, direct operations, and gain support because, in addition to being an authority in the spiritual sense, he was one in the practical sense. He represented a unique and powerful union between principles and practice. When these elements are joined, the church appears real and caring, while life seems infused with religion. As the nature of crises and problems changes, so do the criteria for choosing leaders, and so does the meaning of whatever religious ideas and values are invoked to cope with and explain crises. In this way a continual union is maintained between religion and the demands of daily life. Mormons find their religion effective in solving everyday problems because the leaders are professional problem-solvers, who are convinced that those very problems are the main business of the religion.

Whereas the leadership structure of the church holds only a small fraction of the male members, all other Mormon men are organized into the priesthood. This divinely established category, along with the Mormon idea of the family and the mystical blood tie of every Mormon to ancient Israel, conceptually unifies the whole body of believers.

When founding his church, Joseph Smith employed an organization that he regarded as identical with the early Christian church, which he called the priesthood. To Mormons, the priesthood is both an organizational and a mystical category: priests govern because their power is from God. Since the priesthood had existed at various pre-Mormon times, God, in ordaining Joseph Smith, merely refounded the institution, making its benefits available once more to mankind. There are two basic priesthood orders:

Aaronic and Melchizedec. The first is mainly for inexperienced males, usually youngsters, and the second is for
mature adults. Both orders are subdivided into three grades,
most of which a Mormon passes through during early life,
entering the highest grade at the time of full adulthood,
which coincides with setting up a family. Every priesthood
order has prescribed duties, as expected in a church without
a professional clergy.

The total priesthood is regarded as the whole of the
church leadership. It begins to absorb a Mormon early.
From twelve to eighteen, a young man belongs to the
Aaronic order, where he progresses from deacon to teacher
to priest. Originally these posts had the important function
of keeping harmony in the church, but today they are
mostly apprenticeships. Under the supervision of adults,
boys and young men are taught the functions of church leadership in the great variety of tasks that a lay clergy in a pragmatic church must know.

Most young Mormon men go on self-financed missions for
two years in an area selected by the church. When they go
on a mission, they are ordained elders and enter the second
major priesthood category, called Melchizedec. This happens somewhere between eighteen and twenty. After elder,
the two higher orders of the Melchizedec priesthood are seventy and high priest, and these are not entered on the basis
of age. All of the church's highest administrative posts are
held by high priests. A seventy is a more specialized category, usually involving adults who are missionaries at home.
All these priesthood types are represented in each ward, and
the priests meet by rank on a weekly basis for instruction in
doctrine and other church matters.

For Mormon women the major organization is the
Women's Relief Society, founded by Joseph Smith's wife
Emma. This is one of the general welfare arms of the church,
which works with the local bishop overseeing family welfare, poor relief, and similar tasks in the ward. Neither this
nor any other women's organization gives any clue to the
central conceptual role of women, especially as wives and
mothers, in the church. The highest heavenly rewards are

predicated on a married life that produces children. Given the singular emphasis on the family in Mormonism, both now and in the hereafter, the centrality of women in the religion is inevitable.

All ranks of the church's priesthood are put to work in the ward. All ward organizations, male and female, have a head appointed by the bishop and usually two councilors chosen by the head, who is a priest unless the group is presided over by a woman. Of the many different organizations found in a Mormon ward, some of the more basic are the Sunday School, which includes the whole population; the Young Men's and Young Women's Mutual Improvement Associations, a YMCA-YWCA variant; Boy Scouts and Girl Scouts; weekly doctrine classes, including Primary for youngsters and Seminary for junior high school and high school students; Home Teachers, who visit all ward families in the role of home missionaries and handle local disputes. These and at least a dozen other organizations keep Mormons continually busy in church-related activities. Church organizations encompass all of life, excluding not a single organizable domain, and every effort is made to include as much activity and as many people as possible, so that the church will be as embracing as a society and as caring as a family, upon which it is modeled.

Running parallel to the priesthood is a category both more abstract and more universal. All Mormons, whether born or converted, belong to the House of Israel. They are all new Israelites, or new Jews. A Mormon learns which part of the House of Israel he or she descends from during a Patriarchal Blessing, which is a personalized revelation, usually for a teenager, which identifies his or her spiritual inheritance from Israel. This common heritage establishes an ancient heritage and a unique modern identity, which unifies and homogenizes the diffuse membership of the church.

Cutting across these three categories—church organization, the priesthood, and the descent from Israel—is the Mormon family. Family organization, according to Mormons, is the basic building block of the church. It is divinely instituted. In it the organizational categories of the church are realized as well as taught. Every family member belongs to the ward and stake organization, every member has his or her House of Israel blood revealed, and every male is a priest and every woman allows him to fulfill that priestly role. The family thus vivifies the organizational structure of the church even as the church legitimizes the family. Here then are both the social and symbolic organizations of Mormons.

3

Tithing: The Regulation of Ecological Diversity

Starting in 1876 and continuing through the next decade, Mormons from central and southern Utah went south in wagons and on foot down into Arizona, crossing the Colorado Plateau. A huge table land, the Colorado Plateau extends along the western edge of the Rocky Mountains from southern Utah and Colorado into northern New Mexico and the northeastern third of Arizona. Averaging 6000 feet, the plateau gradually rises as it goes south, reaching its maximum height along its southern rim in central Arizona.

On entering Arizona proper, the Saints had to cross the Colorado River. Although they accomplished this feat at the Mormon outpost called Lee's Ferry and not at the Grand Canyon, which is one mile deep and thirteen across, the Mormons nonetheless negotiated one of the major physiographic barriers of North America. They then traveled the southern rim of the plateau to enter the vast drainage of the Little Colorado River. Tributary to the Colorado proper only in a technical sense, the Little Colorado drains almost the entire northeastern quarter of Arizona. Rising at 11,000 feet in the mountains that form the southern edge of the plateau, it flows northwest to join the Colorado itself just before that river enters the Grand Canyon. But long before it joins the Colorado, this sister river forms a series of shallow valleys which are studded with mountain ranges and, in the south, with lava flows and cinder cones of recent origin. The valleys are often filled to great depth with eroded materials such as sand, gravel, and clay. This typically Southwestern landscape is composed of brilliantly colored and sculptured sandstone, eroded mesas, volcanic tuffs, and box canyons. It is, in short, a desert.

High in the southern part of the region rainfall may reach 13 inches a year, and lower in the north it may reach 8 inches. Given that the Little Colorado is a year-round stream only in its upper reaches, this small amount of rainfall provides a frail ecological setting for both farmers and cattle raisers. Added to the scant moisture is the high variation in frost-free days per year: "There are, on the average, 140 days between the last frost of the spring and the first frost of the fall. This figure has varied from 90 to 210 days for the years for which records exist" (Martin and Plog 1973:38–39). Because most cereals take four months to mature, agricultural existence on the plateau is problematical from the standpoint of temperature alone. The higher altitudes, though better watered, are colder. As a result, the number of locales suitable for farming are rare indeed.

The Mormons entered this grand and complex geography with almost no prior knowledge, with meager provisions, and with horses and a few iron tools as their only equipment for harnessing a region whose own well-adapted aboriginal population had been shrinking steadily since the fifteenth century. Initially, the Mormons faced at least as hard a time as they had upon entering the Great Salt Lake valley thirty years earlier. An account of their situation in 1878 at the end of the first winter on the Little Colorado tells the tale:

> The Brethren had been laboring in the United Order and many of them (or all) were poor and spring found them destitute of both clothing and provisions, their slender stocks that they had left Utah with were entirely exhausted. This with their scanty numbers compelled them to postpone their labor on the dam for the season, and to scatter in different directions in search of work. Some went on the road freighting. Joseph S. Gordon and others made a trip to Elmoro, Colorado with horseteams freighting wool, others scattered in different places working to obtain bread-stuffs for themselves and families for the season (History and Settlement of the Snowflake Area 21).

The intense privations experienced by Mormon settlers had to some extent been foreseen by church authorities like Brigham Young, who clearly intended that the practice of communal living, including eating at a common table, was to alleviate the harsh conditions. This foresight paid off, for while the best locations were being scouted, successful wheat harvests were soon produced in the United Order settlements. These had the double effect of attracting more people from Utah and ensuring further colonization within the Arizona Territory.

Four United Order towns were founded, the most prominent being Sunset and St. Joseph, the others being Old Taylor and Brigham City. These towns were often used as stopover sites for the peopling of the rest of the Little Colorado area. For example, land on Silver Creek, a southern tributary of the Little Colorado, was bought by a well-to-do Mormon, James Flake, from a recently settled non-Mormon rancher, James Stimson. This land, which included several well-watered valleys, proved to be the best in the region. Called Snowflake, it was the biggest Mormon settlement in the region and within ten years held around a thousand people. Its effect on the first settlers was electric:

On July 21st, 1878, Wm. J. Flake and James Gale with their families moved into the valley. The hardships and trials that they had undergone since they left Utah caused the sisters to shed tears of joy when they came in sight of the valley covered with its mantel of green, and they realized that they were again to have a home and a resting place. They had been nearly one year moving about in their wagons and had worked exceedingly hard for a short time at Old Taylor trying to make a home but had failed, and now that they had found one they were overjoyed (History and Settlement of the Snowflake Area 25).

Initial settlement throughout Arizona was hard because the area, though already occupied, was in a state somewhere between ongoing frontier exploration and the arrival of civil order. People were scattered across northern and eastern Arizona: the Apache, Navajo, and Hopi Indians; Mexicans near the New Mexico border; a few Anglo farmers; an occasional Jewish trader; the U.S. Army overseeing the

Apaches; a few railroad people arriving with the Southern Pacific in the early 1880s; and a smattering of merchants and still fewer civil administrators. The railroad soon brought cattlemen, sheepmen, horse and cattle thieves, gunmen, murderers, thugs, and the whole spectrum of economic pirates that naturally springs up in areas where wealth is available but there is no real sovereign power. Northeastern Arizona at this time was a no man's land, to be either taken by the powerful—Congress simply gave away thousands of square miles of it as bounty to the railroad—or held by the persistent, such as the Indians. Although the Mormons encountered only a few of these forces when they arrived in the late 1870s, they met the rest as soon as the railroad moved through in 1881. Despite competition among these groups, two conditions prevailed that were essential to Mormon operation. For all practical purposes, the population of gentiles was so small and scattered that Mormons lived in isolation. Further, no one power was dominant in the area, which meant that any group with sufficient resources could carve out a domain. The domains were of two kinds: solid, compact areas, such as Indian agricultural lands and Mormon villages, or networks of raiding vectors, such as those used by the Apache or by Anglo horse and cattle thieves. Until the late 1880s all these groups were jockeying with each other for position, none of them able to become dominant. Each had a measure of autonomy in its own area, which derived in part from keeping out competitors. Thus the frailty of the setting on the Little Colorado had as much to do with social as with environmental factors.

When any one of the social groups joined with any other, as several did against the Mormons in the late 1880s, the result was persecution. For the better part of their first decade in the area the Mormons were hounded, having once again raised fears of clannish action or peculiar practices. Their opponents turned what little political power there was against them. In describing such moves made by a group of gentiles composed of Anglo businessmen, cattlemen, Mexicans, and railroad interests, the Mormons reported:

They have stuffed the ballot boxes. They have thrown out our votes without counting them. They have deprived our people of holding office when elected, and of voting at the polls. They have raised our taxes higher than assessed without our knowledge. They have squandered the public funds. They have instigated the Indians and Mexicans to prey upon our stocks. They have called our most respected sisters prostitutes [referring to plural marriage] and our children bastards. They have advocated lynch law and the use of the rope and shotgun upon our best and most worthy citizens and for no other cause than that they were "Mormons" (History and Settlement of the Snowflake Area 84).

The Mormons were also caught between the warring sheep and cattle interests. Their position was difficult, not because Mormons had strong affiliations with either side —although they themselves usually raised cattle not sheep —but because they suffered from the depredations of the outlaws whom the war created:

During the fore part of the year 1887 . . . strong feeling sprang up between the sheep men and cow boys in the west part of the country, this had been increasing for some time. The seat of this trouble was west of us and between the Tweeksberries and the Grahams [both non-Mormons], the former being sheep men. One or two sheep herders had been killed and the cow boys had gone so far as to offer a reward for the scalps of sheep herders.

About Aug. 9, 1887 some of the cow boys went over in that district and were fired on, two being killed. The notorious Payne of black snake and pistol notoriety was one of them, which made all honest men feel more safe. This trouble increased until several others were killed; all had characters.

About Sept. 4 Sheriff A. R. Owens attempted to arrest one of this lawless gang, a man who was known as Andy Cooper. He refused to give up and the sheriff killed him and two others, wounding the 4th in the struggle. The sheriff from Yavapai [County] killed two of the gang in Pleasant Valley, this made about 21 that had been killed in a very short time which improved things very much for the honest stock raisers.

About August 11, 1888 James Scott, James Stott and Jeff Wilson were hung near the Verdy road on the mountain by a party supposed to be a vigalent committee of some thirty men mostly from the Pleasant Valley district. The bodies hung there about a week when a party from Holbrook went out and buried them. This may have been a high handed piece of business but it certainly had a good effect as many who were implicated in stealing left the County (History and Settlement of the Snowflake Area 155–156, 169).

The relative absence of all forms of power over the natural and social environments extended to other areas. Not only were there only three steam engines, almost no steel, and no modern technical knowledge about arid area farming, but there was also no civil bureaucracy, no police, no army, and no court system. When the rudiments of these last did appear, they were weak, being used punitively by whatever local power could maneuver them.

Technological backwardness and the unfamiliarity of conditions on the frontier—new climates, foreign land-scapes, exotic flora, dangerous fauna, and difficult living conditions in general—increased human suffering in the area well beyond what is normally associated with the life of the period. The toll of epidemics from smallpox, influenza, and diphtheria was especially high in Arizona. Some of this was owing to the fact that no medical service was available until the turn of the century, which was another aspect of having no control over the environment:

"During the months of September and October [1887] there was a great amount of sickness in and about Snowflake. Many of the children died with what was supposed to be a form of diptheria. Z. B. Decker lost 4, Leroy Beely lost 3, all he had, and many others lost some one, some two. These sad losses cast quite a gloom over our settlements" (History and Settlement of the Snowflake Area 156).

Conditions like these, added to the difficult ecological circumstances, produced a continually shifting and even transient population in the Mormon communities:

The crops for 1880 were very light and that of Brigham City almost an entire failure. The saints there became so much dissatisfied that some of them moved to the upper Gila country in

Pima County, others located in the settlements of the Eastern Arizona Stake.

There have been quite a number of men called to St. Johns [from Utah in 1885–1886], of whom perhaps about two thirds have come, numbering about 250. Of that number there are about 140 remaining, some being dissatisfied with the country and some with the people ... about this time the feeling was so bitter against the saints that they felt the necessity of carrying fire arms (History and Settlement of the Snowflake Area 16, 96).

This combination of factors was sufficient to make settlement precarious and life dangerous. It was also more than enough to bring out the not-too-deeply buried Calvinism in Mormonism. There was much talk of trials sent by God to purge his Saints, who retained their faith probably because it was all they had to keep them alive. That it did just that in a material sense is clear

The first towns settled by the Mormons were the United Order forts, which were palisades along whose inside walls were lean-to apartments for each family. All the apartments looked onto a central courtyard. Later settlements were laid out according to the Plat of Zion, which gave them the same general appearance: broad streets arranged in a regular grid near the center of which was a meetinghouse; rows of trees bordering the streets and fields; canals running beside them; and gardens.

In the first decade life in these towns was neither comfortable nor beautiful. The early houses were wagon beds set on the ground with canvas covers, which were used while log houses with pole and dirt roofs were being built. These too left much to be desired:

"After a dirt roof had weathered one or two wet years, its supports became rotted and it 'falls in' when least expected. If the family on such occasions was wrapped in profound and peaceful slumber, the rude and sudden awakening caused considerable excitement. The family immediately commenced to 'dig out' emerging in all kinds of evening attire. If the family was outside on such an occasion, they immediately commenced to 'dig in' " (Coleman in Peterson 1973:260).

Such an environment created a niche for more than just human inhabitants:

> The "Parson" had several vacant houses and we moved in rent free. Those were built of cottonwood logs, chinked, and dobed, dirt floor and roof and consisted of from one to three rooms. We moved in immediately and set up housekeeping. Next morning we moved all the beds out, set the wagon boxes off the wagons and used them for bed rooms . . . the bed bugs were so bad that we just couldn't sleep in those houses. We finally had to take our meals outside. The bed bugs would fall down into the vittles when we were eating (Coleman in Peterson 1973:259).

This fragile and uncomfortable world of the Mormon pioneers, which required bravery and dedication, produced personalities to match its demands. Mormon diaries, journals, letters, and newspapers are full of such people. The leader who engineered the initial success of the effort to colonize Arizona was Lot Smith. Smith was chosen by Brigham Young to lead the first settlers into Arizona and to establish them in communal towns. Using unremunerated human labor maintained at subsistence levels, coupled with leadership that was autocratic even by Mormon standards, Smith between 1876 and 1886 built a successful network of four United Order towns and their associated enterprises, which underwrote all further development along the Little Colorado. He supplied grain and feed in hard times, lumber for new houses, cattle to pay for land purchases, and all from the property produced and held in common under his direction. His care for the newer, noncommunal towns in their infancy was often their sole guarantee of continued existence. His storehouse was used by Salt Lake head-quarters as the source of goods for distribution to needy set-tlements which would eventually outsize and outlast his own. By the mid-1880s when the other towns were be-ginning to blossom, the United Order communities were failing for the same reason that they had worked in the first place: they taxed individuals to their material and emotional limits.

Smith was the kind of leader whom utopias often produce.

He was a tyrant, who used exhortations to prayerful humility to produce self-induced submission in his subordinates, and when that failed, he used violence. He had much in common with other barons of his age: he amassed a fortune by Mormon standards, and he ruled large numbers of people for a time. But he had one option denied to all other contemporary buccaneers: he could legitimately have many women as his wives, and he had eight. Not satisfied with collecting cattle, money, subjects, and women, he seems to have treated the last so poorly that Wilford Woodruff, a friend and an apostle who was soon to be president of the church, admonished him continually:

Now Brother Lot I see you make a [slighting] remark concerning your wives and family. I want to say a few words upon the same subject. Now I think you have got 8 as good women as your wives with you as the Lord or any body else made in our day and generation. They are good virtuous women and have always been true to you, and the women righteously demand at your hands, love, affection, and kind treatment. And it is not a weakness in any good man to manifest these principles to his wives and children. And I have thought with other of your friends that this was (frequently?) the fault of Brother Lot Smith (Woodruff 1882).

The towns led by Lot Smith eventually failed because he was too hard on people, who could see no improvement in their individual lives, and because more productive towns had been established. These other settlements were led by Jesse N. Smith, no relative to Lot Smith, who entered the Little Colorado area shortly after Lot and was charged by Brigham Young to set up the major settlements along the Little Colorado. He founded two dozen noncommunal towns and guided over three thousand people spread out over thousands of square miles. He led the colony for thirty years, holding it together through more adversity than God ought to have inflicted on any one people, let alone those who were supposed to be his chosen.

The specific circumstances encountered in maintaining life on the Smiths' frontier scenario did not differ much from the rest of the Western settlements, for the Little Colorado River of Arizona is a variant of the Western desert that stretches from the Canadian border into northern Mexico. The region can be divided into zones according to topography, soil type, and climate, any one criterion being fairly crude as a measure of environmental variety, but all together revealing the natural complexity of the area. The borders of the Little Colorado region enclose about 12,800 square miles and contain eleven different environmental zones. The whole area, including its extension into New Mexico, is roughly an oval, with a long axis of about 160 miles running southeast to northwest along the Little Colorado River, and a short axis of about 80 miles running northeast to southwest.

The first Mormon settlements along the Little Colorado were only along the river itself and consequently only in one or two environmental zones. But within four years there was a town, or at least a cluster of families, in all of the major zones of the region. Even as an initial settlement was made along the alluvium of the river, a seasonal camp would be set up thirty and more miles to the west in forested country, where a sawmill and dairy industry would almost immediately be established. Mormon colonizers adopted an ecological strategy that attempted to utilize the resources of all of the major environmental zones and to disperse groups of families throughout the different zones as soon as they had been scouted out. Such scattering occurred for two reasons. The population limit in the original towns along the river was very low, so these towns had to become donor populations. Second, no single locale was much more favored by nature for farming than any other, and each was deficient in some major commodity, so that maximum exploitation could be achieved only by spreading the population over as wide a range of environmental zones as possible.

Once set up, every Mormon town produced essentially the same items. There was some specialization, but by far the greatest source of variation in produce sprang, not from a town's gearing itself to the produce of its own zone and excluding items grown better elsewhere, but from its producing more of what it naturally grew best. All towns produced hay, grain, livestock, dairy products, and vegetables. Many also produced molasses, lumber, and an assortment of homemade craft items like shoes and brooms, looms and farm implements. While these items varied from year to year and from town to town, they could always be found somewhere in the towns of the area. The towns exchanged products among themselves to compensate for the annual variation produced largely by environmental vagaries like rainfall and temperature. The real staying power of agrarian Mormonism in the Great Basin derived from the way in which the economic imbalance existing in any given town during any year was balanced through systematic exchange with surrounding Mormon towns.

The key to harnessing ecological variation was the tithing system, and the key to the tithing system was its place in Mormon religion. Its economic function cannot be understood apart from its religious meaning. Tithing was a divine institution and, as such, ensured the church's economic strength while guaranteeing a full share of blessings to those who paid the full tithe:

"By this principle it shall be seen whose hearts are set on doing the will of God and keeping his commandments, thereby sanctifying the Land of Zion unto God . . . By such obedience he gains the spirit of inspiration in temporal and spiritual pursuits so that in the end he is ahead financially and temporally, to say nothing of the spiritual growth that always attends such a course" (Joseph F. Smith in McConkie 1966:797–798).

Despite its complexities, the nineteenth-century tithing system followed the same general pattern all over Mormondom. The idea behind the law was that the whole community of Saints could benefit all of its segments if each individual paid an annual sum to a central point. This increment would then be used to benefit those Saints and Saintly projects most in need.

The Mormons effectively defined religious experience in

terms of managing ecological problems. The corrective
measures that are an inevitable part of any subsistence
pattern were called religious actions, and when these led to
agrarian success, it was called a religious experience,
affirming Mormonism's capacity to guarantee survival.
Seeing the desert bloom was seeing the truth of God's
working through his church. Tithing, in this context, was
the proof of a person's faithfulness, the witness of God's
blessings, and the effective means of financing crucial
activities. Obeying God's law helped to ensure the productivity of daily life, and the resulting productivity was
a guarantee of God's involvement and of the consequent
veracity of the religion.

Tithing has come to be one of a handful of official marks
of Mormon worthiness. The centrality of this institution in a
person's life is even more marked today than it was in the
nineteenth century. Part of the explanation is that, as the
accepted stereotypes of proper Mormon behavior became
broader and consequently harder to codify and measure, a
set of rational criteria was needed to identify the faithful.
Money, expressed as tithing, became one of those rational
criteria. One's standing in the church today, including
admittance to the temple, is therefore measured by tithing.
It is a precise measure, and although the information is
not directly available to one's neighbors, they do, being
neighbors, have a sense of it. So within the Mormon
community, among the hierarchs who run the church and
also among one's neighbors, the quality of the tithe is one of
the marks of the Saint.

In cash-poor Arizona in the nineteenth century, about 90
percent of the annual tithing was in kind. Tithing in the
bishop's storehouse, which usually represented what was on
hand in a farming family at any given season of the year, was
fairly representative of items that were common or scarce in
a town at any season, since people tended to turn over their
surpluses. Generally tithing also represented the best
produce available within a town at any specific time. If a
Mormon gave the choicest to the Lord, it would not go
unnoticed by God, who kept an eye on the trials of his

Saints, especially in this marginal agricultural land. Tithing demanded that one be fair with the Lord, and in small towns everybody knew who was being even-handed. But more effective than the public eye and the bishop's annual assessment of the fullness of a person's tithe was its internalized value. There was thought to be a definable relationship between giving the choicest produce as tithing and receiving the choicest of the Lord's blessings. The literal Saints had exacting expectations of the Lord's performance. And the blessings followed, in large part because of the way the Lord's anointed leadership handled the liberal tithing that was passed on to them.

Tithing, the chief means of capitalizing the economy, had two meanings for every Mormon. First, tithing gained favor with the supernatural. It was one of the major keys to the next life for, among other more spiritual requirements, without a full tithe one could not enter the temple to receive one's endowments. Second, tithing was a key to success in this life. The relationship between the tithe and worldly well-being was apparent because the feedback loop between taxation and the security it provided was short and direct.

The material benefits from tithing were visible at several regional levels. The General Tithing Office in Salt Lake City bulged with everything that could be bought or sold on the far side of the Rocky Mountains:

Here are piles of rawhide, both cow and mustang, or even pig-skin; bins of shelled corn, and cribs full of corn in the ear; wheat and rye, oats and barley; casks of salt provisions; wool, homespun, yarn, and homewoven cloths in hanks and bales; indigo; cocoons and raw silk; butter, cheese, and all manner of farm produce; even the most destructible of vegetable growths—not only potatoes, turnips, and other root crops, but green peas and beans; fruit, and young cabbages, hay, carpenters' work, boys' caps, slop-shop overalls; hemp-rope, preserves, tinware, stogies, confectionery, adobe bricks and tiles, moss and gramma mattresses; buckskin leggins, gloves, moccasins, hunting shirts, and complete suits ... These are but a minute fraction of the contents of the church Tithing Stores (Ludlow in Arrington 1958:141).

The General Tithing Office handled tithing from the whole church. It received income from every ward, which in Arizona meant every town. A bishop collected the tithing and assumed the responsibility for disposing of it as the church directed. Since most tithing was in kind, it was impossible in Arizona, as in many other places outside the valleys of central Utah, to send goods the 700 or 800 miles to Salt Lake City. Cash alone was wanted at church headquarters, so the bishop was required to dispose of the tithing in such a fashion that the flow of cash to Salt Lake would be as large a part of ward tithing as possible. In Arizona and much of Mormondom, only a fraction of tithing, 10 to 25 percent in cash, actually found its way to church headquarters, so that in the process of disposal the bishops had tremendous surpluses, which they funneled into a massive, although local, redistribution network.

The records to keep track of the variation list the tithes of each individual as well as the total amounts produced by each town annually, thus forming a long record of production, marketing, and consumption for all the colonies of Mormondom including the towns along the Little Colorado River (see Appendix). The tithing records from these towns, representing the forced savings of the Mormon communities, are an index to the amount of local, self-generated capital. They show that surplus appeared almost exclusively in kind, not cash. They indicate the relative proportions of produce and livestock in any one town in any year. Finally, they show the variation among towns as well as the fluctuation in any one town over the years.

In Pinedale, for example, a town in the forested zone over 6000 feet high with about a hundred people in twenty families, livestock, one of the principal sources of income, shows great variation over ten years (table 1). The variation resulted from a number of factors. The drop between 1893 and 1897 was a result of severe overgrazing of range land, drought, cattle thieves, and a disastrous drop in cattle prices in the national beef market. The national market did not normally play a significant role in the Mormon economy, since Mormon farmers did not produce for it, but the stake

Table 1. *Livestock Tithing in Pinedale, Arizona, 1888–1898.*[a]

Year	Dollar value[b]	Percentage of total
1888	44	28
1889	75	23
1890	17	4
1891	35	14
1892	27	11
1893	15	9
1894	0	0
1895	13	10
1896	0	0
1897	12	4
1898	58	18

Source: Record of Stake Funds 1882–1901:89–91, 170–174, 245.

a. The only available figures show that in 1879 church officials set prices for cows at $14.00–20.00 per head and yearlings at $6.00–7.00. (Smith, Lot 1879: October 29).

b. Dollar fractions are rounded.

maintained a cattle herd of beef received in tithing, and this was sometimes sold on the market. These particular historical factors, however, should not mask the fact that variation in this major resource would have occurred for one reason if not for another.

The figures for grain in the same town show a similar fluctuation over the same ten years (table 2). Grain included wheat at $2.00 per bushel, barley at $1.60 per bushel, oats at $1.75 per bushel, and corn at $1.90 per bushel. These prices were normally set by church officials to discourage private trading among the Saints: there was to be no market speculation, no price cutting, no catering to demands outside the community, and no producing of unusual quantities for profit (Smith and Woodruff 1879: October 29). With prices regulated for the whole region, there was little possibility of buying cheap and selling dear so as to make a profit on one's coreligionists. Furthermore, there was little incentive to hold back any goods from tithing so as to make a profit by disposing of them on the equivalent of a black market. Although some of these practices undoubtedly existed, judging by the harsh words recorded in meeting minutes, those same words vied successfully with the profit motive to

Table 2. *Grain Tithing in Pinedale, Arizona, 1888-1898.*[a]

Year	Dollar value	Percentage of total
1888	21	11
1889	69	21
1890	214	52
1891	137	53
1892	143	60
1893	78	47
1894	132	59
1895	39	30
1896	68	32
1897	121	43
1898	91	28

Source: Record of Stake Funds 1882–1901:89–91, 170–174, 245.

a. For 1890 and 1891 the record-keeper coupled hay with grain.

control such behavior. As a result, the figures for cereals are a fair reflection of the variation in prices and percentages of the actual volume produced by a town.

The grain and tithing figures from St. Joseph, later called Joseph City, show similarly unstable conditions over an eleven-year period (tables 3–4). This town, situated on the bank of the Little Colorado River at 4200 feet, had about 110 people in roughly sixteen families. Its most productive crops

Table 3. *Grain Tithing in St. Joseph (Joseph City), Arizona, 1887-1898.*

Year	Dollar value	Percentage of total
1887	157	25
1888	217	29
1889	268	31
1890	376	31
1891	97	16
1892	183	27
1893	171	23
1894	100	16
1895	76	10
1896	117	16
1897	119	13
1898	103	19

Source: Record of Stake Funds 1882–1901:104, 106–111, 113–119, 213.

Table 4. *Livestock Tithing in St. Joseph (Joseph City), Arizona, 1887–1898.*

Year	Dollar value	Percentage of total
1887	229	37
1888	228	30
1889	339	39
1890	243	20
1891	199	34
1892	161	24
1893	41	6
1894	26	6
1895	64	8
1896	60	8
1897	122	13
1898	112	9

Source: Record of Stake Funds 1882–1901:104, 106–111, 113–119, 213.

were grain (mostly wheat) and livestock, which included a large number of dairy cattle. At Woodruff, situated in the same ecological zone as St. Joseph, there was a similar variation over the same period in vegetables and dairy products (table 5). In 1888 and 1889 no vegetables at all were tithed, just dairy products.

The figures for Taylor provide another illustration of the variation in basic foodstuffs from year to year in the

Table 5. *Vegetable and Dairy Tithing in Woodruff, Arizona, 1887–1898.*

Year	Dollar value	Percentage of total
1887	19	5
1888	20	5
1889	49	8
1890	32	4
1891	34	4
1892	48	6
1893	57	10
1894	140	24
1895	107	16
1896	106	17
1897	125	17
1898	107	12

Source: Record of Stake Funds 1882–1901:160–165, 178–187, 250.

Mormon communities. Taylor and its sister town, Snowflake, both of them located on Silver Creek, a spring-fed, nonsilty tributary of the Little Colorado, are in the most favored area of the whole river system, having plentiful water and a reliable growing season. Snowflake, in fact, the most prosperous of the two dozen or so towns, shows a far greater stability in its annual tithing, item by item, than does any other town. But comparatively well-endowed Taylor shows considerable variation in hay, one of its main crops (table 6). The figures from Taylor are indices to the annual production, since they represent between 10 and 15 percent of the total livestock, wheat, feed, and any other crops produced in any specific year, thus demonstrating the annual variation and the unpredictability of the contents of the storeroom.

Rearrangement of the tithing data by product shows a similarly sharp seasonal variation over the whole region during a four-year period (table 7). Two patterns emerge from a comparison of the figures. First, in dollar values, there was a production rise from 1888 to 1889 and a decrease in 1892 and 1893. Apart from this trend, the history of grain production in any one town was independent of the history of production in any other. When paired by similarity of ecological zone, the matching towns are St. Joseph and

Table 6. *Hay Tithing in Taylor, Arizona, 1887–1898.*

Year	Dollar value	Percentage of total
1887	295	30
1888	312	24
1889	0	0
1890	493	29
1891	658	48
1892	470	30
1893	325	29
1894	439	35
1895	318	32
1896	461	40
1897	270	24
1898	280	23

Source: Record of Stake Funds 1882–1901:140–147, 152–156, 158–159, 220–222.

Table 7. *Grain Tithing in Little Colorado Towns, 1888–1889 and 1892–1893.*

Ward	1888		1889		1892		1893	
	$	%	$	%	$	%	$	%
St. Joseph	217	29	268	31	183	27	171	23
Woodruff	131	32	219	36	139	15	52	9
Taylor	375	29	617	40	283	18	190	17
Snowflake	537	18	989	35	503	15	427	15
Showlow	67	24	148	36	139	25	75	29
Pinedale	21	11	69	21	143	60	78	47
Total	1348		2310		1390		993	

Source: Record of Stake Funds 1882–1901:89–251.

Woodruff, Taylor and Snowflake, Showlow and Pinedale. Even within a pair, the produce from a crop could vary widely from year to year. For example, St. Joseph tithed $183 in grain in 1892 and $171 a year later, staying practically constant, whereas Woodruff produced $139 in grain in 1892 and dropped to $52 a year later. Rises and declines were not related to each other and thus posed two problems. The most common problem was the scarcity resulting from low yields. The other problem was the difficulty of turning a surplus into cash or into the produce needed because it either could not be grown or had not been grown in sufficient quantity. Insufficiencies regarding some item or other faced every town at least once a year, as illustrated by livestock production between these Arizona communities over a four-year period (table 8). Livestock was the prime commodity produced by these towns and the most negotiable commodity possessed by Mormons in dealing with the rest of the world.

The exchange network which handled cattle and all other goods, scarce or plentiful, operated at three different levels: within a town, between towns, and between Salt Lake City and the Arizona communities. At the most local level, family heads tithed, and others in a family were encouraged to participate. Children and teenagers could contribute their own labor; a housewife, who regarded eggs and butter as her province, could tithe them. A commodity was tithed as it came available: eggs and butter were brought to the bishop's

Table 8. *Livestock Tithing in Little Colorado Towns, 1888–1889 and 1892–1893.*

Ward	1888		1889		1892		1893	
	$	%	$	%	$	%	$	%
St. Joseph	228	30	339	39	161	24	41	6
Woodruff	84	21	78	13	259	30	136	24
Taylor	115	9	74	5	165	11	105	10
Snowflake	652	22	593	21	739	22	459	16
Showlow	33	12	18	4	139	27	98	37
Pinedale	44	24	75	23	27	11	15	9
Total	1156		1177		1490		854	

Source: Record of Stake Funds 1882–1901:89–251.

storehouse daily or weekly, crops when they ripened, pigs when they littered, and sheep and cattle once a year at lambing and roundup. People rarely waited for the end of the year to divide their increase, and with the possible exception of cash, tithing was paid at the season of abundance. Fall produced the largest stores in the local tithing office. In general, this method of payment meant that tithes represented a direct proportion of what every family produced.

Once the tithing was contributed, it had to be distributed in order to be useful, and several institutions served as an effective network through which goods and labor flowed in and out of all the towns along the Little Colorado. At the local level a town's tithing offices consisted of storage cellars, bins, barns, pens, and yards. They usually occupied a central location in town, were often manned on a daily basis, and were open to the public. Although selling was not their expressed purpose, any bishop would willingly accept cash for any product on hand and would commonly exchange one kind of product for another.

Beyond this sort of exchange, there were a number of standard uses for tithing and procedures for redistributing it. Before tithing left a ward, 10 percent of the annual yield went to the bishop for his family's personal use. Depending on the town and the circumstances, from 1 to 25 percent of a year's tithing went to the poor, usually widows and families struck by disaster. Poor relief was usually negligible, hovering much closer to 1 percent than to 25 percent. This was not an index to stinginess but reflected the personal care that Mormons took of each other—care that was face-to-face, not institutional. Bishops paid out a portion of tithing to the local ward for public works and to other wards in times of disaster. They also systematically exchanged plentiful goods for scarce ones in surrounding towns.

These redistributive institutions were not responsible for informing the bishops or the people about which products were either plentiful or scarce throughout the region, but without some systematic knowledge of such variation, exchange would have been either impossible or inefficient. That information was provided systematically and accurately by the bishop's reports at the Quarterly Stake Conferences. These reports, read publicly, provided precise information and, because of their sacred context, guaranteed that people were neither hiding surpluses nor covering up failures to produce. Such reports spread the information needed to make distribution effective and were necessary both to even out and to counterbalance the self-sufficiency that each family and every town aimed at by religious directive.

All families and towns raised the same basic foodstuffs as a matter of course. Thus the question is not how religion promoted zone specialization but how religion redistributed the products of a naturally variable region. The information reported in rituals guaranteed that any storehouse, public or private, was optimally balanced.

Mormon rituals have two aspects which make them useful in agrarian regulation. They are geared automatically to the agrarian round, and their temporal content makes them responsive to the economy. The most important ritual tied to agriculture was the Quarterly Stake Conference. From early church times, the practice of gathering the faithful four times a year served to channel information about the condition of the people to church leaders and to reinspire, redirect, and reunify the people. Quarterly Conferences in Arizona attempted to bring together everybody in the stake;

out of a population of about 3000, they often managed to assemble 500 people. There were two stakes along the Little Colorado, and they held conferences close together, generally in January but sometimes in December, April, July or August, and October, thus coinciding with crucial parts of the agricultural cycle and allowing leaders to attend both conferences so as to cover the entire area. These events were so important that often one or more of the Twelve Apostles was present. A typical schedule of area-wide meetings for the Snowflake Stake in 1898 brought together people from every town in the stake:

February 17–19, 1898: Apostles from Salt Lake City make rounds to St. Joseph and Snowflake preaching.

February 22, 1898: High Council meets with Apostles in attendance.

February 27–28, 1898: Quarterly Stake Conference at Snowflake and simultaneously meeting were the Stake Board of Education and officials of the Young Ladies' Mutual Improvement Association.

May 27, 1898: The High Council meets.

May 28, 1898: The semi-annual conference of the Stake Primary organization and the Ladies' Relief Society.

May 29–30, 1898: Young Men's and Young Ladies' Mutual Improvement Associations officials meet in conference in Snowflake.

August 26, 1898: High Council meets.

August 28–29, 1898: Quarterly Stake Conference.

November 12, 1898: Primary and Ladies' Relief Society meets.

November 13–14, 1898: High Council meets.

November 13, 1898: Meeting of the Stake Priesthood.

November 15, 1898: Meeting of Stake Seventies.

November 27–28, 1898: Quarterly Stake Conference (History and Settlement of the Snowflake Area: 222–225).

Conferences lasted two days, with meetings of the Stake Presidency and bishops preceding and succeeding the main events. Quarterly Conferences were to some degree stage-managed. Late on the Friday preceding a conference that was to open the next morning, the Stake High Council met. A stake president and his two councilors, forming the Stake

Presidency, were the most powerful men in any given region. They, with the other dozen men or so who made up the High Council, wielded the greatest local power. This group met before a conference to make the major policy decisions to be presented during the next two days. If any policies had been issued by Salt Lake, they had to be adjusted to local conditions, but more commonly the High Council set prices, decided on contracts for public works, or organized goods and labor to be sent to a town experiencing a specific problem, such as a dam washout. These problems were presented to the High Council both for its general knowledge and explicit ratification.

Priesthood meetings involving smaller groups of local leaders were held in conjunction with Stake Conferences and could make specific economic decisions concerning exchange possibilities. A report on the St. Johns Stake Priesthood Meeting held at Alpine Heights, Arizona, on June 8, 1890, shows how quickly information was made available for general use:

> Vice President S. D. Moore reported the Tannery Company had secured the services of a tanner and had procured pine bark for a year and were ready to receive the subscription, and were desirous of obtaining good hides.
>
> Subject of the road from Alma to Luna considered. Moved and seconded that we pay $.20 an hour for work on the road in produce at cash rates. Moved and seconded that we pay $.35 an hour for man and team. Agreed that work begin in two weeks from tomorrow . . .
>
> Benediction given by L. H. Marble (St. Johns Stake Historical Record 1887–1915:103).

Even though policy was decided by the hierarchy, it was never so presented to a conference. Policy emanating from Salt Lake was simply announced, but in all other matters a conference, representing the mass of the faithful, was asked to express its will or, in Mormon terms, "sustain" a policy of the Stake Presidency and High Council. In no case do the conference minutes reveal that any open discussion or disagreement was expressed. These meetings in fact supplied audiences for the pro forma ratification of decisions made behind the scenes by the leadership.

At the most formal Mormon rituals today there is still no give-and-take discussion that leads to a decision that did not exist before the discussion began. Mormons do discuss freely about unresolved issues and all the other ambiguous problems that any group of people is bound to have, but not in the chief ritual contexts. Such discussions occur in small groups among people who know each other well, such as Sunday Schools or Family Home Evenings where unity is not the chief goal. Mormons are allowed in any service or ritual to offer solutions, personal or joint, but in the largest rituals no one, regardless of the level of disagreement, may dispute a solution. This prohibition provides an index to how rituals enforced pragmatic decisions among nineteenth century Mormons and shows that sanctity and dispute cannot exist in the same context: the latter robs the former of its power.

The Stake Conference itself consisted of four major public meetings: Saturday morning and afternoon, and Sunday morning and afternoon. These were interlaced with meetings of the High Priests' Quorum for leading men, the Primary for Sunday School children, the Women's Relief Society for all women, the Seventies' Quorum for home missionaries, and the Young Men's and Ladies' Mutual Improvement Associations for adolescents. Usually a dance was held on Saturday night, and there was ample time for socializing and business.

The conference involved hymns, prayers, and benedictions, administration of the sacrament, and exegeses on doctrinal points, as well as reports on practical matters. Although all conferences were religious services, their economic content was manifest, as shown by a report of Bishop Kempe from Erastus (later Concho) in the minutes of a June 1887 conference: "Our prospects for a harvest [wheat] are quite good, the brethren have built a good fence and have thus preserved their grain; our fruit looks good, except the peaches" (Snowflake Stake Historical Record 1886–1889:

126–127). Crop conditions, good and bad, informed people in advance who could provide help and who would need it.

On the 30th of September 1895 Pres. L. H. Hatch returned home from the ward conference at Tuba City. He reported good prosperity among the Saints of that ward. Said the Bishop there had raised 1200 bushels of wheat this season.

At this Conference [Nov. 23, 1895] the bishops reported general good health and prosperity although crops were light. At some places in the forest there had been a little neglect to plant, at Snowflake and Taylor a disastrous hail storm had destroyed a great deal of produce in the field, at St. Joseph water had been uncommonly scarce and a very early and killing frost in September had greatly damaged crops in all this section of country. (History and Settlement of the Snowflake Area:207–209).

Minutes, which are actually summaries of the reports read to the people, show the details made available about economic conditions:

The usual good brotherly feeling prevailed [Sept. 9–10, 1900], and the usual instructive council was given. A fair degree of prosperity was reported, although in some of the wards, crops had been damaged or entirely cut off by the heavy and long-continued drouth which has prevailed in this part so long. The range is almost a complete failure until September this year.

The reports [May 16–17, 1903] were favorable. Apostle M. F. Cowly and Elder L. A. Kelsch [?] attended [and] spoke very earnestly. Weather is cold and crops are backward. Most of the fruit is killed by hard frost. But an abundance of moisture in the mountains promises good crops of grain, etc.

The season [August 18, 1906] progresses nicely, crops are good, even dry farming has been successful. Though no heavy rains occurred and no serious floods, signs of frost appear early, about Sept. 18—and earlier.

Pres. Smith in reporting [November 1908] the condition of the stake said that altho some have not reaped abundantly as common, yet as a whole we are prospering. The health of the people

is good; the Academy is better than ever before, 112 are now en-
rolled [in primary and secondary school] ... we are supporting
20 missionaries (History and Settlement of the Snowflake
Area:236, 255, 292, 312).

Crop conditions, the weather, the state of irrigation systems,
local political affairs, ward organization, sickness, and many
other matters affecting the economy, including the general
morale, were summed up and appraised at conferences and
then commented on by the stake president. A Quarterly
Conference report submitted by a bishop often included a
census of every ward, including a count of the men, women,
children, new births, deaths, missionaries, tithe payers, and
so on:

Dec. 1905. Heavy storms continue through December and the
weather turns desperately cold. Dec. 23 to 26 the thermometer
registered as low as 11° to 15° below zero in different parts of the
country. A protracted cold spell followed ...

In January diptheria broke out in Show Low. Three children
died before it was checked ... Construction was begun on the
Woodruff dam in the middle of January.

Yearly reports for 1905 show an increase in population of 42
souls, total 1612 [for the eight towns composing the Snowflake
Stake].

Tithing decrease $262.88. Total [tithing] for year $9541.55.
Average tithe per capita of population $5.91. Non-tithing-
payers—increase 12. Total 64 (History and Settlement of the
Snowflake Area:285).

Land ownership, a frequent topic at Quarterly Conferences, usually involved, not exchanges of land within the
community, but obtaining possession of land from outsiders
who claimed control of the acreage on which Mormons had
settled. Stake leaders used a religious context to bolster their
role as the settlers' chief negotiators with outsiders, to describe their progress in outside negotiations to the people,
and to assure them that their land was secure. This made the
decisions affecting the future seem more plausible and hope-
ful than they might otherwise have seemed while hiding the

powerlessness of the Mormons and their leaders. Ritual made it easier for people with limited real power to make and enforce decisions in their own community:

> Pres. Jesse N. Smith said [he] ... spoke ... with Mr. Bevins, (U.S. Government) Land Agent. Gave him a history of the purchase of land from the rancher previous to any survey of the land, or railroad grant. He considered we had rights in equity in our case. He advised that we communicate with the officials of the Aztec Land Company. They were fair men and he would aid in what he could and move quickly while they were in office to obtain our rights. If we fail with them, then appeal to the Government whose officials were good men and he felt they would do what was right. Compared the situation of the Saints with Israel when in bondage in Egypt ... [and] of the unjust laws passed against the increase of male children, of the birth of Moses and the Exodus of Israel from bondage (High Priests' Quorum Minute Book 1866–1892:19–22).

At this time the Mormon lands, already paid for once, were in danger of falling into railroad hands, having been preempted by Congress for award to the railroads as a bounty for construction. When the Aztec Land and Cattle Company, a massive speculative scheme dealing in land and cattle, bought most of the lands awarded the railroad, the church in Salt Lake came forward with funds to purchase them. This second payment for their lands, made by the church, was subsequently repaid to the church by local Mormons by reinvesting the repayment as improvements on their own lands: "Early in 1894 the Saints in this stake were made to rejoice by the leading brethren of the church Authorities giving people in Snowflake, Taylor and Woodruff the privilege of gaining title to these lands which they occupied by applying the price thereof in labor, upon dams canals, reservoirs, etc., with a view of storing and controlling more water for irrigation" (History and Settlement of the Snowflake Area 1870–1912:201–202).

Because Mormons did not isolate religion and economics in exclusive contexts but combined them into a single category, the religious flavor of conferences was strong, as shown in the minutes of a conference held on June 3–4, 1911:

> Pres. Smith reported our agricultural interests not so bright on account of winds and late frosts.
>
> All the wards and auxiliary associations have sent in written reports. Dangerous speculations in livestock are growing.
>
> The Apostles felt to sympathize with us in the loss [by fire] of our Academy and cited the trials of Job and the early drivings of the saints as examples worse than ours, for our solace. Proper sanitation, and salvation for the dead were among the subjects dwelt upon (History and Settlement of the Snowflake Area: 339).

Mixing sanitation and salvation for the dead was predictable and even essential in a religion governing reality with sanctity. The logical extension of this mixture occurred at a conference on May 16–17, 1908:

> Pres. Samuel F. Smith reported the people as a whole in good health. Fruit prospects destroyed, yet we should thank the Lord we still have sufficient time for a bounteous harvest of grain, etc.
>
> There was a splendid turn out during the 4 meetings of the conference (A.M. Sat. 190; P.M. 253; A.M. Sunday 422; P.M. 510) and although none of the General Authorities were present, the spirit of the Lord was manifest to a marked degree (History and Settlement of the Snowflake Area:307).

The feeling of fellowship indicated by the presence of the spirit of the Lord closed the loop between subsistence success and religious experience. The reports of likely success produced emotional and spiritual satisfaction, while the reports of actual successes, given their practical exchange value, were guaranteed to lead to greater success through balanced redistribution. This furthered satisfactory religious experiences. Summing up the reports for the 1887 conference, Stake President Jesse N. Smith said: "I have listened to the reports that have been made and see that there are a great variety of circumstances—some are prosperous, some are not, this is the condition of the Saints. We have to study the nature of the soil—as we become acquainted with the nature of the soil we may possibly improve it" (Snowflake Stake Historical Record 1886–1889:126–127).

Implicit in Smith's comments was the suggestion that, as the potential of the various soil types and their relation to moisture and temperature came to be understood, appropriate crops could be fitted to them. The tithing records make clear that after broad trial-and-error experimentation in every new settlement, the range of produce was narrowed to that best suited to the locale, and then the surplus was systematically exchanged. Within a theological context, improving the soil refers to the Mormon idea that, under the ministration of the Saints, the natural environment would change for the better: "the earth itself is subject to certain laws of progression and salvation because of which it eventually will become a fit abode for exalted beings" (McConkie 1966:210). The earth is a living entity, a spirit with an incarnated form. The earth and humans, each in their respective progression or evolution to perfection, work together so that the improvement of the earth helps people to achieve their own improvement.

So theology became ecology, and experience in the latter was defined as the validity of the former, completing the circle. Mormons had become acquainted with the nature of the soil, both the dirt of the ground and the environment writ large, and the products of the land had been evened out among themselves through the church's institutions with enough success that the chief priest could realistically sum up his people's condition as prosperity. Religion through ritual had governed the economy successfully and thereby produced the conviction of religious truth.

Information was passed around during and after a conference, which allowed essential exchange to take place. Presumably each family coming to a conference would bring with it detailed crop information from its own and neighboring farms. A well-informed family might know about conditions in its whole town and maybe a neighboring town as well. The conference provided an occasion for the family to use that information to its own advantage, but if information had been no more generalized than this, the conference would have been little more than a fair. However, the Mormon bishop attending a Quarterly Conference not only knew the condition of all crops for his whole town but after the conference knew what was scarce or plentiful in the storehouses of the whole region, as well as the condition of what was being raised in the fields and pasture lands. His information was both accurate and general. So while a conference brought together many individuals with limited information and with specific goods to sell or supplement, it also provided the rituals through which exchange could transcend uninformed bartering and become effective redistribution.

Although neither the meeting minutes nor the journal entries illustrate specifically how the information picked up at a conference was used, widespread exchange of goods clearly occurred. The exchange, though initiated by conferences, did not always depend on the content of the rituals. Conferences held at Snowflake or Taylor in October or November had people coming from St. Joseph and all other grain-producing towns to bring their grist to the mill at Shumway near Taylor. The grain was ground during the conference, thus producing a family's flour, a portion of which could be tithed and some of which could be exchanged readily in the course of the conference. Since it was regarded as almost a duty to patronize Shumway's grist mill instead of a gentile's, the fall conference saw tremendous amounts of grain and flour exchanged in the Snowflake area.

In addition to grain, people brought melons and other portable items to exchange. People now in their eighty's and ninety's have told me that the exchange of goods accompanied a conference and that the information picked up on the spot facilitated this trading. Over the next several months such information must also have influenced the trading among bishops' storehouses all over the Little Colorado area. This accurate, region-wide information allowed people to plan. The fact that they planned and that the planning netted them survival is the sum of the Mormons' history.

The information reported at a conference was used by the

leaders to benefit public works. The tithing office and barns at Taylor were built with tithing monies, and a road to St. Johns was paid for with tithing produce. That is, Mormons who did the labor were paid in kind, which they received at the tithing office. They thereby earned back their own taxes, only distributed among needed commodities. The tithing barns at Woodruff, the granary at Taylor, the brick telegraph office at Snowflake, and half the annual pay of the telegraph operator came out of tithing funds. The major portion of funds to build the Stake Academy, a church-run elementary and high school, came from tithing. Moreover, the effective absence of state and county government in this area of Arizona meant that no public improvements would have been built if the Mormons had not undertaken them themselves.

A large amount of discretionary power was placed in the hands of bishops and stake presidents in managing crises. A bishop controlled the use of tithing at the ward level, while the stake president controlled it for the whole region, and much of the redistribution in Arizona was done by these church officials to aid their respective constituents. In Arizona the Mormons had to put up with an entire catalogue of natural and human caprices. Frost at the wrong time, thaws at the wrong season, floods, insects, hail, torrential rain or not enough rain, erosion, salt deposition, horse and cattle thieves, marauding Indians, the railroad leeches, the land and cattle companies—a legion of evils appeared to face the Saints.

Floods were probably the most frequent and devastating natural disaster that could hit these towns. A bishop had the authority to ship supplies from his ward's storehouse to the stricken community and offer tithing labor to help reconstruct the public works. Aid was always given: the Saints seem to have been free with their goods, at least with other Saints.

Without much doubt, the most ingenious device available to Mormons to repair public works in times of disaster was tithing labor. This labor, valued at $2.00 a day, was contingent upon a man's feeding himself on the job, and if he brought his team, he was accorded a higher value but had to feed the team himself. Tithing labor did not involve much redistribution, being generally used as a standby or in times of unemployment or disaster. In Arizona, labor was in short supply in any one town, and a dam required a gigantic amount of man-hours to build or repair. It was therefore possible for both the people living in a community hit with misfortune and the people coming from other towns to supply labor to consider the time spent as part of their annual tithe.

To some degree the value of labor was set by demand. When demand was high, so was the value, but since labor was generally thought to be an inexpensive way of tithing, its use was restricted. As much as this may sound like true market conditions, it describes a premarket economy. When a person had nothing to offer but labor, it was accepted as being just as negotiable as money, and its price did not fall. By giving labor a fixed value and by allowing it to be a commodity in the tithing system, the community guaranteed itself both a labor supply at peak demand points and no unemployment.

Labor tithing was never more than 4 or 5 percent of a town's total annual tithing. Among themselves, the Mormons never sold labor as a commodity. In times of stress, Mormons could work for wages in gentile towns, but the reduction of the value of labor to a salable commodity subject to the whims of a market never occurred. One of the means guaranteeing the integrity of labor derived from the source of its value, the religious system. When labor was given a wage value, it was within the tithing system and, as a result, was attached to religious rationales, not to profit and market forces. When labor was considered a commodity, it was also a religious act and was used almost entirely in crises under conditions governed by the hierarchy.

From 12 to 25 percent of the total annual tithing in the Little Colorado area was exchanged "for better kinds," that is, goods more useful to a ward than what they had in surplus. More acceptable to a ward was cash or genuinely scarce food stuffs. The records show that the goods received in exchange were usually items showing a decline from previous years. Most towns exchanged in kind and invariably paid with surpluses; goods that were scarce by the previous year's measurements were generally not traded. Trading went on throughout the year, and during the winter and spring a ward would have a large amount of stored products on hand from the previous fall, specifically from the previous December 31, when a family was obliged to settle its tithing for the year. Tithing records show that a season's surpluses provided the goods "paid out in exchange." Goods received on exchange were mostly determined by looking at what the current year's produce showed would be scarce. Regardless of seasonal variation, and sometimes regardless of the immediate condition of a crop, the crops most favored for paying out were those that the community always grew in quantity. Grain was always used as a medium of payment at Taylor, and stock at St. Joseph; the poorer towns often chose to pay in labor.

Snowflake provides a typical example of tithing exchange. In 1891, Snowflake's total tithing receipts were $5172. Tithing paid in exchange was $825, and that received in return balanced at $825. The tithing exchange can be broken down into categories from the records (table 9). Exchanges often took place during a time of year when last year's tithing could be drawn on but when the coming year's crops and tithing could only be guessed or calculated from the quality of the season. After the bulk of tithing was spent or forwarded to Salt Lake, the balance on hand in Snowflake carried over into 1891 from 1890 was $1433 (table 10). The

Table 9. *Tithing Exchange in Snowflake, Arizona, 1891.*

Item received	Dollar value	Item paid out	Dollar value
Cash	404	Dairy and	
Merchandise	33	vegetable	75
Stock	388	Grain and hay	750
Total	825		825

Source: Record of Stake Funds 1882–1901:125–126.

Table 10. *Tithing Balance on Hand in Snowflake, Arizona, December 31, 1890.*

Product	Dollar value
Dairy and vegetables	116
Grain and hay	1110
Stock	33
Miscellaneous	174
Total	1433

Source: Record of Stake Funds 1882–1901:125–126.

town converted part of this unusually high surplus of grain and hay into cash and the rest into livestock, the surplus of which had shrunk from $1037 in 1890 to $33 during the course of 1891. Tithing in livestock for 1891 itself fell to $730, a drop of 25 percent from the previous year. The drop, which is an index to the amount of meat and medium of exchange available to the town could probably have been forecast from spring births and was insured against further increase by exchanging a plentiful commodity to compensate for the scarcity.

Exchange between tithing offices in the stake involved about 20 percent of a year's tithing. Assuming that this represented between 10 and 15 percent of a community's output counting all kinds of required extra donations, between 1 and 2 percent of a town's production was traded. Though not large, this was a significant figure, given the marginal nature of these economies. Moreover, all towns produced the same basic products and were usually concerned with balancing ratios between crops, not with importing a totally missing item.

One of the most ingenious parts to tithing exchange was the transfer of tithing credit over long distances. The Arizona colonies were only one of several sets of towns established on the peripheries of Mormondom, and in order to finance them, a large store of financial devices took advantage of the central tithing resources of the church. One commodity unavailable for use in colonization was cash. For most of its period of effective political independence, Mormondom had an imbalance of payments with the Eastern

United States from which it derived most of its manufactured goods and where it was obliged to spend what cash it had. To avoid sending cash into areas where it would be hard to spend anyway, the Presiding Bishop's Office, the central office in charge of tithing, invented a system that allowed tithing deposits in Salt Lake City to be withdrawn at the tithing offices in Arizona. The key to the system was that the transactions could take place in kind: $200 worth of cattle deposited at the General Tithing Office yards in Salt Lake could be taken as $200 worth of grain from the local tithing office in Arizona. The system worked as long as there was a reasonable supply in the local Arizona tithing houses.

It is unclear how widespread this system of credit was, and from the complaints issued by some Arizona leaders, one of the major problems was the difference in price between Salt Lake and Arizona. Local leaders were quick to notice that goods were cheaper in Utah and dearer in Arizona, which put a tax on local storehouses. A head of cattle or bushel of grain cost less in Utah, where supply was better, than in Arizona, where supply was short and prices correspondingly higher. As Lot Smith wrote on July 12, 1879, to President John Taylor about the discrepancy in prices: "I have written to you twice on tithing matters, asking how you wish it disposed of. Whether it is fair to the church for persons to pay in tithing in the north and draw here where it is worth more. Some have already done this, and it seems a little one sided." A few months later, Wilford Woodruff wrote from Arizona to the bishopric on the subject of tithing wheat: "It does not seem proper for men to deposit wheat at Salt Lake and draw the same amount here for while wheat is not worth more than $1 in Salt Lake, it is worth $2 cash at the mill here."

Anywhere from 20 to 40 percent of annual tithing in Arizona was disbursed locally on orders from the Presiding Bishop's Office in Salt Lake City. The wards received orders from church headquarters to distribute goods locally, and the local wards disbursed in kind accordingly. These goods went to the local population, and the ward charged the disbursements against the stake. In other words, in theory all tithing went to Salt Lake via the stake. When tithing was disbursed locally by order of Salt Lake, the disbursals were represented as a contribution to the stake and hence to Salt Lake. For example, in 1879 John Taylor wrote to Lot Smith from Salt Lake City about expending local resources:

> We fully approve of your course in loaning your tithing wheat to the brethren of your adjoining settlements in their necessities caused by the loss of crops by floods, etc., and recommend that you have them return for the grain so borrowed into the Tithing Office where they reside in conformity with your arrangements with them; a statement of such deposit should be forwarded to you as your vouchers, and in your reports to this office. The same can be drawn on from those offices as may be required.

In writing to Lot Smith in 1880, Wilford Woodruff clarified the system of credit operating within the tithing system and added a word about conditions in Arizona:

> The Apostles seem to appreciate what assistance you are rendering to the *needy who want bread.* I wish also to say in this connection that the mother of Joseph H. Willkins of St. Johns, she lives in Ogden. He is one of the carpenters we took dinner with at St. Johns. His mother has heard that he had nothing to eat but black beans. She wanted to know if she could not deposit 25 or 30 bus. of wheat in the Tithing Office and let him [draw it] and he said he would do it. But I did not know where he could get the wheat in Arizona, except it was of you. So I told her to deposit some wheat in the office and I would send the order to you and I hope you will do what you can about it. I think you took a bucket of flour to him when we went.

However, if the mother deposited 30 bushels of wheat worth $30 dollars in Salt Lake City, what could be received in Arizona? Could her son take 30 bushels or $30 worth of wheat regardless of the amount that $30 would buy? The resolution of this issue is not recorded.

In the decade 1888–1898, about 25 percent of the income of the stake was sent as cash to the General Tithing Office in Salt Lake City. The rest stayed in Arizona among the towns where it was collected. In 1888 the total income to the Snowflake Stake, the aggregate of all its eight wards, was $11,839. Of this amount, $3419 was sent to Salt Lake; the rest stayed home. Ten years later, in 1898, the total stake income was $19,908, of which $4,264 was "forwarded to the Trustee in Trust," that is, to Salt Lake City. By the late 1880s the church was no longer sending huge resources to Arizona but was directing the use of local savings for the same purposes of community support for which it had originally sent capital.

The Little Colorado region had no central redistribution point, no commercial banking or credit institutions, and despite conferences, no periodic market or bazaar. In place of these the area had the Arizona Commercial and Mercantile Institution (ACMI), which was the church's general store and which, in tandem with the tithing system, handled most of the redistribution made necessary by differences in production and needs.

The ACMI was a true cooperative store. When it was first set up, stake leaders followed the injunction of church leaders in Utah and dispersed the ownership as broadly as possible throughout the local population. Stock in the store could be had initially at very small denominations, but within a decade most people had sold their stock for badly needed goods or cash, and only the smallest, richest fragment of the population held ownership. The remaining owners were also the chief religious leaders who, from the beginning, had made all the managerial decisions for the ACMI. It was church policy that the president of the stake be chairman of the Board of Directors of the store.

The store was capitalized in another way besides stock, in a fortuitous case of forced savings. John Young, one of Brigham Young's more adventuresome sons, held the major railroad contracts for building the first rail lines across northern Arizona in 1880 and 1881. The church in Utah had decided over a decade earlier to bid for the rail construction contracts from the roads themselves in order to avoid the influx of rail camp laborers who would, it was feared, profane Zion. By handling the contracts, the church had also guaranteed its people and itself the income from the labor. In Arizona, much the same rationale held. The local settlers were almost destitute during the earliest years of colonizing, so John Young hired Mormon men and began to grade the route, cut the ties, and build the railroad. The rail companies themselves, as became their custom, failed to pay in full for the labor, which left Young in no position to reimburse the workers. A year or so after the rail line had been finished, Young raised the money he owed the workers and arranged with the church to have it deposited in the form of goods in the ACMI, which could be drawn on by individuals, depending on how much they were owed. Acting as middleman, or holder of forced savings, the ACMI could realize a profit in handling the goods by adjusting the prices.

Although initially there was an outlet of the ACMI in nearly every settlement, the area's central store was soon located in Holbrook on the Little Colorado River, the railroad head and a gentile town. Its records have been destroyed, but two ledgers from the Snowflake branch of the ACMI covering the years 1890–1892 and 1901–1903 survive. They reveal an institution of extraordinary complexity. The store's most obvious function was to serve as middleman in the trade between the local population and the Eastern manufacturers who shipped goods to Albuquerque and St. Louis. The store was open to any bishop to exchange his tithing for cash or kind, depending on the circumstances of the store and his ward's needs. Individuals could pay their tithing into the store and have it credited to their ward account. To this end and also for purposes of their own exchange, the local wards of Snowflake, Taylor, Pinedale, and Showlow kept accounts with the ACMI branch in Snowflake, where they could unload surpluses and receive individual tithes. Because the ACMI was open to private individuals as well as to bishops, it catered to the exchange of all parties and thereby operated as the major node in redistribution.

The Snowflake Stake also kept an account with the ACMI. This account was probably the General Tithing Storehouse for the stake. Since there is no record of an actual

complex of buildings at the stake center in Snowflake, aside
from the bishop's storehouse, and since the available records
of the ACMI show fragmentary dealings with the stake, it is
quite possible that the stake simply banked with the ACMI.
Money for tithing expressed either as cash or goods could sit
in the store's accounts until its periodic forwarding to
church headquarters. Evidence for this hypothesis comes
from Jesse Smith's statement to John Lathrop at a High
Council trial that his fine paid to the stake would be put to
interest in the ACMI. Not only did the stake keep an account there, but it received interest on it as well.

The banking aspects of the ACMI were considerable. The
store was one of the main exchanges for converting goods
into cash. During the polygamy persecutions of the late
1880s its paper stock, when cashed in, underwrote the flight
of many stake leaders like Jesse Smith to Mexico and their
subsequent expenses. Beyond this, the ACMI functioned as
a bank insofar as it accepted personal credits and debits that
were independent of the trading accounts it held. The books
were set up so that individuals and institutions had separate
accounts. These seem to show that individuals were charging goods against the accounts of other individuals and were
making deposits into the accounts of others. If this is the
proper way of reading the data in the ledgers, which are un-
accompanied by the rules used to keep them, then the
ACMI was running private checking accounts and paying
interest on deposits for the bulk of the population, and all
the transactions were done in kind, essentially with produce,
merchandise, and livestock.

This system would have enormously simplified all forms
of exchange: individuals would have had a central, well-
stocked storehouse-bank with outlets in every town. Since
the ACMI was a church-run institution owned by the whole
population, its profits were immediately available to the
community and its motives above suspicion. Its religious
sanctions may also have allowed it to operate effectively
without heavy financial backing.

Since the branch offices of the ACMI in every town over
the Little Colorado were tied to the central store in Hol-

brook, and since all Mormons were under explicit, enforced obligation to trade with the church store in preference to the few private stores, the network facilitating regional interchange was more efficient than that usually existing on the frontier. Moreover, when compared to modern conditions on the Little Colorado, trade and banking in the nineteenth century were not subjected to the rake-off in sales taxes, service charges, and interest rates that they are in that area today. Whatever profit was made by the tithing houses or the ACMI was reinvested directly into the Mormon community.

The Board of Trade was a central device for regulating all aspects of exchange and controlling the effects of both market forces and competition. Set up in the first years of the Arizona colony, it was consciously modeled on Zion's Central Board of Trade in Utah. The function of both was to unify the prices that Mormons charged for their produce when marketing it to the world. As a result, the Board of Trade regulated the prices of goods Mormons sold each other as well. Price-fixing eliminated price-cutting and guaranteed that Mormon farmers would not undercut each other. Given the uniformity in the kinds of products raised, a surplus or a deficit of a specific product over the whole Little Colorado would at times lead to price instability. A Board of Trade made up of local leaders could provide a flexible means for imposing uniformity within the local area. An early example of the imposition of such uniformity imposed by the Stake High Council appeared in Lot Smith's letter from one of his United Order towns, Sunset, in 1879:

There will be a considerable tithing [in] flour which I expect will sell for some $5.60 a hundred [pounds] here. On the following page you will find the tithing price list .. as we arranged it in Council.

Wheat per bushel		$2.00
Barley	"	1.60
Oats	"	1.25
Corn	"	1.90
Potatoes	"	1.00

Carrots	"	.25–.30
Beets	"	.25–.30
Onions	"	2.00
Cabbage per pound		.02–.03
Beans	"	.04–.05
Peas	"	.05–.06
Turnips per bushel		.25–.30
Cheese per pound		.15–.20
Pork	"	.12½
Mutton	"	.05–.06
Beef	"	.05–.06
Sole leather	"	.05
Wool	"	.05
Salt	"	.02–.03
Squash each		.05–.20
Chickens	"	.25–.30
Pigs—5wks. old		2.00–3.00
Upper leather per kit		5.00
Hay per ton		15.00–20.00
Cows per head		14.00–20.00
Yearlings		6.00–7.00
Sheep		1.00–2.00
Tithing labor per day		1.50

Ritual can be used to make men transcend narrow self-interest, and it was so used to resolve an internal conflict that developed between the church's Board of Trade and the ACMI, on the one hand, and the mercantile houses privately owned by Mormons on the other. In the Quarterly Stake Conference held at Snowflake May 31 and June 1, 1896, the board's role was revealed, as was its conflict with private interests:

For 2 or 3 years past this Stake has undertaken to maintain a Board of Trade. There has been some ill feeling between the Board and other individuals—some of the brethren engaged in merchandising being particularly blamed by the Board, but at the High Priests' meeting of this Conference held on the evening of May 31, there was rather an exceptionally peaceful feeling manifested, and the head men of the three principal mercantile houses

were unanimously sustained as the Board of Trade for the ensu-
ing year. These men were R. Hulet [manager of the ACMI],
James M. Flake, and Alma Z. Palmer (History and Settlement of
the Snowflake Area: 213).

This decision placed the board in the hands of professional
wholesalers and retailers, the self-interested parties; at the
same time, it unified the whole formal redistribution network under church authority, thus offering some price protection to the Mormon population. Such a solution, which
mediated between private profit and socialized surplus, was
possible and effective because all those involved were priesthood members and the arrangement was made at a High
Priests' meeting where the decision had religious meaning.
The solution redirected the self-interest of individual wholesalers and subordinated it to the community as a whole.

The arguments of Ray A. Rappaport, which tie ritual to
ecological management, are helpful in understanding the
Mormons' use of ritual to run their lives. Rappaport described sanctity as the chief quality possessed by religious
rituals:

> Propositions such as ["Hear, oh Israel, the Lord our God, the
> Lord is One," or "In the name of the Father, the Son and the
> Holy Ghost, Amen," or "Joseph Smith is a prophet of God and
> the Church he founded is true"] are peculiar. Since their terms
> have no material referents, they are not amenable to verification,
> but neither are they vulnerable to falsification. They are, in a
> strict logical positivist sense, nonsense. Yet they are taken to be
> unquestionably true. This characteristic, I believe, is the *sine qua
> non* of sanctity. I take the term "sacred" to refer to the quality of
> unquestionable truthfulness imputed by the faithful to unverifi-
> able propositions.

Sacred sentences can be used to give a quality of unquestionable truthfulness or certainty to

> sentences containing information upon which societies operate.
> In the liturgical aspect of religious rituals ultimate sacred proposi-
> tions are periodically reaffirmed and may, outside of rituals,

sanctify sentences directly important in the regulation of society. Thus the sacred escapes from strictly religious contexts, and sentences concerning economic arrangements, political authorities, and other social conventions may, in fact very likely will, be sanctified (Rappaport 1971a:29).

Although sanctity is used universally, Rappaport suggested that technologically primitive and underdeveloped societies use it as their chief source of power. In the absence of any other kind, power derived from unempirical beings can be used to govern society. Mormondom was technologically underdeveloped and even primitive, both because it was situated on a frontier and because it deliberately excluded some aspects of industrialism.

The ritual contexts used by Mormons, such as the Quarterly Stake Conferences, were powerful multiple contexts, involving apostles, a large group of the faithful, the sacrament, discourse about truth, and discussion of the ultimately necessary. The major function of the conference was to carry messages from the leaders who were close to God to the people. Those messages were sometimes about theological and hence unempirical matters and sometimes about earthly and hence measurable concerns. At the time it could not have been shown that Mormons in Arizona had a better way to live on a frontier than anyone else, and from a contemporary perspective their way offered real disadvantages. But the use of power derived from imaginary sources created the material success represented in these tithing figures. Success happened by making economic and political decisions, which were often difficult or trying, calling them religious necessity, and defining the resultant material success as religious experience.

4

Water Control: The Origins of Dynamic Adjustment

To farm a desert, Mormons had to irrigate. As a result of that necessity, the control and management of water was a central part of their existence. Given that they had no experience with wet farming before entering the desert West, and given that they were used to resolving all problems through their religion, it was inevitable that the problem of learning how to farm a desert was handled through rituals. As a result, irrigation, the one aspect of the farming system most crucial to existence and most prone to crises, was balanced through the operation of sanctity. Ritual contexts directly and consciously juxtaposed the ultimate but unverifiable truth to matters of planning, building, and operating dams, measuring and distributing water, and maintaining canals. The record of this relationship is available from the people who experienced it and who passed on to us their efforts, their emotions, and their spiritual history. The records drive home the capacity of religion to govern economic and social reality in the absence of other, more concrete sources of power. The history of water control provides a firm basis for understanding nineteenth-century Mormon communities since such control was one of the main contexts for the development of Mormon society in the West and one where the shaping of Mormonism can be plainly seen.

The earliest known use of irrigated farming in the desert West, as evidenced by archaeological remains in the southern Arizona desert, was by the Hohokam culture for almost its entire history, 200 B.C. to A.D. 1200. Every settled group in the prehistoric Southwest that used agriculture also shows traces of irrigation. The Mormons did not think of either their settlement pattern or their system of water control as a systematic strategy for survival in this harsh environment. Although conscious of the interdependence of resources in a town, they were much less aware, if at all, of the kind of insurance they purchased for their collective survival by the diversity of environmental variation that they harnessed over the whole Little Colorado area. Yet such a strategy undeniably existed, as it had existed among the prehistoric inhabitants as well, although not over such a huge area.

In the broken and environmentally varied area of the Little Colorado River, a variety of survival strategies has been used through history. The archaeologists who discovered the prehistoric irrigation networks of the area suggested that the system was tailored to fit the requirements of each particular zone (Plog and Garrett 1972). It included the strategies of check dams on hillsides and diversion dams leading to canals and fields, combined with dry farming and planting along stream banks. Despite some differences in the water control techniques and a different land unit, the Mormons used essentially the same strategies on a bigger scale.

Even though a more efficient technology was available to Mormons than to the Indians who had irrigated between A.D. 700 and 1300, including the availability of surveying equipment, Mormons found that to build their canals on top of prehistoric ones was invariably less chancey than to rely on their own surveying equipment. Mormons had to dig their ditches by hand and to quarry and place stones for their dams with the aid only of iron tools and horses; no jackhammers, no cranes, and at first no cement were available. Mormons nonetheless fitted a series of canals, settling ponds, and dams to the idiosyncrasies of a variety of sites, juggling the technical repertoire at their command. Since most sites had to be fitted out with dams several times, the trial-and-error process yielded an ever better fit between the rivers and the installations.

The first Mormon settlers brought along a surveyor, who examined all or most dam sites and was especially attentive to canal construction. Major Ladd was not, however, either a hydrologist or a civil engineer with dam-building experience. The first recorded professional engineer equipped with a knowledge of dam construction and water control experience showed up in the area in 1904. In the meantime, Mormons built at least three dozen dams at seven Little Colorado towns, and like all of the prehistoric water control devices, these were constructed without benefit of professionals and depended solely on local ingenuity tempered with increasing experience. The most prominent dam-building towns were St. Joseph, Woodruff, Snowflake, Taylor, and St. Johns, two lesser towns being Hunt and Round Valley.

The irrigation system was operated and regulated through the use of religious rituals. Rituals and beliefs thereby combined to aid in the continual improvement of, and hence effective control over, the environment. Effective control constituted the first phase of the church's success.

Religion ruled the economic life of the Mormons from their arrival in the West partly because they deliberately fostered such a primitive way of life in the technological sense that religion was the only available source of power, and partly because nobody knew how to farm a desert. The absence of much concrete power dovetailed with the Mormon rejection of capitalism and most of the industrial world to guarantee to their religion a virtual command over subsistence practices for many decades.

The Mormons serve as eyewitness guides to the privations of struggling on the margins of existence. From the first dams built along the Little Colorado in 1876 to 1923 when dam-building was abandoned, the entire effort was plagued by failure. While dams washed out with regularity from the beginning, and were just as regularly rebuilt, the best and most typical descriptions of the rains, floods, washouts, and human reactions to them come from accounts close to the turn of the century, which stand for all the events over this forty-seven year period:

On the 4th of October 1895 one of the largest floods known in this land for many years passed through Woodruff, Holbrook and St. Johns valleys. The county bridge over the Little Colorado River three miles above Woodruff was lifted bodily and floated in a whole and complete condition to the Woodruff Dam. It went over the dam like a great streamer, but a few seconds later the ruins in a thousand pieces appeared in the torrent below.

During August [1904] very heavy rains fell and the washes were so greatly swollen that very heavy floods resulted.

President D. K. Udall of St. Johns Stake with others had labored several years to construct a reservoir about 40 miles above Woodruff ward on the Little Colorado River. There was a large body of water stored there covering 2500 acres of ground and in some places 20 feet deep. On the 26th of August this heavy levee was swept away turning this heavy body of water wildly down the [Little] Colorado River towards Woodruff and other settlements below. President Udall, feeling that the Woodruff people especially were in great danger . . . . rode all night and very nearly lost his life while crossing the Little Colorado River about 3 miles above Woodruff. However, he warned the people of Woodruff about 8 o'clock on the morning of August 27th.

The flood gradually grew higher and higher all day on the 27th at Woodruff, until the town was seriously threatened. About 10 o'clock at night, August 27, 1904, the ninth Woodruff Dam was swept away. This is regarded as a great calamity especially to the people of Woodruff and at President Udall's place in the St. Johns Stake.

November 26 [1905] a steady rain began and lasted for about 16 hours, causing terrible floods in all this country. Indeed the heaviest floods ever known, causing great damage to dams, bridges, fences and cultivated land. The dams at Snowflake and Taylor were taken out and also the Taylor bridge.

March 23 [1907] a freshet [flash flood] raised the water to the top of the dam at Daggs [reservoir] and took it out to the bottom, carrying away about one third of the dam. Considerable damage was done along the creek bottom (History and Settlement of the Snowflake Area 208, 271–272, 284, 296).

Mormon dams got stronger with each succeeding attempt to erect a permanent structure. But at the same time that Mormon technological skill in impounding water increased, flood conditions actually worsened, owing to the heavy overgrazing in an area already delicately balanced as a succulent desert. The Mormons were not aware of the cyclical dynamism of conditions around them, but their records show that the worsening environmental conditions kept pace with and may even have outrun their own growing competence in water control. This is part of the reason that the Little Colorado towns built and rebuilt so many dams and yet disasters remained so unremitting. In their desperation, the Mormons were forced to accept a particularly hard-driving deity behind these conditions, one continually testing his Saints.

Dam disasters fill the pages of the Little Colorado histories (table 11). Until the 1920s, when permanent dams using modern engineering and reinforced concrete were built, the disasters and the spiritual "testing" they represented continued unabated. Until then all Mormon dams were built in essentially one of two equally unstable ways. One type involved mud, sand, and stone piled in and around a maze of logs and brush; the other was a solid earthwork. Both types stretched across a stream. On the Little Colorado River itself, as opposed to its smaller tributaries, it was necessary to raise the level of the river water with a diversion dam so that the water flowed into an irrigation ditch placed above the dam. A pond existed behind every dam, but only those ponds on Silver Creek and at St. Johns on the upper Little Colorado were turned into reservoirs, and these required impermeable dams.

All the early diversion dams leaked as a result of the way they were constructed. Later leak-proof dams were made of earth, as in the Snowflake-Taylor area, or of stone and cement, as at Woodruff and St. Joseph. All had spillways, which were supposed to keep floods from piling up behind a dam and spilling over the top in an unselective fashion. But the spillways were never adequate, and when a flood came, the dams were too limited for the volume they were forced to handle. Moreover, dams often were not provided with adequate foundations. This factor, coupled with inadequate spillways, meant that dams frequently gave way in a flood.

Table 11. *Dam Washouts in Little Colorado Towns, 1876–1923.*[a]

Year	Woodruff	St. Joseph	Taylor	Hunt	Snowflake[b]	Round Valley	St. Johns[c]
1876		7/19					
1877		x	x[d]				
1878	4/24	x	x[e]		Fall		
1879		x			Spring repair		
1880	5/18	x					
1881	9/	3/					
1882		x					
1883	7/26	x					
1884	1/29						
	4/19						
1885	7/24						
1886							x
1887		x					
1888		x					
1889		x					
1890	2/21	2/21	2/21		2/21		
	11/8						
1891	2/17	2/17	2/17		2/17		
1892							
1893							
1894							
1895							
1896							
1897							
1898							
1899							x
1900							
1901							
1902							
1903							8/8
1904	8/27						
1905	5/2		11/26	x	4/23	3/8	4/23-26
1906			3/		3/		
1907			3/23		3/23		
1908			3/4-5[f]		3/4-5[f]		
1909							
1910							
1911			3/1-7[g]		3/1-7		
1912							
1913							
1914							
1915	x			x			x

Table 11. (*Continued*)

Year	Woodruff	St. Joseph	Taylor	Hunt	Snowflake[b]	Round Valley	St. Johns[c]
1916							
1917							
1918							
1919							
1920							
1921							
1922							
1923		x					

Source: History and Settlement of the Snowflake Area: 1870–1912. Data on Joseph City provided by George S. Tanner.

a. Letter *x* means no day or month is available.

b. First irrigation ditch in Snowflake area was built by James Stinson, a non-Mormon, in early 1870s.

c. First irrigation ditch at St. Johns was built by non-Mormons in 1873; first dam was built in 1880.

d. Five dams were built and washed away in one year at Taylor when that town was located on Little Colorado River.

e. First dam at Taylor after the settlement was moved from Little Colorado River to Silver Creek above Snowflake.

f. Floods with heavy damage.

g. Damage to Daggs Reservoir.

Dams also faced the process of aggradation. Waterborne silt did not pass through a dam; it settled behind it. No engineering device has yet been designed to solve this problem. Silt rose behind a dam in layers that were thickest just behind the dam and thinner further from it. Even on small dams the level of the stream bed might be regularly affected for several miles above the dam. As the river bed rose with the deposition of silt, a pond stretched out further, becoming shallower with distance. As the water-covered surface expanded, the water tended to spread laterally along the face of the dam and, if not checked, would run around the sides, leading to partial collapse.

When a dam washed out, a certain portion of accumulated silt flushed out. But even if washed out regularly, buildup would always be faster than any washout could counterbalance. As aggradation continued, the level of the riverbed would be permanently raised, creating a flat, broad plateau of silt, which could only be avoided by moving the location of a dam. In leaving behind some of the deposited silt, one washout played a role in hastening the next one. To deal with this problem, the people of St. Joseph built their dam at six different locations over a period of forty years, selecting spots not artificially widened by the river, or with a firmer bottom, or above recent sediment buildup, or nearer the canal's juncture with the river. This process also allowed downstream locations to continue to erode earlier accumulations of silt.

The pattern of destruction and rebuilding as revealed in the long list of washouts is so extensive as to suggest something more than tragedy. The Mormon documents from the era are eloquent about the meaning of the disasters to the local population. When a community stood watching its dam collapse, it was witnessing the destruction of thousands of man-hours of work, hundreds of dollars of hard-earned cash, and the visible symbol of existence itself. The records are clear that, when a dam went out, the world seemed close to going to pieces. But the world did not fall apart, and the dams were rebuilt so consistently that one is forced to wonder about the internal dynamics of the washout-rebuilding process.

It appears that the basic pattern of Little Colorado washouts in the nineteenth century was actually essential for the successful operation of the irrigation system. While all did not necessarily have salutary effects on the water control system, many probably did. In order for the system to function, dams had to give way with some regularity. In fact, when permanent dams were installed throughout the Little Colorado area in the 1920s, they were soon silted up and became useless, as at Woodruff, or caused massive aggradation and flooding upstream, as at Joseph City. After the 1920s the population of Woodruff turned from irrigation to wells attached to power-driven pumps set down into the water table. The dam at St. Joseph backed up so much silt that the town of Holbrook ten miles above the dam is now continually threatened by flooding as a consequence of the rise in the river bottom. Once permanent dams replaced the collapsible system, the irrigation network became increasingly useless and even dangerous.

Fully half the washouts happened in the winter. Snows in the White Mountains south of the Little Colorado melting in the spring or in an unseasonable thaw would swell the river, and if the rise were sudden and high enough, the waters would sweep over any dam. Summer floods during the thunderstorm season of July, August, and September also posed threats to the water control network. Thunderstorms throughout the desert West dump huge amounts of water in a very short time. Unable to penetrate the ground quickly, the water runs off and swells the streams. Depending on the fierceness of the flood and the condition of the dam, a flood could completely wreck the system, damage it, or pass safely through. Not all the recorded washouts were complete; some heavily damaged the irrigation system or the fields but did not destroy the dam. There was a continuum in the degree of damage inflicted. However, the process of washout and rebuilding involved in any of these events was more or less the same.

When a dam collapsed, the flood waters poured through the gap created, often taking along large sections of the dam. Sometimes nothing would be left except the abutments. With the opening of a dam, the torrent would begin to erode the silt, continuing to do so after the flood subsided until the dam was raised again. A dam burst did not guarantee that fields, crops, and town would be safe from flooding; it only gave a better chance that they would be spared. Occasionally everything was hit and the disaster was unmitigated.

However, if no dam collapse took place, the likelihood of flood water pouring through the canals and over the fields was greater. Then flood waters would erode the canals and drop their load of silt over the fields. Silt suffocates the ground with small round soil particles which plug and solidify the looser soil, making it difficult for water and air to penetrate and for plants to come up. In addition, water left to evaporate on the ground leaves mineral salts which raise the soil's salinity. They lower the yield and require flushing, which in turn depends on the operation of the irrigation system.

One of the major functions of a dam on the Little Colorado River was to settle silt before water entered the canals. The greater the velocity of the water, the greater the quantity of silt suspended. If silty water is stopped in a pond, the silt will settle out before the water is led along the canals into the fields. During the summer rainy season today, the Little Colorado River bears a 25 percent load of silt by volume. At such a rate, a settling pond would fill up rapidly. This condition is not so marked along Silver Creek, although during the rainy season it can easily carry a 10 percent load of silt. The more successfully a dam operated to provide a pond, the less successfully it could handle a substantial flood because it quickly built up a load of silt which, by raising the river's bottom, made it possible for a flood to run around the dam's sides or over its top. Since many later dams were meant to hold back all water in a stream, they invited an even more difficult time. They had been trapping all the silt and were suddenly forced to hold a mass of extra water. The greater the inability of a dam to handle a flood, the greater the danger that flood waters would erupt into the canals and fields if the dam itself did not give way. With a break, flood waters rushed by the town and fields instead of through them, cleaning out the load of silt which had been compromising the dam's usefulness. This feedback accounts for the rapid succession of dam destruction in the early period of Mormon settlement. It probably accounts for many of the later washouts as well and helps to explain their periodicity.

There are no contemporary figures on the rate of silt aggradation behind these dams. It is, therefore, difficult to know what a maximally efficient rate of washouts would be, but some hint is gleaned from the regularity of destruction in the earliest years of Mormon dam-building. Maximum efficiency would have required an annual clean-out except in drought years. Efficiency would have dictated dams that could be opened at the bottom, allowing the river to flush its own bed, and annual flushing was exactly what the Mormons allowed in their first ten years and what they had to put up with periodically until the 1920s.

Not every washout, however, was efficient. Occasionally there were two or more floods in one year, each damaging or destroying a dam and its connected system. There was no way to avoid seeing these as disasters. Nonetheless, given the primitive technology and semiarid farming conditions, the system worked. It produced neither equilibrium nor plenty; it was a marginal success.

A flood that produced a dam disaster, damaging the water control system and the fields, precipitated action affecting the whole town and the entire set of Mormon communities in the Little Colorado area. The loss of a dam meant starvation for the community unless its people took a number of steps, which after several repetitions became routinized. First and foremost was rebuilding the dam. But to do so, capital had to be raised, supplies brought to the town whose potential surplus had been destroyed, and labor for the actual rebuilding of the dam recruited and organized. These and other major activities had to be initiated if the stricken town were to survive.

Two-thirds of the towns dependent on water control for survival have in fact survived. There was grief when a dam burst, but nobody ever starved and nobody ever lacked help. One of the first events in a town after a dam disaster was a visit by a member of the area's hierarchy or by one of the Twelve Apostles. The apostles, traveling members of the governing body of the church, were often present in the Arizona towns, especially through the first twenty years of their existence. They might be hiding out from federal polygamy hunters, but they still served as a powerful, sensitive link to Salt Lake City. As a result, a disaster in one of the towns would immediately come to their attention, and aid for the disaster victims would be prompt and many-faceted.

The usual pattern after a disaster was a two-sided program of relief and rebuilding, both carried on under the aegis of the church, particularly through its rituals. Shortly after a disaster, the leadership assessed the damage, the immediate needs of the community, and the requirements to rebuild the dam and repair the damage. Then a sermon was preached to the townspeople about the trial that God had just visited on his own people to make them more worthy of his imminent second coming. There was no doubt that the washout was God's way of showing the Saints that they had imperfections displeasing to him. And just as clear was the washout's message that further effort was needed by Mormons to prepare the earth for God's coming. The desert was to be overcome, and the overcoming was concrete proof that God was coming again, this time through the agency of his appointed church. Through a series of such sermons, the hierarchy explained the event to the people, who thus explained it to themselves, and the world view of defeat was transformed into the world view of another chance to show their worthiness to be God's chosen:

President E. N. Freeman of the St. Johns Stake said . . . We cannot see the advantage of trials until we pass through them. If we put off the time to do a thing when called on, we do not gain by it. The Lord's ways are not a man's ways. We sometimes feel that we are harshly dealt with, and these trials have taken some out of the Church, but they are to prepare us for something better. Some of us do not profit by what we pass through. Our Savior had charity upon the cross, he said Father forgive them for they know not what they do. All our trials are for our benefit. We are to be saviors to all mankind. We have been sent out to these desert places to prepare us for this great work. Some have order about their labor, while others do not have this order; we need to use the blessings that surround us. When the Prophet had his vision, his friends tried to convince him that it was delusion. We have no reason to complain. Let us look at the trial the Prophet had to pass through. No matter what we pass through, we know the Lord lives. If we put dams in the river and they never washed out, we would not be tried by putting them in again. It seems that the fires are being lit up that are to try us. It is said that the Lord would raise up a man to lead his people out of bondage. If we were not in bondage, we could not be led out; the Lord will bring something to try each of us. If we are faithful, we will meet our friends again. We lose our dearest and warmest relatives, these trials come but we should say: thy will be done, O Lord. (Historical Record, Snowflake Stake 1890–1892:14–15).

As the persecution of Mormons rose, the world view of trial-by-ordeal came to characterize their beliefs. This ideology, which was not native to Mormonism and certainly was not consistent with what Joseph Smith had hoped to accomplish in terms of earthly liberation for his people, grew especially strong in Arizona and on the fringes of Mormondom. It was deeply instilled in Mormon colonists and was perpetuated by them. It kept people persevering at difficult tasks which were thought to be essential to building up the kingdom in general, and eventually it produced a world view of permanent subordination, as reported by a contemporary Mormon diarist:

> The Church authorities were practical and philosophical. For example: the people on the Little Colorado were having a hard time, especially at Woodruff and Joseph City. They just couldn't keep those dams in, and a couple of the Apostles came down to look things over and give encouragement and aid to those people.
>
> Those Apostles came on up into the more prosperous communities and at meetings asked us to donate. Quote: "Brothers and Sisters: You know the extreme difficulties our people are having along the Little Colorado. We must not let those settlements be broken up. You more prosperous people must help them. Donate of your cattle, horses, grain, wagons—anything you can spare that they can use ... Listen (and the speaker lowered his voice), if we can just keep those old people there till they die off and the young ones grow up, it will be home to those young people. And when the dam goes out, they will be just like a bunch of beavers. They won't know anything else but to go and put it in again. They will be permanently located—rooted into the soil" unquote. Good philosophy, no? Who else would have thought of that but a Mormon colonization promoter? And, the people of the more prosperous communities contributed liberally (Coleman in Peterson 1973:188–189).

Rituals based on this kind of philosophy can be used to present arbitrary, even fallacious logic as acceptable truth. They can also reduce skepticism to irony—at least for the Mormon diarist—and turn irrational moves into plausible acts of faith. This ideology produced Woodruff's thirteen dams, sustained its population around a permanent core of families, and made everyone give to support the town's needs—all this despite the demonstratively unproductive nature of the place.

After the immediate psychological and ideological ministration to the community, an organized effort was made in the other Mormon towns to assist the one losing its dam. The Stake Presidency had authority to ship supplies from local tithing storehouses all over the stake, to divert funds, and to direct people to tithe in labor by working a number of hours on the reconstruction. A wide spectrum of religious meetings rallied and enlisted the cooperation of the whole population.

A dam disaster affected all levels of Mormon life, and almost every primary effect produced a feedback. For example, in order to ensure an income to themselves after a washout, some members of the stricken town would work in nearby gentile towns. One mother and her elder daughters from Woodruff worked in the hotel in Holbrook. Men worked for cattle-raising outfits or on a dozen other jobs. Such laboring among the gentiles was explicitly discouraged as a means of earning a living for the Saints. Not only did wage work throw Mormons into contact with the outside world, but it adjusted them to the idea of wage labor, a concept foreign to farmers oriented to cooperative efforts. Yet in emergency such work brought much-needed cash into the community and provided it with a base to consider reconstruction.

Often a disaster would force Mormon children into the local public schools. Yet Mormons were excluded from teaching in the public schools, usually by local, unconstitutional rulings, and the presence of Mormon children in them violated one of the principal guidelines of a saintly life. Education in gentile schools was a major threat to the homogeneity of the Mormon way of life.

The instant a dam broke, the carrying capacity of the immediate area was vastly exceeded. If a family could support itself on wage labor during the period when its town had no dam, the chances were high that it would not have to leave its home. Usually, however, such a disaster was the prelude to migration from the stricken community. It was also one of the major factors acting as a check on the number of people coming into the Little Colorado area. Breaks, regardless of their supposed advantage, often produced a year without crops. Under such constraints, the whole population of the Little Colorado area climbed to little more than 3000 by 1890, though many more people entered the area. The primitiveness of the irrigation system kept the population so low, and two-thirds to three-quarters of those who stayed were supported by the irrigation system. The paradox is that the system would not have functioned at all without periodic washouts.

Dam disasters limited the population from expanding beyond the point Mormon leaders would have favored, but the disasters also kept the population in any one town so low that no catastrophic disaster could level a population too big for the weak economy to support. Just as dams operated under a natural system that automatically precipitated washouts, so a washout also initiated an outmigration from towns that were overpopulated. Some of the population returned to Utah; some went to southern Arizona, either to Mesa or to the Mormon towns in the desert; a few went into northern Mexico; and many went to other towns on the Little Colorado. Often they brought needed skills to a community that could afford to support them.

These various demographic patterns reflected the extreme mobility of a segment of the local population. Shifting between a core of settled towns was a population remnant made up of families who tried to settle in one or more locations over a period of years. In addition, the entire population was subject to a very high infant mortality rate and a depressingly high accident rate, which meant that mobility, accompanied by a fairly high death rate, severely limited population growth in an area whose economy was overextended from the beginning.

Not one of the Mormon towns on the Little Colorado could support even a thousand people. The average population was in the low hundreds throughout the nineteenth century and by the mid-1880s was fixed. After that date the carrying capacity could be expanded only by founding new towns. This became increasingly hard to do, since in one form or another new towns had to be capitalized by Salt Lake and by the mid-1880s the church was engaged in a battle with the outside world for survival as an institution. It no longer had adequate resources to found new towns on the fringes of its empire when it was under attack at its center. The floating population survived by floating, not by settling down. People shifted from locale to locale, abandoning some towns and founding new ones. The largest shifts occurred in the late 1870s and the first half of the 1880s; by 1886 half a dozen towns were dead. Down to the present day, a segment of the local population readily moves from one town to another depending on the demands of the economy.

To prevent the whole population from becoming one large migration when disaster struck, the role of the church management was central. To cope with disaster in long-range rather than immediate terms, the church used the Quarterly Stake Conference. A dam disaster was never more than three months away from a conference, of which it automatically became the subject. The conference was used as a managerial device for sustaining the affected community and for organizing supply and rebuilding activities. The bishops' reports given at a Quarterly Conference between 1890 and 1892, for example, included notice of a recent serious flood and appraised the whole community of its damage:

Bp. John Hunt said . . . The flood that has come upon us [Snowflake] has injured us quite badly, it has me . . . Our ditches are somewhat injured, our dams of this ward are not injured much, our lands are damaged some . . .

Bp. John Bushman said, in regard to the settlement [St. Joseph, later Joseph City] where I reside . . . We have suffered a loss, the water having washed around and taken a part of our dam. Our people are poor but we have a desire to establish a little ward. We have inducements, there is plenty of land and it produces fairly.

Bp. E. M. Webb said . . . The dam that has gone out does not discourage me. I never have been satisfied to stay at Woodruff until this dam went out and now I feel to stay (Historical Record, Snowflake Stake 1890–1892:16–18).

At a meeting of the High Council during the Quarterly Conference, the leadership of the stake and any of the visiting General Authorities faced the basic problems raised by these reports: whether or not the town-site should be abandoned, how much annual tithing could be diverted to dam-rebuilding, and whether or not a new bishop was needed in the community to pull it together for a new effort.

During the conference rebuilding also began. Cooperative action, for example, was taken at a priesthood meeting during a Quarterly Conference on November 18, 1904, after another washout at Woodruff:

> Through the appeal of President Jesse N. Smith and other leading brethren the Priesthood Meeting voted to assist the people of Woodruff Ward to rebuild their dam which the flood destroyed last August.
>
> An allotment to the wards was made to contribute to the Woodruff Dam Fund as follows:
>
> | | |
> |---|---:|
> | Snowflake was asked for | $ 650.00 |
> | St. Joseph ” ” ” | 400.00 |
> | Taylor ” ” ” | 400.00 |
> | Show Low ” ” ” | 50.00 |
> | Total | $1500.00 |
>
> Pinedale ward was excused and a part of the people of Show Low ward because they had lost their crops of 1904 through the severe drought.
>
> Pres. Smith explained that the church had contributed $500.00 in cash for the Woodruff Dam Fund. He also stated the contributions named above, he wished to be first used to assist the sick, the widows, and the more unfortunate of the Woodruff people in paying their dam assessments (History and Settlement of the Snowflake Area 276).

Another conference saw Jesse Smith, stake president, organize three or four dozen men who volunteered their labor to rebuild the dam at Woodruff. Under the president's leadership, their six weeks of work represented one long uninterrupted Mormon act of worship. When a bishop led the reconstruction, the whole of Mormon religion was present.

Contemporary documents show that daily labor was an act of worship and that, in the case of critical projects, worship was filled with an unusual immediacy because one had to search for God's will in current events. Was the washout a sign to leave the town? Was periodic disaster a message to abandon the spot as a place to settle? Should they or should they not seek an alternative to the whole effort? These questions occurred to every family about its relation to the town, the dam, and settlement in Arizona, and it occurred to the whole people as a people about its common effort.

The trial, thus expressed, presented a major difficulty in management. The question was who should determine God's answer. The rigid hierarchy of decision-making prevented atomization, but the notion of testing that accompanied this hierarchy and worked throughout the whole population allowed the people to convince themselves: the Saints could expect to be forever subject to God's efforts to perfect them through the fires of adversity. At a Quarterly Conference around 1890 Jesse N. Smith, in enunciating the decision to push ahead with another dam at Woodruff, explained what meeting the latest disaster would produce:

> Some in certain districts find themselves stripped of all they possess by floods . . . those who struggled . . . are the ones in whom confidence can be placed . . . those who become strong making each failure a success. There is no one prominent among the Latter-day Saints who has not struggled with poverty (Historical Record, Snowflake Stake 1890–1892:4–5).

When a decision to rebuild a dam had been made and a plan of action set up, doubts were alleviated at the communal level. Doubts could never be entirely eliminated, however, despite the taken-for-granted stance enunciated by the hierarchy. Since the resolution of doubts and the forming of decisions took place in the various types of worship service, those services themselves took on the character of forums for confronting the pragmatic in the context of the sacred.

On the surface it appeared that rituals acted to maintain equilibrium, as was the case with the redistribution of tithing. The functioning whole, a combination of ecological management and religious action, is illustrated in the minutes of a priesthood meeting sometime between 1890 and 1892 where, amid prayer and hymn-singing, the actual rules for allocating water were laid out and agreed on by the leaders of the community:

House called to order by Pres. Jesse N. Smith.
  Singing by the Brethren.
  Prayer by Ninian Miller.
  Singing by the Brethren.
  Pres. J. N. Smith said: It has been proposed that the 2 wards, Snowflake and Taylor [cooperate] in the work of our dams and ditches.
  Pres. L. H. Hatch said: as he understood it had been decided that we work equally according to acres on the dams, ditches and reservoirs.
  Bro. N. Miller favored the proposition to make a general cause on the ditches.
  Bro. Jenning favored it. Some others spoke on the subject.
  On motion it was carried that we have a committee of 4 to adjudicate this water matter.
  On motion it was carried that John H. Willis, Alof Larson, Jas. H. Lewis and Willard Hatch be this committee.
  On motion it was carried that we have a general water master.
  On motion it was carried that Alexander Steward be the chief water divider.
  On motion it was carried that A. Stewart ... appoint all the sub-water masters for the 2 wards.
  On motion it was carried that the water be measured by the Leffeill system or plan.
  On motion it was carried that we have a general recorder to record these claims, etc.
  On motion it was carried that John H. Willis be the general water recorder (Historical Record, Snowflake Stake 1890–1892:10–13).

This is how a system operates that calls all members priests and all actions sacred. In larger rituals, "ditch-cleaning was a job that settlers knew well, returning to it in a dogged annual rhythm punctuated by periodic repairs necessitated by floods and washouts. Water assessments and work schedules announced from church pulpits were frequent ceremonials as the cycle of maintenance went on" (Peterson 1973:180).

The whole area's participation in dam maintenance and reconstruction guaranteed that the benefiting community would reciprocate when any other town needed cooperative labor in its turn. Since nearly every town could count on a mishap sooner rather than later, and since there was some periodicity to disasters, crises were staggered throughout the area. That staggering allowed time for a town to recoup its economic position before being called on to contribute part of its surplus and labor to a newly unfortunate neighbor. Rituals kept the dams maintained and rebuilt, while dams provided the empirical content for rituals which, as soon as they had the appropriate content, acted to care for the dams. Besides these two factors, a third variable was introduced into the system almost from the start. Dropped into the reciprocating interaction between ritual and dam-building was success itself.

Just as Mormonism had developed under an extended series of crises before settling in the desert West, the crises continued and became more varied after Mormons got there. Even in a single domain like water control, an evolution took place in the kinds of problems that Mormons had to face. Because the nature of their technology and the realities of gaining a living were changing, changes were also introduced into the rituals. Mormonism generated success, but that success was also to change it.

The changes in technological problems were noticeable in the dams on the Little Colorado and Silver Creek:

The first dams were not large works, rising no more than twelve feet. As a lift of more than a few feet was usually avoided, it was hoped that such modest barriers would be adequate. Hard experience soon proved that the happy combination of conditions under which the small dam sufficed was limited indeed. Larger works or continuing reconstruction were consequently required.

All of the earliest dams were constructed of dirtfill, bound and stabilized by rock, cedar brush, and logs. In time settlers learned to lay them with the side fronting the water rising at a gentle pitch so that the flood swept up and over, leaving the dam intact. Before the turn of the century, more impressive works had been made on the Little Colorado, but Silver Creek was still controlled by a series of these earthen and rubble diversion dams. For decades it proved necessary to replace them with heartbreaking regularity. Later a degree of permanence was achieved by pouring concrete shells over the dams and laying aprons downstream onto which flooding waters fell as they came over the dam.

After the earliest years, efforts were made to impound unused water in reservoirs to supplement the natural flow of the streams during periods of heavy irrigation. Between Snowflake and Taylor, for example, three such reservoirs had been constructed by the early 1890s. Dams or levees ten or twelve feet in height and two hundred yards in length were built, generally at sites removed from the direct path of the river. One of these was said to have "about 4550 yards of earth work in the bank besides rock and brush." Its capacity was estimated at "enough water to irrigate 1000 acres over once" (Peterson 1973:178–179).

Mormons dealt with different kinds of dams, which in turn had different rates of replacement and were perfected at different rates. This variability was successfully handled, even though it meant several different solutions to the same problem. The first eight dams built at Woodruff, for example, on the Little Colorado River between 1878 and 1890 were increased in size and strength each time; the next two, built in November 1890 and February 1891, were also washed away. "As engineering skills increased and the weather moderated, [an] eleventh dam, now flagged by stone slabs, held until 1904." The twelfth collapsed in 1915. Then, "Weary, but this time with substantial state and church aid, Woodruff turned to dam number thirteen. Engineers now determined that ditches could be chiseled along the canyon side making feasible the construction of a dam on Silver Creek just above its confluence with the river. Escaping the silts and minerals of the Little Colorado as well as its fierce floods, a permanent diversion dam was completed in 1919" (Peterson 1973:185–186.) The sheer scale of the changes made to guarantee security was evident by the turn of the century:

About the 10th of January 1904 James G. Camps, Asst. Engineer of Boise Idaho, in the Reclamation Service, U.S. Geological Survey, came into our Stake, and after looking about for a time proceeded to survey a dam site and reservoir site in the box canyon about one quarter mile above the Woodruff Dam. The dam if ever built will be 90 ft. high and hold the water back up the Colorado about 6 miles.

During the Conference [May 1904] Pres. Jesse N. Smith announced that the First Presidency will encourage both by influence and substantial means to build the Lone Pine Reservoir; with the object in view of reclaiming several thousand acres more land.

Oct. 16 [1905] a Brother J. Fewson Smith arrived on the same train with Pres. Smith coming for the purpose of surveying the dam and reservoir sites claimed by our people and make reports and recommendations at headquarters according to his findings.

He visited the Woodruff Dam site and suggested a much stronger and heavier dam and the main body of solid masonry. Later he proposed a pumping plant for the time being for the purpose of irrigation (History and Settlement of the Snowflake Area 263, 296, 282–284).

Technological, economic, and social changes which resulted mostly in improvements brought concomitant changes in skills, jobs, modes of organization, and ways of thinking. One of the implications of success, as Rappaport recognized, was the degrading of sanctity by sources of power more empirically predictable than the supernatural:

When, because of technological development, it became possible for authorities to stand upon power rather than upon sanctity, they did not dispense entirely with sanctity. Rather the relationship between sanctity and authority changed. Whereas the unquestionable status of ultimate sacred propositions previously rested upon affirmation through the religious experiences of the faithful, it now came to rest, overtly or covertly, upon force. Whereas previously authority was contingent upon its sanctification, sanctity now became the instrument of authority (Rappaport 1971a:41).

The Mormon leaders understood that their authority as religious figures would be undermined by certain forms of technological development and that, for their rituals to retain the power to regulate the society and economy, some forms had to be kept out. Hence their explicit fears of the railroad, cattle-raising, mining, timbering, trading, and any undertakings that brought them into close contact with gentiles. The church's capacity to govern depended on a basically cooperative and predominantly agrarian way of life in which God, through his church, not through the techniques of strangers, was the problem-solver and regulator. Mormon rituals worked because the frontier and the hierarchy had combined to ensure that anything which would solve their problems differently was unavailable. In short, they lived in and partly created a state of technological underdevelopment.

But Mormons also believed in perfectibility. They wanted nothing of magic and everything of rational control over human progress; they not only anticipated earthly improvement but guaranteed it. Their continued improvement of water control technology was one indication of this commitment. But such improvements guaranteed success to some and wealth to others. Success and the security it gave, as shown by the tithing and irrigation systems, represented the kind of power that ultimately undermined the role of religion as the chief source of power in Mormon society by providing alternatives: "There was never a time when this Church has so many members as today. We did not all embrace the Gospel at the same time or under the same conditions: some are tried with wealth, this is the case in Salt Lake City and Ogden, some there who have a small piece of land ... soon find themselves in possession of property to the amount of $100,000" (Historical Record, Snowflake Stake 1890–1892:4).

This is what success looked like in the Salt Lake valley forty years after the Mormons moved there. Their success had been produced by an economy governed by religious sanctions issued through rituals, and the same process produced the same result in Arizona. Dependence upon unempirical power soon produced a kind of power which was quite empirical. Improved technology and expertise formed one source of security, which Mormons cultivated and utilized. In turn, these produced and maintained the surplus wealth expressed as tithing and as private profit, an allied source of power. Yet another source of power was rationalized knowledge, expressed in technical know-how, as opposed to inspiration or revelation. These three forms of power, which were not exactly independent of each other, represent the success of sanctity but are qualitatively different from it.

Religious power was further weakened by being linked too closely to the directives that governed action: "As water matters came to take a large part of his [Jesse N. Smith, stake president] time, stake gatherings increasingly assumed the character of staff meetings from which water policy and administration issued. One Danish settler uttered a truism when he remarked from the pulpit that all that was talked about in worship meeting was 'Vater Ditch! Vater Ditch! Vater Ditch!' " (Peterson 1973:183). The Dane's complaint shows that Mormons linked messages about the supernatural to directives on subsistence within their rituals. The link diluted the sacred by making the unempirical real and measurable, limiting God's measure to whatever material aim was in sight. By pragmatizing rituals, Mormons came to understand God by whatever goal was handy, but because their world was changing rapidly, so did God and all he stood for. While such pragmatism was useful and even necessary in the early phases of settlement in Utah, Arizona, and elsewhere, it was not justified later when other sources of power beyond Mormon control had come into existence. When that happened, practical issues were still dealt with in rituals, and pragmatized rituals often just masked directives coming from elsewhere.

The history of the water control system is linked by three factors: religious government based on primitive technology, the search for worldly success, and the identification of success with religious experience. These made the efforts at water control an open-ended spiral of interactions leading to continual change because improved technology, although satisfying in religious terms, made religious government unnecessary. Later, when the Mormon world became owned by outside powers, Mormonism's close linkage of improved circumstances to religious experience meant that when its people worked for others, they thought they were still working for God.

5

Ecclesiastical Courts: Inventing Labels and Enforcing Definitions

The Mormons in Arizona managed to achieve harmony, establish community, and set up a working society, but not without strenuous efforts. Those who moved into Arizona came from all parts of Utah; some, in addition, were converts from the South. Most were total strangers, having never seen or heard of each other before. Though they shared Mormonism and farming, privation and persecution, they had never lived as neighbors, never shared the same immediate leadership and the same land, water, cattle, or enemies. Even if they were agreed on Mormonism, they had not worked out the meaning of their religion when applied to concrete situations. United in ideas about God and life as encoded in Mormon doctrine and traditions, they did not begin life in Arizona with an understanding of what Mormonism should look like on that ground. However, they did have an institution which allowed them to invent the agreement and understanding needed to create a working community: the High Council, whose fifteen men acted as legislature and court. It became the community's instrument for establishing normative behavior. Through the operations of the council the community defined itself and established its own rules.

The council minutes record the practical decisions made during the first twenty-five years of the community's existence (table 12). In them are accounts of court trials, revealing how issues changed as the community matured. In

Table 12. *High Council Trials in Eastern Arizona and Snowflake Stakes, 1884–1896.*

Date	Offense	Decision	Comments
Mar. 1884	Jumping (illegal settlement) a ranch and killing 35 sheep in the process	Case dismissed	
Sept. 1884	Drunkenness and profanity	Reversed ruling of Bp. Ct.[a] for disfellowshiping	
Mar. 1885	Drunk and bringing disgrace	Excommunicated for apostasy, drunkenness, unchristian conduct	
June 1885	Profanity, whoredom, apostasy	Upheld ruling of Bp. Ct. for excommunication	
Sept. 1885	Adultery, unchristian conduct	Disfellowshiped	
Sept. 1885	Cattle-stealing	Charge not sustained	
Sept. 1885	Adultery	Decision deferred	Case too complex for decision because involved a rebaptism in 1881, requiring consultation with Salt Lake City
Dec. 1885	Adultery	Excommunication deferred from Sept. 1885	Rebaptism rejected
June 1886	Punishing an Indian	Reversed ruling of Bp. Ct. for disfellowshiping	
Sept. 1886	Appropriating mission property (Hunt *v.* Smith & Hatch)	Case continued from earlier unrecorded date	Discussion

Table 12. (*Continued*)

Date	Offense	Decision	Comments
Sept. 1886	Hunt *v.* Smith & Hatch	Case continued	Continued discussion; Hunt called to "make the affair right before the people"
Dec. 1886	Drunkenness and Stealing	Upheld previous disfellowshiping	
Dec. 1886	Hunt *v.* Smith & Hatch	Hunt indicted	Confusion surrounding Hunt case was termed "unsatisfactory"; Hunt called to stand trial
Dec. 1886	Bestiality	Charge ruled unfounded; case dropped	Option to charge the charger was stopped "lest more trouble be made"
Jan. 1887	Cutting lucerne, taking unmarked cattle and yearling, neglect and exploitation of bro.'s wife and family	Settled item by item	Case on appeal from St. Johns
Jan. 1887	Two appeals	Upheld two previous excommunications	
Jan. 1887	Hunt *v.* Smith & Hatch		Smith wanted to have Hunt step aside
Mar. 1887	Hunt *v.* Smith & Hatch	Hunt disfellowshiped	Hunt: "Smith has been tyrannical"
June 1887	Adultery, on appeal	"Present self to people and ask for forgiveness"	
June 1887	Defrauding U.S. Post Office of $5000	Excommunicated	

Table 12. (*Continued*)

Date	Offense	Decision	Comments
July 1887	Hunt *v.* Smith & Hatch on appeal	Reversed disfellowshiping	Hunt reinstated by 3 apostles; no significant difference seen between Hunt's and Smith's opinions on the dispute; Smith gently chastised in private; no public display
Dec. 1887	Default on debt of $20	Upheld previous ruling to pay back	
Mar. 1888	Theft of child	Upheld previous ruling for excommunication	
May 1888	Theft of government flour in freighting	Upheld ruling of Bp. Ct.	
Mar. 1889	Liberties with a wife and unchristian conduct	Not guilty	Established court's right to "ferret out sin and iniquity and expand charges"
May 1889	Partnership responsibilities and profit-sharing (H.L. Hayes *v.* L. Smith)	Referred to Pres. Woodruff for disposition	
June 1889	Improper disposition of property	Refund money; no church penalty	
May 1890	Complaint claiming $95 on note	Pay back in 6 mo. with 10% interest	
Feb. 1891	Betting and racing	Stand before people and confess wrong	J.N. Smith: "This thing of getting something for nothing should be frowned upon"

Table 12. (*Continued*)

Date	Offense	Decision	Comments
May 1891	Bringing falsely before the law (L. Smith *v.* H.L. Hayes)	Decision deferred	Major issue: better to take a loss than to sue before the law
Feb. 1893	Unchristian conduct	Pay penalty of one cow or (?) one yearling	
Aug. 1895	Default on note of $1000	Pay back	
Aug. 1896	Adultery and incest	Upheld previous disfellowshiping with excommunication	
Nov. 1896	Hurt feelings because forbidden by Bp. to speak at meeting	No official ruling; Bp. (offender) told to forbear	Apostle J.W. Taylor defended free speech

Source: High Council Minutes, Eastern Arizona Stake and Snowflake Stake 1880–1898, 1898–1907.

a. Bp. Ct. stands for Bishop's Court.

the cases reported here, names of the accused, accusors, and witnesses are changed, but the names of High Council members are not. The data exemplify how Mormon culture became established in Arizona—how, through the labels given to events and the definitions imposed on reality, a system of common meanings manifested itself as a smoothly working system. The court system gave itself the right to handle all but the most serious crimes. There is no record of murder, for example, but should such an event have taken place, it would have been referred to the distant civil courts.

To assume that this group of people, heretofore strangers, had only to decide to cooperate and then to invent a social contract would be to oversimplify the problem. For agreement to be reached, there had to be disagreement; for disagreement to be resolved, there had to be a mechanism for arbitrating disputes. This mechanism was the High Council. It initiated, heard, resolved, and utilized disputes and dispute management. Its authority, like all contemporary Mormon institutions, which were heavily dependent on sanctity, stemmed from its ability to define the nature of a dispute in such a way that the whole community saw what the issue was and agreed on its solution.

Because the needs of a new religious community differ from those of a modern nation-state, some of the matters discussed and tried before Mormon courts might seem strange, or trivial, or even painfully beside the point. But they all rested on one or more of the three central issues that were neither trivial, nor strange, nor beside the point and which dominated nearly all business of the High Council in Arizona from the early 1880s well into the early twentieth century. The first and most important issue was to secure the unity of the community: gaining support from people inside and exclusion of those outside. Mormons had to set the boundaries of their community. The second issue was to define the nature of authority, identifying who would have power over whom in the hierarchy. As the nineteenth century ended and the community grew better established, a third issue emerged. Mormons had to reconcile differences between the traditional, cooperative Mormon economy and the increasingly important capitalist economy which was absorbing them. These three issues usually underlay the range of disputes discussed in or tried before the High Council, including theft, adultery, indecent behavior, default, fraud, and insubordination.

Given the fact that deviance is not an absolute category but is defined and redefined by a society, its definition may be achieved by the settlement and arbitration of disputes. When the council issued a decision, it established one range of behavior that would be punished and another range that would be tolerated. Since Mormonism never developed a code of canon law, even though it had an elaborate court system, it was able to tolerate variations all over the kingdom. While the variations matched the wide range of novel circumstances that Mormons were getting used to, they also meant that no body of law serving as precedent was carried into a new community as a foundation for resolving the inevitable disputes. Mormon communities established rules for normal behavior, not by deducing them from scripture, but by reacting to particular events and setting limits for what would be tolerated in each instance. This meant every time Mormons settled down, they had to reinvent much of Mormonism, and the reinvention did not necessarily duplicate what they had been familiar with. The process of inventing and reinventing community life with all its meanings, feelings, and rules kept pace with the continuing process of technological experimentation. Both processes predisposed Mormons to adjust, adapt, and continually change the meanings and definitions that they applied to the whole of life.

Because the High Council handled that part of change known as deviation, the balanced part of Mormon society could continue to operate effectively. In large part, the equilibrium and balance manifested in local Mormon society were possible because the High Council listened to problems arising from the minutiae of everyday life. It showed individuals how to arrive at solutions in the midst of ambiguity; it worked because it plunged into this ambiguity and handled it in a decentralized, sensitive way. The council routinized novelty and, by giving it definition, made it a normal part of Mormonism and contributed to the efficient operation of the system.

The High Council was composed of the most important men in the community. The minutes from Arizona show that the council always met on the Friday before a Stake Conference and that decisions made then were often presented for public ratification the next day; the council frequently met on a monthly basis as well. It could be called into session whenever a difficulty arose. Regardless of whether the council acted as a court or as an adviser to the Stake Presidency, its decisions amounted to prescriptions. Because there was a tendency for the council in its role as court to deal with novel and critical issues, it became the central stage where new meanings were invented. Once the council as court had invented the new labels, the council in its role as a deliberative body routinized its own definitions by repeatedly applying them in other areas.

When the council sat as a court, it was part of a larger set of courts within the church, and this elaborate system had a detail and comprehensiveness that was not paralleled by the council's organization as a deliberative or advisory body. Mormon church courts were originally founded for relatively restricted uses. Their real florescence occurred in the Utah period of the church and ceased when the United States set up fully operating civil courts in all Western territories by the turn of the century. The church had, and maintains, a hierarchy of courts consisting of three levels. The lowest was a Bishop's Court, composed of a bishop and his two councilors. Since every ward had a bishop, every ward also contained a Bishop's Court. In these, the majority of the cases took place. The records for these courts in Arizona have not survived.

The second and most important court was that of the High Council. Throughout the desert West in the nineteenth century, the High Councils had both original and appellate jurisdictions, the latter covering the Bishop's Courts. The third court, the one of last appeal and potentially open to all, was the First Presidency of the church. The president and his first and second councilors sat for the rare cases brought to this court from the High Council.

Of these three courts, the High Council heard all significant cases and, because of its authority, could effectively turn court decisions into legislation. The High Council was more than a court: in the nineteenth century it was entrusted with the spiritual and temporal well-being of the stake. Within the council, the stake president was also president of the court and had responsibility for appointing the twelve members of the High Council. When all acted together as a court, the president, after consulting with his two councilors and engaging in private prayer, passed judgment. The two major penalties open to him at his discretion were "disfellowshiping" and "excommunication." Disfellowshiping meant the loss of standing in the community. It could be reversed by public confession or by fulfilling whatever sentence the court handed down. Excommunication meant expulsion from the church but could be reversed under some conditions. These penalties were powerful social tools in the small towns of nineteenth century Arizona, but even more powerful was public confession, which enforced the decisions and was a prelude to reinstatement in the community's grace. In confession, the convicted individual stood before a congregation, admitted guilt, and requested forgiveness. With so mighty a tool, a stake president or bishop could reduce an individual to compliance. However, it was the court's policy to restrict the apology to those who already had knowledge of the offense. If only the priesthood knew about it, for example, forgiveness was required only of the priesthood.

When a case came before the High Council either for trial or on appeal, certain procedures were followed. Upon appointment, every high councilor was given a set position, numbered from one to twelve, and for as long as he was on the council he held the same number, although later in the century in Arizona the councilors chose lots numbered to twelve for each new case. When a case came up, the president decided how serious it was and appointed two, four, or six councilors to speak for a defendant and an equal number for the plaintiff, the even-numbered councilors standing up for the accused to "prevent insult and injustice," and the odd-numbered councilors standing up for the prosecution. The issues were argued by the councilors after the evidence had been presented. In practice, the arguments were presented alternately—one for the accused, then one against—all taking place before the public. After the arguments, the president and his two councilors retired to consider the evidence, to pray, and to make a decision. Their decision was announced and then sustained by a vote of the twelve high councilors and the whole audience. If one or both of the president's two councilors dissented, the decision still held, for the president's decision was thought to be a manifestation of the Holy Ghost.

Whereas the president's power was not circumscribed by his court, it was considered essential that a public vote of all present, both councilors and audience, be taken to sustain the announced decision. Sometimes at this point there was dissent, but not often, since such action could be looked upon as insubordination. Since the chief penalties available to the court were disfellowshiping and excommunication, and since these depended on a cooperating public, the vote of as many people as possible to approve the decision was crucial. Such stringent social control had to depend on community acquiescence, and this was obtained through the public vote of approval when the High Council originally made its decision.

Both church courts and the High Council had their powers diminished during and after the 1890s with the establishment of civil courts and secular government. Neither courts nor council disappeared, but both became limited solely to affairs internal to the church. The courts continue to hear cases on moral issues down to the present. Sexual offenses like adultery and homosexuality, violations of church policy like keeping plural wives, sustained belief in doctrinal principals opposed by the church, and dishonesty of all sorts are dealt with by ecclesiastical courts, which still use confession, disfellowshiping, and excommunication as their main penalties.

During the court's period of greatest importance in nineteenth century Arizona, the issue that returned most consistently to the council both as court and as deliberative body was a tough, two-sided one: how to behave toward those who were in and those who were outside the community. It was easy to distinguish a Mormon from a non-Mormon. What was hard was to know how to *behave* to a non-Mormon. How far away were others to be kept? Given the vulnerability of the Mormons, where was the line to be drawn between exclusion and hostility? Or, in terms of behavior, how were others to be handled without provoking dangerous opposition? Within the community, the problem was not so much uniform behavior to outsiders as to each other. In a heterogeneous group of three thousand people, what variation should be tolerated and what prohibited? What should these people be unified about? What were the key agreements needed for community harmony and survival?

The Mormons did not live in a vacuum. The *Book of Mormon* and Brigham Young, for example, defined their relationship to the Indians. This issue was raised in court in June 1886 when a Mormon was tried and convicted for "punishing an Indian" (High Council Minutes 1880–1898). Mormon problems with other neighbors never reached court, although from time to time the High Council attempted to keep cowboys from attending Mormon dances:

> President Smith then urged that we have an unwritten regulation to the effect that we would not join with outsiders in our dances. Now if this is a good regulation let us carry it out; if not then, let us drop it and say no more about it. After some talk by the brethren, President Smith said it is worse to go to the dances of the Gentiles than to have the Gentiles attend our dances. I do not feel we are going outside the spirit of the Gospel when we ask the people to do that which is for their own good. So far as I can see, brethren, there is nothing to be gained by throwing down the bars and going back to the old condition.
>
> It was then moved that we maintain our regulation, viz: to exclude rough cowboy elements from our dances, also to discourage round dancing in all our wards. Vote was unanimous in favor of the motion (High Council Minutes 1898–1907: 19–20).

Looming above all these outsiders was the federal government, hardly to be called a group like the Indians or Anglos, but certainly a neighbor. Mormons already had a long, ambivalent relationship to the federal government. All living American Mormons shared a conscious disdain, even hatred, for the civil authority which had upheld their persecution, refused to protect or compensate them when they were murderously attacked, and continually uttered threats against the saintly community. Despite this ambivalence, the Mormons on the Little Colorado River brought one of their own to trial in June 1887 for defrauding the

U.S. Post Office of $5000. The council also kept watch over
the Mormons who freighted for the U.S. Army at nearby
Fort Apache to see that their brethren gave the government
all it had paid for. Postal service, and especially the cash
made in hauling freight for the army, were too valued by the
Mormons to be jeopardized. However much Mormons ex-
coriated the federal government by principle, good business
relations had to be maintained for their survival throughout
the area. In establishing its rectitude, the community separated Robin Hood-economics from ideological distaste for a
capitalist government: no Mormon was to steal from the government for personal benefit or the supposed benefit of the
community.

Mormons could and often had to come and go among gentiles, but Mormons also did a lot of shifting among their own
and other communities. The High Council spent most of its
efforts in defining membership inside the community. Every
Mormon town had permeable boundaries. Economic frailty
created a floating population which had to go from ward to
ward, that is, from town to town. The dual problem of defining relations with the outside world and of establishing a
coherent community made the task of defining who was in
and who was out doubly hard. Every decision was several
decisions: one about the inside, one about the outside, and
one about the effect of the interaction.

To define boundaries, the High Council in 1898 formalized a system of internal passports, or "recommends," that
had already been in use for some time. The leaders decided
to use the recommends, which were written statements from
a bishop of a person's worthiness to enter the temple, as a
check on unwanted mobility between towns. With this decision, every good Mormon could be known: "It was then
stated by both Pres J. N. Smith and J. H. Richards that a
recommend should be sent to anyone who moves away from
a ward and is too indifferent to ask for a recommend. But if
such persons should return to the old home after a lapse of
half a year, they must bring a recommend with them,
whether they took one away or not" (High Council Minutes
1898–1907:4). This ruling kept track of the membership

of the community, put a defining fence around a town and stake, and homogenized the population.

The ruling of 1898 amplified the council's expressed concern for community unity, which was the subject of its first recorded business in Arizona. In September 1880 and again in December 1883 Stake President Jesse N. Smith stressed both the unity of the Saints and the unity of the council. Since theoretically Smith could rule alone, his insistence on the backing of the council indicated the frailty of his actual power and the resultant need for unanimity among the leadership and populace of the area. Smith defined unity as uniform agreement and, in so doing, revealed how crucial consensus was to maintaining authority. The leaders could define who was inside and who was outside only when backed by consensus, and this in turn could come into being only when discipline exercised through recommends unified the community.

In order to maintain their coherence in the face of powerful dissolving forces, Mormons had to make concrete decisions about what to tell and what to hide. In September 1884, for example, the High Council discussed what to keep secret from outsiders, making explicit reference to plural marriage, which was engendering opposition. But even without persecution, it is plain that during the founding and solidifying of any community, secrets bind: "Bro. Smith instructed the councilors that they as missionaries among the people should seek to sustain our organization; and it is your duty to spread the views of the Stake Presidency. We have not the right to reflect evil upon our organization; none of this council have the right to speak the truth ... when it does not reflect credit" (High Council Minutes 1898–1907: 337).

Beyond secrecy, which was a passive form of identification, the community defined itself through a unified relationship to its land. Land became the most concrete symbol of what was inside and what outside. It was also the community's most tangible asset. Mormons had to fight the railroad, cattle companies, and Indian reservations to preserve their boundaries against competing claims to various pieces of their property. In light of the exorbitant payments that Mormons had made for their land and the improvements needed to make it arable, such threats intensified the land's value, giving it a depth of meaning unknown elsewhere on the frontier. Since land was not held in common but could be alienated, the High Council addressed itself to this problem several times. In 1895 it issued its most explicit statement: "The propriety of saints selling their town property to persons not of our faith was called up. After some explanation and considerable discussion, for and against disfellowshipping a man for selling to an 'outsider,' Pres. Smith said, 'We should endeavor to protect this community; and we should say that any person in this stake who sells his land to outsiders places his fellowship in peril' " (High Council Minutes 1880–1898:331).

To lose one's fellowship, although the milder form of expulsion from town life, was not a light matter: it meant spiritual death. The ban could be lifted by public confession which, to be accepted, required a vote by a show of hands from the congregation. Such a system could work only if the community was almost unanimously agreed. On the subject of alienating its land, there was substantial agreement in the community. As a result, today most land still remains in Mormon hands.

The system of recommends, the support of their leaders, and the refusal to alienate land comprised the public side of Mormon unity, all of which involved joint actions and shared conclusions. But the other side of the system, its private and intimate aspect, was probably the more important key to the system's success. Public penalties were not as effective throughout the community as was private arbitration, by which most disputes inside the group were resolved. Mormons had sufficient experience and pragmatism to know how frequently disputes could arise in any group. Although preaching safeguarded against controversy much of the time, Mormons, to their credit, realized that dispute was inevitable, and they met the problem head-on by establishing an elaborate, workable method of handling disputes among neighbors. Home teachers, adult men who visited every family in a ward once a month, handled many family and neighborhood problems. The home teachers received strict injunctions to keep all that they heard confidential; they were not even to tell the bishops of the problems they encountered: "Pres. Hatch said ... we should settle our difficulties among ourselves. It is not right to be too technical with each other. We should honor the beautiful organization that we have, using our officials [e.g. home teachers] instead of resorting to the Law of the Land" (High Council Minutes 1880–1893:350).

This kind of internal arbitration preserved the community's unity by ensuring privacy and guaranteeing sensitivity to grass-roots difficulties. But while it kept many crises from occurring, it smothered others. To counterbalance such a tendency and to silhouette issues that might be of general importance, the High Council meeting in March 1889 established its right "to ferret out iniquity and sin and therefore expand the charges" against anyone brought before it (High Council Minutes 1880–1898: March 1889). Through this process, many issues came to light that solidified unity and coherence inside the community.

Ferreting out iniquity was a delicate procedure. If what was exposed were not appropriate, the issue might become too big and backfire by polarizing opinion into undesirable camps. An underdog might attract support per se, or someone really powerful might flaunt the council. Even more important was selecting a culprit who would stick out the barrage and not just pick up and move on to avoid the difficulty. The matter had to be timed so that it offered an opportunity to test and strengthen council authority, an authority based solely on common agreement.

The case of John Lathrop is instructive. The High Council deliberately identified his case as insubordination in order to highlight the importance of consensus, or the basic need for the individual's will to bend to the community and its representatives. To remain an insider, one could not have reservations on certain subjects; unity was all important. The very triviality of the matter in the Lathrop case points up the frailty of the community's balance among citizens who shared in bartering or dam building but who occasionally broke the common belief. Brother Lathrop was a member of the High Council who chose not to pay the $1.50 that the council had voted as an assessment on all families toward building the Brigham Young Monument, to be erected in Salt Lake City on the fiftieth anniversary of the Mormon entry into Utah. Jesse Smith charged John Lathrop with contempt of the council for his act. Lathrop said he thought it a free will offering, not compulsory, and he initially refused even to give the money as contrition when requested by Smith:

> Bro. Littleton L. Perkins plead that we should act very generously toward Bro. Lathrop, and not be too technical.
> Bro. Lathrop said he had never intended to treat this body of men with contempt . . .
> Bro. Lathrop then paid over $1.50 cash . . .
> Pres. Smith thought an apology was also due.
> Pres. Smith D. Rogers said the amount of money was not the only question to be disposed of, for Bro. Lathrop's single vote [against the assessment] was overruled by the council, therefore he was in contempt and an apology was due from Bro. Lathrop.
> Pres. Smith said that Bro. Lathrop had also placed his bishop in contempt.
> Bro. Lathrop said he had admitted all that the brethren here accused him of—he had not however intended to treat this council with contempt and said: "What more can I do?"
> Pres. Smith said that Bro. Lathrop had placed every man in this stake in contempt. [Smith] continued saying his apology was satisfactory and proposed to forgive Bro. Lathrop. Council voted unanimously to forgive Bro. Lathrop (High Council Minutes 1898–1907:51).

This matter indicates how one man's reasoned opposition and consistent disapproval were enough to threaten the basis of the leadership's power. That power was thought to stem from its access to divine favor:

> President L. H. Hatch said on account of the great familiarity existing between us we often forget to attach the importance that we should to our positions in this council . . . I believe everyone of us in this council has been called as Aaron was called—by rev-

elation. If one of us thinks that he has not been called of God by revelation, then faith immediately flies away and the ability to accomplish good will ceases. The Lord does not always speak loudly in thundering tones, but often he speaks with a still small voice to the man who is called to nominate officials (High Council Minutes 1880–1898:356). At one meeting of the council Hatch remarked: When we used to meet one of the early members of the High Council in Nauvoo we greatly appreciated them, almost felt that the leading elders were supernatural beings—some were looked upon almost as gods.

Now the calling and positions of you High Councilors and the leading brethren are just as sacred, just as responsible and just as honorable now as those of the early days of this Church (High Council Minutes 1880–1898: February 1897).

Brother Lathrop's $1.50 reveals that the High Council's way of dealing with novel events and unsolved problems complemented the rituals that regulated much of the rest of society. Because of the resolution of disputes in the High Council, there could occur the unanimity about rituals and the balance stemming from their smooth operation. The $1.50 was important, as Hatch told the very men whom he had helped to appoint, because they were actually appointed by God and were themselves almost like gods, and one could no more sustain reasoned disagreement with them than one could with God. Each individual had to internalize the unity that was essential to the community's existence.

The High Council trials and debates allow a rare glimpse into the processes that changed individuals into citizens, Mormons at large into residents of a specific town, and people with prior identities into subjects of a new order who quickly fitted in without having to be coerced or forced into a regimen. The minutes offer a small example of the process whereby a Mormon community took its members and its newcomers and made them work in the system, or socialized them. The court did not perform an incidental socialization process; it deliberately highlighted lapses from order and failures to conform, as with Lathrop. By this means individuals were turned into subjects, and unity was created. The central strategem was to achieve self-policing: "Do not wish to beg a man to do right," said Jesse Smith in desperation in

one case, suggesting that the defendant should discipline himself because ultimately no one else had the power to do so.

For self-policing to work, individuals had to see themselves as free to answer or not when arraigned. That is why
individuals were called by name, and responded by name
and other identifying traits. The church in the person of
Brigham Young, or Jesse Smith, or the High Council, could
call an individual to go to Arizona, to build a dam, or to be
tried for an alleged infraction. And amazingly, without any
visible means of coercion, such as police, sheriffs, jails, or
armies, individuals did go, build, or confess and beg forgiveness. Because individuals recognized themselves in Mormonism and had their whole being in it, they could be
summoned successfully for one duty or another. Brother
Lathrop was called before the council as a brother and a
member of the High Council, and he recognized himself as
such when called. The community, which had given him
these identities among many others—adult, husband, father,
Mormon—at this juncture chose to use only these few.

Ordinary subjects are possible only if there is an absolute
other to which to be subject, and in Christian life that other
is God. God calls people to come to him freely. He does not
beg; they come of their own accord. In coming, people subject themselves to the ultimate authority and freely obey his
will—more specifically, the will known as conscience instilled in themselves. This is a straightforward understanding that society creates its own reflection in God and then
makes individuals in that image. They are given free agency
or free will so that this process may appear to happen
voluntarily.

This seemingly simple process has another aspect. The
subjects are always provided with a model and with its rewards. The ultimate model is Christ. God not only duplicates himself in many subjects but also produced a peerless
subject for all to duplicate. Since in Christianity the model
to be followed is God's son, and since all subjects see themselves, their present and future, as God's concern, they are
guaranteed that all will be well, or will achieve glory.

Brother Lathrop, like anyone arraigned, faced some of the

deepest human emotions. At the same time as these were being stirred, he had to admit to being subject to a higher authority and to abide by its will. When God, society, and Jesse Smith agreed to forgive him, he was told that all was well, in other words, that he was a member of society in good standing once again. In the process, Lathrop had been further socialized and his unity with the community made more complete. So had every man and woman who watched these emotionally trying events and voted on guilt and voted again on forgiveness. They too were identifying with the will of God by acting as God's instrument, but they were also learning from Lathrop's example how to bend themselves before that same instrument.

The High Council thus reinforced society's image of itself by defining its rules in novel situations. The council dealt with ambiguities, disentangling them to create order. The members of the council and the people who appeared before it served as models for each other to emulate. The council was a divine creation, and the behavior and opinions of those serving on it were images of required thought and action. The people and rules were real, immediate, intricate, local, and certified. Those called before the court also modeled, pointing out what not to emulate and how to confess and request forgiveness or to carry out the stipulations of more complex decisions. All this for $1.50.

In the course of welding a group of disparate families and individuals into a coherent unit ruled by a single hierarchy, the church court defined the nature of the family, including sexual relations. A new group must define family life to survive with any coherence. Additionally, marriage practices involve the external world through the reputation that they create; they are an obvious boundary, separating insiders from outsiders. New forms of marriage need to be closely defined, or the unity for which they are designed can just as easily invite disaster.

All American utopias faced the problem and the possibility of redefining traditional family relationships and sexual activities. The Shakers adopted abstinence, the Oneida community changeable partners, and the Mormons adopted plural marriage, openly for thirty or forty years and in secret for longer. Experimentation with an institution as central to social life as the family gives a community tremendous freedom to rework much of the structure of human relationships, while it releases people from the traditional bonds governing behavior. In other words, any group redefining the family and sex has to state what it refuses to tolerate as well as what it wants to support. Among Mormons, the instrument that watched over the limits of sexual freedom, authority, and responsibility within the family was the court system.

Plural marriage, the key effort made by Mormons to redefine traditional family relationships, was a closely watched institution. Nothing directly involving plural marriage ever came before the High Council in Arizona, but during the 1880s and 1890s Mormons were prosecuted intensely by the federal judicial system because of plural marriage and were fully aware of the picture that the national press and Eastern society had painted of them. Mormons were regarded as libertines whose gluttonous sexual appetite matched the political hunger of the church, both of which were condemned as grossly un-American. To avoid justifying the image of sexual barbarity and to maintain order in their own house, Mormons took sexual offenses seriously; they used trials to establish and enforce the behavior that they thought proper, which in retrospect was at least as proper and standard as that found in the rest of Victorian America.

Almost one-third of the cases brought before the High Council between 1884 and 1896 in Arizona involved sexual offenses, usually charges of adultery. This was a serious sin, and conviction meant excommunication. The wronged spouse was also excommunicated if, after discovery of the adulterous behavior, sexual relations continued. The tension created by a trial for adultery is evident from a report at the conclusion of one such trial in 1886: "The people were scandalized by the disgraceful proceedings first coming before the world by an Indian reporting the case to [a non-Mormon]. After being asked several times by Bishop Standifird and Bro. Hatch to let them rebaptize the [offending couple,

Pres. Smith] did consent but with the understanding that their priesthood was not to be restored. This was before it was made known to him that adulterers could not be received back into the Church again" (High Council Minutes 1880–1898:27–33).

Letting any knowledge of adultery seep outside the fold was inexcusable, since the scandal compromised the community. The harshness of the penalty, perpetual loss of priesthood status, effectively cut off participation in the church and thus barred the affected parties from access to the temple and its blessings. This was a form of spiritual death. Jesse Smith's curious ignorance of the procedure in adultery trials could only mean that the church as a whole was in the process of redefining its attitude to the problem. The harsh penalty indicated that the church was deeply concerned about adultery at this time. There were several reasons for concern. When this trial occurred, the external pressure on plural marriage, felt indirectly in Arizona, was reaching its peak. Moreover, the church had increased self-confidence in governing its large and loyal population. It was also aware of the sexual mishaps that could occur in empty areas with few people and little supervision. All these factors inclined the church to stronger discipline.

The same region in which this discipline was meted out saw the High Council preoccupied with urging young people to marry as part of an effort to hold onto as much territory as possible. This policy conflicted with the rules for strict sexual control. Mormon girls "must not be sent away to work—they become whores if they do. Marriage must be made simple and cheap" (High Council Minutes 1880–1898: February 1898). Jesse Smith urged "that the young people—especially the young men—marry. The Kingdom is almost waiting for the young people to marry. The indifference to this important step is a matter of great heaviness to the leading brethren" (High Council Minutes 1880–1898:357). A tension must have existed between the exhortations for quick and early marriage and the strict prohibitions against experimentation beforehand or departing from complete faithfulness between the partners afterward.

This tension was made public at any trial where the rules for sexual behavior were discussed.

For example, the community's priorities emerged as it resolved such a conflict in a case in 1888 (High Council Minutes 1880-1889:201-214). In this case the community arbitrated parental authority, the duties of children to parents, the propriety of early marriage, and the place of the court to rule on these matters. The case revolved around the elopement of a young man of twenty-one and a girl who was "not of legal age," that is, under eighteen. The young woman's father brought suit against the young man's parents for "theft of my child." The court tried the accused parents and then the groom's younger brother for helping with the elopement. The parents were accused of aiding their older son with his plans. The younger brother was tried separately for his part in the affair. The eloping couple, however, was never tried for anything.

Amid a large amount of inconclusive testimony, only one statement from Jesse Smith concerned the elopement itself: "No young man or maiden twenty-one or thirty years of age was warranted in disobeying parents." This was the closest he came to criticizing the elopement. The parents of the new groom were quickly exonerated, and the father of the bride was then accused of vindictiveness and of forceably preventing his daughter from seeing her young man. Even though the bride's father had denied her permission to marry, her disobedience was not considered serious since he was using the wrong means of controlling his daughter. What the proper means were was not specified. The role of the groom's parents was actually unclear, but they were absolved of any responsibility for the deed. The admittedly guilty younger brother was excused as too young to be responsible since "his inexperience is some defense for him . . . it [being] natural for the younger to follow the older."

A major leitmotif throughout the trial was the contemptuous attitude of the boy's parents to the lower court which had tried them earlier. The boy's parents had ignored the Bishop's Court by not showing up when it met and were clearly at odds with their bishop. He had disfellowshiped them on several grounds, but he had not found them guilty of the bride's parents' claim. For their alleged contempt of the Bishop's Court, the accused couple received universal disapproval from the High Council, which made it clear that regardless of the truth of the other charges against them, this was the insupportable behavior.

Jesse Smith's decision was remarkable for its evasion of the specific charges and of the elopement that had caused the affair. On other matters, he was quite precise:

> I want all those parties who were wrong to get right. I am of the opinion that no good result will come from carrying out the decision of the Bishop. The disfellowship of [the groom's parents] will be removed and they . . . received back into the fellowship of the ward for the reason that there was no evidence against them. The boy [groom's brother] was young and somewhat excusable on that account; [Smith] did not feel to make an example of the young one. The first two charges [against the groom's parents] had not been sustained and as to the third thought it proper to accept his confession and let him go free with the rest . . . Pres. Smith did not feel in the least to censure the Bishop in the course he had taken.

In ignoring the elopement, the fact that the age of the bride required parental consent (in civil law), the indifference of the boy's parents, the outrage of the girl's parents, and the severe action of the bishop, the stake president chose to avoid many facts that he could clearly have used to reach a different decision. He chose to make two points: the young must be allowed to marry, and the courts must be respected. In stressing early marriage, he was supporting the very basis of the community's existence. Its essence was kinship expressed through the family, whose members extended back into the preexistence and forward into the future through Celestial Marriage. Family continuity guaranteed unity in the earthly present. It was the only acceptable form of social life, regardless of whether it involved the plural families of one husband or the impatient efforts of an eloping couple.

Since authority was insecure and of necessity hierarchical, any community ruling itself by sanctity had to relegate interpretive power to a few hands lest everyone listen to God directly. This requirement led to the second major theme dominating the High Council in nineteenth century Arizona. Mormon hierarchical authority is best illustrated by the long, tough struggle between Jesse Smith, a stake president appointed by Brigham Young, and John Hunt, bishop of the Snowflake Ward. The case defined the limits to hierarchy. Mormonism identified itself as a theocracy with pyramidal leadership, but since it also had an intensely egalitarian caste, as evidenced by its communalism and Joseph Smith's insistence on theological freedom for himself and his people, these conflicting tendencies had continually to be arbitrated. The problem was how only a few people could talk to God on behalf of everyone when religious experience and all aspects of daily life were functions of each other. This is the inherent conflict in government by sanctity.

Jesse Smith, as stake president, was directly responsible to the Quorum of Twelve Apostles and the First Presidency of the Church. John Hunt, bishop of the Snowflake Ward, had been appointed by the stake president and ultimately by the First Presidency of the Church. He was responsible to the stake president. He could also be removed by his ward if even a small minority were sufficiently vocal. The chain of rights and duties at all these levels was clear.

Ambiguity was introduced because Smith and Hunt lived in the same settlement. Starting in 1886, ten years after the founding of the Little Colorado colonies, Smith and his first councilor and stake patriarch, Lorenzo Hill Hatch, decided to remove Hunt as bishop of the Snowflake Ward. To do so, Smith took the unusual step of using the High Council to bring charges against Hunt. The struggle took two years to settle, and the result occupies more than thirty pages in the trial record (High Council Minutes 1880–1898: June, September, December 1886). The surface dispute was over who had the right to preside over the Sunday meetings of the ward in Snowflake, the stake president or the bishop.

The first round, in September 1885, was won by the stake president, who charged the bishop with misappropriating mission property. After discussion in the High Council, the bishop was called upon to "make the affair right before the people." The decision created confusion. In December, four months later, Hunt was indicted and called to stand trial. In January, Smith wanted to have the bishop "step aside," that is, resign. By March, Bishop Hunt accused Smith of being a tyrant. Smith managed to have the High Council disfellowship the bishop, a move which placed undisputed power in Smith's hands. Disfellowshiping a bishop was not a light matter, and Hunt felt sufficiently chastised to make a public confession early in 1886. The sight was startling, with the bishop standing before his congregation, which included both Smith and Hatch. Hunt, who must have had a durable sense of humor, confessed and begged forgiveness for misdeeds that he strongly implied were nonsensical and which were in fact the misdeeds of his accusers. The leadership found the confession unacceptable. In May or June 1886 the matter was taken to Salt Lake and the First Presidency. On June 22, 1886, John Taylor, president of the church, and George Q. Cannon, first councilor to the president, sent their response to the elders in Snowflake:

In reply we have to say that the President of the Stake has the right to preside in every religious meeting in the Stake. If he did not have this right he would not be the President. But whether he will exercise it at all times is another question.

Bishops of wards also have rights; they preside over their wards; and in all meetings in a usual capacity it is their unquestioned right to preside. Should there be a meeting called in the ward by the President of the Stake it would be proper as a matter of courtesy for the Bishop to yield the presidency of the meeting to the President of the Stake, and it would be optional with the latter whether he should preside or request the Bishop to do so. If the President of the Stake should happen to be present at a Ward Meeting, he would treat the Bishop with proper courtesy and would not assume the Presidency of the meeting unless requested to do so by the Bishop or should feel, for any reason, that it would be proper for him to do so. Ordinarily he would let the Bishop preside. On the other hand at such a meeting a courteous Bishop would render to the President of the Stake the direction of the proceedings of the meeting, and would consult him as to how he wished the meeting conducted.

Where men feel as they should do, there need be no collision respecting duties nor no feeling but that of the utmost respect for each other. No wise President will go into a ward and arbitrarily assume control of Ward Meetings when the Bishop is present; neither will a wise, judicious Bishop treat the President of the Stake with the least disrespect. He will honor him as his President and ask his counsel, and seek to obtain from him his wishes, if he have any, respecting the Business of the meeting or the manner in which it shall be conducted. We have mentioned the President of the Stake in answering these questions, but the same remarks and conclusions apply to either of his councilors.

"You say some of the Twelve" have instructed Brother L. H. Hatch that the President of the Stake should preside over all meetings in his Stake where an apostle is not present.

Of course we cannot say how correct this statement is, and if it were not better qualified than it is (which it probably was) it is not correct. A President of a Stake presides over his Stake even when an Apostle is present, and no wise Apostle will go into a stake and assume the Presidency thereof, or of any of its meetings unless called for some special purpose by him, or the First Presidency who may send him.

A Stake organization is a complete organization, and is under the direct control of the First Presidency of the Church. An apostle holds all the authority which man can hold on the earth in the flesh; but he will not interfere with the affairs of a Stake further than to council and instruct unless he sees some glaring wrong which in his authority as an Apostle he has the right to reprove, or is authorized by the First Presidency to attend to affairs there (Snowflake Stake Historical Record 1886–1889: 58–60).

This letter, a consummately political document, eventually righted matters. In July 1886 the disfellowshiping eventually was reversed. Hunt was reinstated, and Jesse Smith affirmed that there was no significant difference of opinion between him and Hunt. A visiting apostle chastised Smith in a High Council meeting, and public display was avoided. The letter from Salt Lake showed an intimate familiarity with local circumstances and demonstrated the high level of administrative rationality at the top of church administration. That the letter resolved the conflict indicates the power of the central church leadership. Salt Lake, however, fully aware that the dust of Arizona might becloud a letter dealing in a sophisticated way with subtle issues of hierarchy, was not surprised when the stake president and bishop disagreed at first over its meaning. Not until the arrival of one of the Twelve Apostles from Salt Lake on an annual visit was the intent of the letter made unambiguous and the limits to the stake president's position enforced.

News of this letter was presumably circulated throughout the community by the high councilors and interpreted in many discussions. The issue warranted such a serious reply from the First Presidency because it definitively established the limits to hierarchy, linking the First Presidency to revelation the same as the stake organization. The episode illustrated the role of the High Council in defining the distribution of power within the hierarchical pyramid. Even though the actual decisions were made and enforced above the High Council, Salt Lake leaders nonetheless used that body to announce its decisions, guarantee effectiveness, and ensure popular knowledge.

The majority of conflicts between freedom and authority among Mormons were probably never publicized or recorded. The structure of Mormon society invited a tension between democracy and hierarchy, and this case illustrates one attempt to resolve that tension. Higher authority, which could be watchful to the point of intrusion, was often confronted by the voice of individual conscience which was a product of free agency. The tension certainly had a role in the struggle between John Hunt and Jesse Smith, and it is a noticeable leitmotif in the memorabilia left by that generation.

In another trial in 1896 concerned with this problem, a charge was brought by an individual ward member against his bishop. The accusation was "hurt feelings because forbidden to speak by his bishop at a meeting." After listening to the case, the High Council quoted Apostle John Taylor on freedom "showing that freedom of speech was or should be allowed." The council decided that there was no cause for

action, and the offending bishop was told to forbear (High
Council Minutes 1880–1898:371). There seems to have been
no trouble among Mormons at all levels to recognize the ideology of individualism—an ideology inherited from the Reformation and republican America—when presented with a
case sufficiently simple and distant to allow perspective on
their own principles.

Thus hierarchy and its powers were delimited, labeled,
and defined, even as those limits and definitions were enforced. There is, however, another aspect to this problem.
The Mormons made all men priests, thereby democratizing
the access to hierarchy while using hierarchy to govern
those same men in all matters. As a result, every wrong,
error, or mistake was an evil committed by a priest and punishable by other priests. As a result, most of the usual ways
of correcting ordinary human error were missing in Mormon society. It must be assumed that many of the disputes
tried in the High Council and the Bishop's Courts were initially the result of mistakes, misunderstandings, and even
chance, rather than of antisocial motives. Many problems
were basically the product of the inexactitudes that occur in
any system. Thus when a carpenter or builder made an
error, Mormon society had no means of treating the error as
a professional mistake or as a financial blunder. Because the
society had defined all life as a religious affair, it was forced
to treat mistakes and blunders as spiritual failings, punishable only in religious terms and hence in hierarchical ones.

In a matter involving a serious miscalculation in the construction of the Stake Academy, the community's school, a
concrete matter was translated into religious and hierarchical terms. The translation enraged both sides because it necessitated an unpleasant examination of aspects of the
accused's spiritual character and imposed a religious penalty
inadequate to the actual offense. The trial took place in December 1899 (High Council Minutes 1898–1907:24–28).
Jesse Smith informed the councilors that, having suspended
Brother Peter Greene as stake chorister, a minor singing
post, he wanted the councilors, "as custodians of the liberties
of the people," to judge the matter: "Pres. Smith then gave

his views of Bro. Greene and his actions: first giving his views of Bro. Greene's virtues and good traits then, on the other hand, stated that he regarded Bro. Greene as a man given to mischief-making and said unfortunately that this evil seems to be growing on Bro. Greene. This is my reason for suspending Bro. Greene and if I am wrong then you High Councilors should correct me." John Hunt, Greene's bishop, responded that Greene "had been remiss in the attendance of Sunday meetings" and had criticized his bishop and president too severely. Greene replied that, although these were misconceptions and he was in fact punctual, he was sorry that anyone thought of him as a mischief-maker and, "If I am guilty I certainly wish to repent and do better and live so that I may set a better name."

Further explanations were requested, no doubt because the proceedings had failed to bring out the real grievance. At this point Smith explained that Green had reversed the floor support beams in the academy building, using those for the first floor on the second and vice versa. Another councilor pointed out that Greene had not paid his subscription toward the academy costs.

Greene offered an explanation for the building error. Then Smith criticized him "upon his unfortunate habit of trying to be on both sides of each question—of wheedling with the sore heads and wheedling with the other side to gain the favor and sympathy of both sides." After more discussion, a vote was taken to uphold Smith's action, and Greene offered his resignation, saying "he had long intended to do so." It was accepted by unanimous vote of those present.

Peter Greene had refused to pay his subscription for building costs, made a construction mistake that was sloppy if not really serious, and criticized the community leaders. He could be punished for the first and last errors through religious sanctions, but these punishments were inadequate to the construction mistake. There were two problems, one manifest, the other latent. A system that equated competence in carpentry with religious posts and behavior would inevitably find its system of equivalencies between offenses and punishments unworkable and inappropriate. An expensive construction error could not be redressed by taking away a minor singing post whose value to the holder was doubtful. The latent problem was the necessity in a religious community that also fostered technological development to extend religious sanctions to mistakes made in every area of achievement. This necessity existed even as the new technology created a class, the children of Greene, who earned a sufficiently secure living from their expertise to declare the system of religious sanctions irrelevant.

The third issue that Mormons faced through their High Council was the reconciliation of cooperative and capitalist economies. Mormons in Arizona lived under three different economic systems in the late nineteenth century. The kinds of dispute handled by the High Council clarify the distinctions between completely communal towns, like those of the United Order, partially cooperative settlements, like most towns in the beginning, and towns immersed in the capitalist economy, which prevailed everywhere else shortly after the turn of the century. Conceptions and definitions of property shifted as conceptions of ownership and private responsibility changed. As private property became more important, penalties were expressed more as fines and less as disfellowshiping and confession. Court decisions became more and more precise as property disputes—land claims, water rights, debts, and thefts—gradually centered around private individuals and privately held property rather than around the obligation of individuals to support church policy or community unity.

Mormons were aware that they were experiencing profound changes in the way their society organized property, but since these changes occurred slowly, no Mormon could be expected to see the matter clearly. However, in two cases the redefinition of economic goals focused the community's attention on what was happening.

One is a property case between the same Lot Smith who headed the United Order enterprise and H. R. Hayes, who came before the High Council charging Smith with a breach of partnership and theft (High Council Minutes 1880–1898:

May 31, 1889). Smith controlled an enormous amount of property in land and livestock, which he treated as his own but which really belonged to the defunct United Order towns. In late 1888 or early 1889 after the dissolution of those settlements Smith, acting as a private individual, transacted some business with Hayes involving profits from the future sale of sheep, wool, cattle, and horses outside the Arizona Territory. The deal's complexity was itself a sign of change, as were its obvious capitalist intentions. Smith refused, for an unknown reason, to pay Hayes for their transactions. Hayes took the matter to the Bishop's Court in Tuba City, which ruled in his favor. Smith refused to move and appealed to the High Council in Snowflake, which heard the case's business intricacies and ruled in sophisticated fashion largely in favor of Hayes. Smith ultimately appealed the matter to his old friend, Wilford Woodruff, then president of the church. The end result of the litigation inside the church is not known, but Jesse Smith's decision for the High Council contains a piece of business philosophy that epitomized the developing Mormon attitude to profits and risk: "Brother Hayes knew what he was about when he went into partnership and he should be willing to take the consequences. Quoted from President Young showing that we do wrong in placing temptation in the way of our brethren. Men when they trade should see the animals they trade for before they trade and thus avoid temptation." These injunctions were completely opposed to those heard a mere five years earlier from the same council when it urged Mormons to have prayerful trust in each other and not to be "too technical" with their fellows. Now the buyer must beware: be watchful first and prayerful second.

Some time between the High Council's ruling and a resolution of Lot Smith's appeal to the First Presidency, Hayes short-circuited the process by suing Smith before the civil courts. The records do not indicate what happened there either, but Smith, seeing this as an opportunity to even the balance, turned around and charged Hayes before the church court for "bringing him falsely before the law." This situation pointed up two problems faced by the Mormon courts: first, they could not enforce their decisions against the rich and powerful, so that aggrieved parties were forced outside the church for redress; and second, they could be used as a weapon to thwart any dissatisfaction stemming from their own inadequacies. The first and basic problem suggested the breakdown of the system, resulting from the approach of a new economic system with its own more rationalized courts, as well as the weakening of religious consensus to the point where a member of the community could not be made to feel obligated to agree to a decision. These trends, one coming from the outside and the other from the inside, coincided to weaken, not the ability to label reality, but the ability to enforce the meaning of the labels.

The second case that focused the community's attention on changing economic goals involved horse-racing for money (High Council Minutes 1880–1898:273–287). President Jesse Smith opened the case by stating that "there had been some racing and some betting and some lying about the collecting of bets. The bishop has called on the authorities for help and we might as well take the matter up and sift it and place ourselves on record. It is whispered that some of our High Council are implicated." The whispers were well founded.

Two sons of a wealthy family in Snowflake were involved. In 1891 one son who sat on the High Council had lent a horse to be raced so that he could improve its reputation in preparation for selling it, and another son had placed a bet on the race. Lots of people made small bets on the race, including some men who sat on the High Council.

The matter came to trial because "the bishop wished this matter talked up to know if people had a right to gamble. Many are not aware of the extent of this evil." The extent of evil included the sale of whiskey, and Smith, among other accusations, charged that if the family of the accused, who owned a general store, "keep this up, they will go under. We should try not to get something for nothing." He also likened racing a horse to selling liquor to a drunkard.

There was a round of discussion at the council during which various members admitted to gambling and said that they felt properly admonished. Everyone but the councilman who owned the horse and whose family owned the store that sold whisky bent to hierarchical authority; he was forced to resign as a home missionary in the face of strong arguments that holding his position under the circumstances would "force a wrong upon the people." However, the accused refused to admit that he was wrong, and in accepting his resignation, Smith summed up the conflict: "Property had been brought into the . . . family [resulting from a younger brother betting on the race]. Still [the council member who lent the horse] says he is not at all responsible for any of this."

If Lot Smith and Hayes could speculate on livestock and wool, and if the High Council could hand down rulings on interest rates, the question is just what "this thing of getting something for nothing was." Smith himself and his family, who became the second wealthiest group of people in the area, opened the region's first private bank. That, like any form of gambling, was making a profit through taking risks. If speculation in livestock and lending money at interest were sanctioned, then why not games of chance? The reason is that public gambling, based completely on chance and thus offering no predictability, could upset the hierarchy since it was a source of power completely separate from sanctity, the acknowledged power base of the community. Gambling in its most public form was not just "evil" but was a concrete threat to the increasingly frail, but established, order of things. Gambling, though not inherently "getting something for nothing," was defined this way by the community. Sudden wealth received, either by chance or by doing "nothing," attacked the bases for order. It attacked hierarchy and the traditional definitions of Mormon economics because it exposed their arbitrariness, the inventedness of the system. "Something" could emerge from "nothing," which did not require God, the church, the hierarchy, faith, or even wits to make it happen. If the world could be governed by chance, then any government was chancy. No practice supporting that insight could be tolerated.

As experimental capitalism emerged from partial communalism, those who already had authority in the religious system attempted to define the social effects of the new economic form in religious terms and thus to maintain the hierarchy intact. When this trial took place, the High Council could still define economic acts like gambling in religious terms for commoners and thus deter them from upsetting the hierarchy by striking it rich through chance. Thus chance was defined as evil, but not every man who took a chance could be made to admit he was evil. The inconsistency left chance open to the rich and powerful, but not to the ordinary man with little power. In the face of a new economic system, Mormon society defined who could keep property, privilege, and power and who would lose the benefits of the old cooperative economy and simultaneously be denied access to the instruments of the new capitalist one.

The separation of religious and economic affairs that had to come to these people started in 1901 when the High Council actually declined to consider an issue that it thought could be handled better by secular authority:

> Elder W. J. Flake stated that some people are branding horses and colts in a rather loose manner—calling them "mavericks." He said he should like the council to take some steps to prevent this practice.
>
> Pres. J. N. Smith stated that he understood the Supervisors properly have charge in this matter and recommended this council and our bishops not mix up with this matter but refer this evil to the county officers. I think as church men we better let this matter alone (High Council Minutes 1898–1907:50).

Smith not only had begun to foster the separation of church and civil domains but also furthered the process by identifying himself and his fellow members as church men. It is not clear whether he was calling himself a man of faith or a cleric, but the fabric of sanctity had been so split by this time that he could think of church and state as separate and could accept the implications of such a bifurcation, the most obvious being the limitation and decline of his own and the church's power.

In contrast with nineteenth-century church rituals, which handled recurrent problems by applying already standardized solutions to them, the council handled new problems or anomalies. The council regulated areas of material concern by defining whom to sell land to, which courts to use, what the nature of insubordination was, what residence requirements were, how to treat Indians, what honesty meant when working for the federal government, what the limits of free speech were, when and how to marry, and what the responsibilities of a business partnership were. In the process, it spread the definition of sin and wrong as well as right and liberty. It not only pinpointed something as good or bad, right or wrong, but also spelled out particulars. In this way, the umbrella of Mormonism was held over a greater part of life, giving it meaning. In this way Mormonism functioned to maintain balance.

To counterbalance change and novelty, the council itself had to be flexible, and its records document rule by revelation and centralized common sense. Devoid of formal systems of law, procedure, and precedent, the courts had two important traits: they were generalized, and they were unspecified. The courts, though autonomous from one another, were arranged in a hierarchy within the continually operating central system of the church. But the central system did not determine the details of the court system; rather it dispersed decision-making. This permitted efficiency, concern for context, and justice as opposed to law. No lawyers as such were ever present at the trials recorded in the nineteenth century. Even though a high councilor was charged with speaking on a party's behalf, he was not obliged to carry such support beyond his own beliefs and convictions. The informal exchanges between the president and the twelve councilors show the president as judge and the councilors as both jury and legal council; their roles and consequently the procedures associated with them varied considerably from case to case. Considerable flexibility was thereby achieved.

The longer the church courts operated in Arizona, the more their decisions came to resemble the form of decisions made by civil courts. They no longer looked like revelations or snatches from the Bible but became specified, naming monetary fines, interest rates, warnings to the buyer, and transfer of matters to civil courts. But while decisions seemed less and less tied to sanctity or inspiration and copied secular form, they were still made on a pragmatic, not a legal, basis. They had secular form but neither secular authority nor the consistency provided by the precedent that civil law must have in order to be rational.

The use of inspiration in sacred government and its courts met the need for flexible responses to the insecurity that was the analytical reason for the use of sanctity in the first place. Inspiration, however, required a short memory, of the sort the Mormons guaranteed themselves by not using precedent, or not considering the context of any past event used as a citation, or not having lawyers. There is no hint that any councilor ever consulted the council's minutes for precedent or guidance. The result, consequently was that a government that used sanctity to rule forgot its own history. In being flexible, avoiding conflict, remaining pragmatic, and requiring consensus, such a government divorced itself from its own past.

The Mormon courts said no to a lot of novelty and, as time went on, became more rational in form. But there was no rational substance to the form since decisions were limited to the case under consideration, not based on the history of similar instances. This method guaranteed swift change or swift counterbalance to change, and added to the guarantee that there would be no knowledge the past had ever been different.

The long-range consequences of the habit of mind which prevented the accumulation of a coherent, systematic interpretation of the relationship between past and present were more general than the absence of precedents in dispute management. Avoidance of precedent meant that the past was never segmented and the segments never could become history; a set of touchstones was not built. Eventually this led to the dissolution of Mormonism's historic critique of contemporary society and to a population without an effective collective memory. These results, when coupled with Mormonism's attraction for rational-looking decisions which are actually spur-of-the-moment reactions, produced one of modern Mormonism's chief traits: a rational population without a memory.

6

Theocracy Transformed: The Separation of Church from State and Economy

Sanctity generated continual technical improvement, concentrated wealth gained from ecological success, and rational though memoryless thought. Each of these products of sanctity acted to transform Mormon society. The search for technical improvement lead to a search for expertise and equipment beyond the borders of the kingdom and thus to a dependence on things and social patterns alien to Mormon life. Wealth did two things: it attracted outside attention, especially in Utah where Easterners wanted a share of success, and it created classes, rich and poor, which compromised Mormon egalitarianism. Secular thought produced not just the familiar business, legal, and organizational rationalities, but it combined with an aspect of sanctity's rule to produce a disregard for historical precedent which led to a kind of memorylessness.

These three processes internal to Mormonism combined with a series of historical events to transform the theocratic state into the church that now exists. The Mormon church was forced to abandon plural marriage in 1890; to dissolve its own political party in 1891; and to divest itself of control over Utah's economy by 1906–1907. These were brought about through effective federal action which gave irreversible momentum to the church's internal transformation. The political and economic character of Mormonism was changed from a theocracy to a church built along standard American lines. In the quarter-century between 1882 and 1907 the American socialist enterprise that was Mormonism was ended by the same nation that had given it birth.

The Mormons and the United States had never been at peace. There had been violence in Missouri and Illinois, and almost as soon as the Mormon population settled in the Salt Lake Valley, trouble resumed. Having arrived in 1847 in what was technically Mexican territory, they found themselves after the Mexican War once more on American soil. This vast, unsettled, and newly acquired area, nearly beyond federal control, was being rapidly colonized by a people who had made their antagonistic feelings toward the United States perfectly clear. The federal government feared that the Mormons might set up a real kingdom in the Great Basin which would constitute a genuine threat to American sovereignty. So in 1857 President James Buchanan sent out an army of five thousand troops to occupy the Salt Lake valley and guarantee United States hegemony. This action started the Utah War, a short, costly, and futile affair for the government, which nevertheless served to let Mormons know that temporal powers were still thinking seriously about them. This was the first and only time that the federal government ever sent an army to Utah, but it was not the only time the government became so frightened that it wanted to subdue the Mormons with outright force.

Instead, legislation and public opinion were used to control Mormonism. The process began in 1856 when the Republican party made its "twin relics of barbarism" statement equating slavery in the South with polygamy in Utah. Then in 1862 with the Morrill Antibigamy Law, Congress sought to control the Saints by making plural marriage a crime punishable by a jail term. While the United States was occupied by the Civil War, Brigham Young and Abraham Lincoln left each other alone, but almost as soon as the war was over and reconstruction begun in the South, federal eyes turned to Utah. The same radical Republicans who had eliminated one of the "twin relics" and imposed carpetbag government on the South, with the intent of reforming the Southerners while colonizing them, then turned their attention to Utah, motivated by hostility to the "peculiar" social institution, political autonomy, and economic independence that characterized that territory. Such a combination presented genuine threats to the integrity of the Union, especially to federalism, and to Eastern capitalism.

In 1874, using a Supreme Court decision that none of the provisions of the Constitution applied to United States territories, Congress passed the Poland Act establishing firm federal control over the courts and juries of the Utah Territory. The earlier Morrill Antibigamy Act had been unenforceable because Utah's local probate courts handled the vast majority of judicial business and no jury of Mormons would convict a fellow Saint for upholding one of the tenets of their religion; no polygamist had ever been convicted. The Poland Act, which gave the U.S. district courts exclusive civil and criminal jurisdiction, thereby eliminating Mormons from the proceedings, began the long process of using federally controlled courts to prosecute Mormons.

In that same decade the national furor over Mormondom took distinct form. A key instrument for reconstructing Utah was the five-man, federally appointed Utah Commission, provided for by the Edmunds Act of 1882. The commission and the governor who were appointed by the President of the United States, constituted the chief power in the territory, apart from the courts. The commission's duty was to regulate all elections in the territory. Test oaths were administered to Mormons, because to vote, citizens had to swear they were neither bigamists nor polygamists. Even Utah gentiles objected, calling the oath an across-the-board infringement on civil rights. As a consequence, the control represented by the commission was not as effective as had been planned.

By the mid-1880s, the forces involved in controlling Utah understood that the fight to strip the church of its power was not working. Polygamists were rarely jailed, the doctrine of plural marriage was stoutly defended by the church, the economy was still securely in church hands, and the

People's party, the party of the church, was still returning most of its candidates to office. This situation provoked the Edmunds-Tucker Act of 1887, which paralyzed but did not kill the church.

This act dissolved the church as a corporation and set up machinery for confiscating all church property valued above $50,000. The church was worth several million dollars. The Perpetual Emigrating Company, an efficient, church-run service that had brought thousands of people into Utah from the East and Europe since 1847, was dissolved:

> The Act also abolished woman's suffrage in Utah; disinherited children of plural marriages; prescribed a comprehensive "test oath" to eliminate polygamists from voting, holding office, and serving on juries; vested all judicial, law enforcement, and militia powers in the Utah Commission and other federal appointees; suspended the territorial school laws, and placed the territorial schools under the control of the territorial supreme court and a court-appointed commissioner. The act required all marriages to be certified by certificate in the probate courts, wiped out all existing election districts, and dissolved the Nauvoo legion [church militia] (Arrington 1958:361).

The act also "provided compulsory attendance of witnesses, stipulated that a lawful wife might testify against her husband, and that commencement of prosecution for adultery should not be limited to complaints of a husband or wife" (Larson 1971:210). In 1890 the United States Supreme Court upheld the act, maintaining that "the church was an organized rebellion against the government, distinguished by the practices of polygamy and ecclesiastical control of its members" (Larson 1971:254).

The Edmunds-Tucker Act was effective in stepping up prosecution of polygamy offenses. By 1893 there were 1004 convictions for unlawful cohabitation and 31 for polygamy under the act. Since the church attempted to fight these cases, its talented men were absorbed in legal defenses for polygamists who were either serving time in prison or avoiding arrest. From 1885 to 1890 the church was escheated of most of its property and, through lack of proper management, fell into debt and economic disarray. Church leaders began to see that the sacred institution they were safeguarding could not survive on righteousness alone; for it to continue, a compromise would have to be reached with the nation and federal government.

The Woodruff Manifesto of 1890 was the compromise. In this document, the head of the church stated, "We are not teaching polygamy or plural marriage . . . my advice to the Latter-day Saints is to refrain from contracting any marriage forbidden by the Law of the land" (Larson 1971:263–264). The status of this document was much debated and to some degree is still. It does not identify itself as a revelation nor is it couched in the form of revelation Joseph Smith received. Yet President Woodruff did not admit that its status was any lower. Most gentiles thought it authoritative, and so did most Mormons. Gentiles interpreted it as a capitulation by the church. Some faithful Mormons, however, regarded the document as subtly distinguishing between advice and revelation and found no guidance in the stance of their leaders who said that it had to be obeyed but did not say whether it was the law of the land or the most recent law of God. Part of the problem in interpretation was that initially neither the church nor the government knew what was the status of already consummated plural marriages. Were husbands of many years now to leave their wives and families as if they had never been attached to them? The courts and, more important, the church seemed to imply this. The problem proved transient. All parties involved understood that polygamy was only an issue to control the church; once the church had dissolved the issue by abolishing polygamy, it no longer mattered whether or not a few thousand married people lived out their lives in peace. Most did.

The manifesto came at a time when Mormons had already been disfranchised in Idaho over plural marriage by a law upheld by the U.S. Supreme Court in 1890. That same year the Cullom-Strubble Bill was introduced into Congress by groups not satisfied with the progress made under the Edmunds-Tucker Act to harness the church. The

Cullom-Strubble Bill would have disfranchised all Utah Mormons regardless of their stance on polygamy. Church leaders reasoned that if disfranchisement was constitutional in Idaho, it would also be constitutional in Utah. They recognized that, despite the stretching of the federal Constitution needed to control them, Congress was not going to let that stop it from achieving its intention in Utah. They further understood that, if the Cullom-Strubble Bill were defeated or vetoed, it would soon come up again stronger and more successful. The church, with its life as an effective institution hanging in the balance, decided to capitulate on what it felt was the strongest weapon held against it. Thus the church renounced polygamy, and the bill died.

Nonetheless, the campaign against the church continued because polygamy was only the surface target for something else. That something else was the church's political and economic power, which had survived intact and untouched despite the campaign against its outstanding social peculiarity. But even though a second major battle to break these sources of church power seemed likely, it did not occur. The threat of disfranchisement never rematerialized because between 1891 and 1896 several processes came together, making further action against the church unnecessary. Its leaders understood that for Utah to gain statehood, the church party would have to be dissolved, which they did; second, the Republicans began to court the church, especially its leaders, because they needed Utah's votes to control Congress; and third, much of the church leadership, which was rich, powerful, and business-oriented, was in sympathy with the general Republican philosophy and saw eye to eye with their interests on the national political level. In the elections of 1896 preliminary to bringing Utah into the Union, church leaders agreed among themselves that those who supported the Democrats would not campaign because the electorate was largely Democratic and the leadership did not want to antagonize the Republicans. They agreed further that the Republican supporters among themselves would try to sway as many people as possible by using the influence of their church positions. The Republicans won, and Utah entered the Union in 1896 as a Republican state, which it has stayed ever since.

In a longer, less colorful process the church was also forced to abandon the economy it had founded and long managed. By 1890 the church had become the home of a network of corporate enterprises which "owned and operated street railways, electric light and power plants, coal mines, salt works, sugar factories, mercantile establishments, publishing houses, and theatres" (Arrington 1958:405). It limited competition among mercantile enterprises, sponsored a political party, and was a major capitalist. The church may not have wanted to be quite so prominent in the world of real power, but by coupling its slender resources with major investments deliberately cultivated among Eastern and European capitalists, it was. As a result, it was pilloried in Congress and the press as anti-American for its participation in business affairs; national opposition to its stance in politics was overwhelming. A United States senator served notice in 1904 "that the institutions of this country must prevail throughout the land" (Arrington 1958:406). Although national institutions meant unregulated free enterprise, capitalism, and competition, they also meant the separation of religious from economic and political power.

Lorenzo Snow, who became church president in 1898, and his successor, Joseph F. Smith, recognized that the growth of the church's business and political power had precipitated the worst crisis in the church's history, the crisis over plural marriage, which had come close to destroying it. These leaders may also have seen that the new Republican and business sympathies of many church leaders pointed to their real commitments, the actual sources of power. Some hint of the disruptive force of business interests in the church appears in a report of Snow's secretary:

> Lorenzo Snow ... was aghast at the heavy burden of debt which had accumulated during the 1890s, and equally disturbed by the financial involvement of the church in business and speculative ventures.

He believed that if half the means used for business enterprises in which the church was interested, had been used in circulating our printed word, a mighty work might have been accomplished. But we were in debt and without money . . . He believed that the Lord was displeased with us for borrowing or going into debt to the extent of nearly two millions of dollars for business enterprises (Arrington 1958:406–407).

Here was the Lord's chief anointed coming to the understanding that worldly power, in the sense of both wealth and the ability to handle it, was deeply embedded in the church hierarchy and consequently in the everyday decisions of church government. The president analyzed the situation as a source of weakness and danger nearly causing the church's destruction. But what Snow could not see was the inevitability of the process as well as its irreversibility.

Both Congress and the church were aware of the danger posed by the sources of the church's wealth, and Congress, acting first with the Edmunds-Tucker Act in 1887, formally divested the church of all its property over $50,000 and appointed a federal receiver to hold and dispose of it. He secured over $800,000 of church property. This confiscation, called escheatment, deprived the church of liquid assets to support its many local communities, compromised its role as guarantor of the population's economic well-being, and put it in debt because of its inability to pay off the interest or capital on earlier loans. The church, on the other hand, also aware of the dangers brought by the growth of its own wealth, was preparing to quit the economy by the late 1880s. It began by urging Mormons to develop private businesses, by cooperating with Eastern capitalists to establish industries throughout its domain, and by divesting itself of ownership and control of many of the enterprises it had founded, nurtured, and matured. Told to dissolve its ties with the economy as early as 1882, the church had gone so far as to encourage private retail and manufacturing businesses:

In harmony with this multiplication of private concerns, most of the so-called church concerns were sold out to private interests or secularized in their policies. These included most local co-operative retailing and industrial enterprises which originally had public sponsorship at the local level; and also such general church concerns as the Salt Lake Street Railroad Company, Salt Lake City Gas Company, Zion's Savings Bank and Trust Company, Provo Woolen Mills, Z.C.M.I., and several land and irrigation projects (Arrington 1958:385).

However, even as the church was divorcing itself from economic enterprises, it remained half in and half out of the economy. The national depression of the 1890s severely affected Utah's marginal agriculture and mining industries, in part because by then its economy was so tied to the nation's that the economic processes of the larger unit affected those of the smaller, and in part because economic support from the church had been diminished and was replaced neither by sufficient Eastern nor by federal capital. The effect of the depression on Utah demonstrated how eroded was the old concept of an economically self-sufficient and safe Zion-in-the-Mountains and how vulnerable was this area without the church as a buffer.

During the depression of 1891 the church moved to correct the severe economic conditions:

> As a result of their concerted efforts, many new and successful industries were initiated. With an investment of about $500,000 the manufacture of sugar [from sugar beets] was initiated; another $500,000 saw the initiation of the hydro-electric power industry in the West; some $250,000 was expended on the development of a salt industry on the shores of Great Salt Lake. The Saltair recreation resort was constructed, as a means of providing employment; railroads were projected; canals were built; new colonies given a start—in short, everything was done to expand the economic base of the Great Basin and surrounding regions (Arrington 1961:32).

Such projects relied mainly on private Eastern capital willing to work closely with the church to expand Utah's economy. Even though the development of industry during the 1890s represented the biggest entry of outside capital in

Utah's history to that date, the church had retained control over most of the newly sponsored industries, thus showing that its leadership still managed unusual economic power.

Financial interests in the East saw this as monopolistic control and questioned the completeness of the separation of church and economy supposedly achieved in 1896 and statehood. The vehicle for a national debate over the continued church financial management in Utah was the trial to seat Reed Smoot in the U.S. Senate, to which he, an apostle, had been elected from Utah. The trial in the Senate lasted from 1903 to 1906, and was over the issue of whether a senator could also belong to an institution that controlled the civil and economic affairs of its people. Smoot was seated by a narrow margin, but: "By the end of the Smoot trial, late in 1906, [Joseph F.] Smith was able to testify that the church did not hold a controlling stock interest in any corporation but the Salt Lake Theatre. By that time, most of its important business properties had been sold to national corporations" (Arrington 1958:406). The trial was as violent an affront to the church as the earlier federal attack over plural marriage, even though legislative action was not at the core of the threat. National publicity labeled the church a giant monopolist trust, an accusation invoking the worst meanings of that term in turn-of-the-century America. Just as polygamy had earlier been a useful handle, now "proprietary monopoly" was a stick used to beat the church in public while limiting its capacity to influence Utah's economy in private. As a result, the church was effectively excluded from controling the resource and industrial development in Utah. Instead, the federal government and private industry dominated Utah's economy. Utah was bought and possessed.

To create a viable, self-sustaining economy and a population with predictable attachments, the federal government then initiated the second stage of the Americanization of Utah: a long-term program of economic aid, which continues to the present. Federal assistance to any state is often given with the conscious aim of securing political loyalty and making the local economy self-sustaining, which was

probably the case in Utah. There was doubtless an understanding that Mormons could be swayed with aid and economic support: "Gifts to the vanquished at the moment of
their defeat . . . can be viewed as the initial pump-priming
step in a dependent relationship, since the 'generosity' of the
conqueror obligates one to reciprocate, to deliver on a regular, periodic basis, the results of one's workmanship"
(Murra 1962:721).

Until statehood, the federal government contributed comparatively little to Utah, but by the turn of the century a
vast array of federal agencies had entered Utah and most of
the surrounding Mormon-occupied areas. These included
the Soil Conservation Service, Corps of Army Engineers,
Bureau of Land Management, Forest Service, National Park
Service, Geological Survey, Reclamation Service, Fish
Commission, Biological Survey, and Bureau of Agricultural
Engineering. Most of these services operated out of the De-
partments of the Interior and Agriculture, but the army and
the Smithsonian were also represented. They indicate the
range of activities—well beyond the church's ability—that
the government could provide to Utah. Once these agencies
began operation in an area, it was likely to receive concrete
services that it could never have provided for itself and
which were likely to enhance its economy. Although government agencies fostered agricultural development more
than industrial, the government put huge investments into
mining surveys, timber management, construction and
maintenance of tourist centers, and range management. Each
of these activities invited private industrial development of
the resources that the government husbanded.

The federal government's greatest contribution to the desert West was its work on irrigation, an effort that began with
the Powell Irrigation Survey of 1888. This massive federally
supported effort, which continued through 1894 under the
auspices of the Geological Survey, gathered information for
the placing of much-needed storage reservoirs in the Great
Basin. Although it did not involve dam-building, it produced centralized information on irrigation, and laid the
basis for renovating the irrigation system started by the

Mormons a half-century earlier, which was inadequate because it provided almost no facilities for storage of water against dry seasons and drought years.

In the twentieth century the federal government organized and financed many irrigation projects in Utah and some in the Mormon area of Arizona as well. These involved not just the survey of locales and the collection of technical information but also the underwriting of loans to communities and even the outright organization of water-control projects when the local area did not have the resources for such an undertaking. The first and one of the biggest irrigation projects sponsored by the government was located south of Salt Lake City. The Strawberry Valley Project was to supply water from the east side of the Wasatch Range to farmlands on the west side near Salt Lake City and Provo by bringing water through the mountains in a huge tunnel. Between 1903, when the Federal Reclamation Service expressed interest in the project, and 1922, when the project was completed and turned over to local users, the government presided over the financing and construction. This enterprise opened up or improved tens of thousands of acres and, though underwritten by the government, was eventually paid for by the water-users themselves.

The government's gifts to Utah almost always remained controlled or owned outside the state. Through the use of long-term loans as well as machinery and technical knowledge with which Utahans were not familiar, dependence was established. In the case of irrigation, the government controlled the construction and long-term financing, and in almost every case it set up a dependent relationship with water-users whereby improvements and extensions of the system would come from the government but were usually paid for by the local people. Only the government had the means to back such large projects and to introduce the technical competence to make them work.

In Utah and all over the Mountain West the government took command of irrigation; it held the church back with a punitive hand while inviting the faithful forward with a beneficent one. Through such pump-priming measures,

Utah's economy was more completely integrated into the national unit.

The ultimate economic effect of the subjection of Utah's economy to the federal government and Eastern capitalism was far-reaching:

> More and more the economic fortunes of Utah came to depend upon decisions and centers of control that lay far outside the confines of the state. The state's economy became "provincial," whereas it had been "metropolitan"; that is, it came to be peripheral to the core economy of the nation rather than being the core of its own regional economy. Many of its basic enterprises were absentee-owned. Its exports consisted increasingly of raw materials and semi-processed goods destined for the East. The rate of growth in manufactures tended to slow down, and the state increasingly imported from the East the semi-processed and finished goods it required.
>
> The culmination of this trend was the Great Depression of the 1930s, from which Utah suffered relatively more than almost every state in the Union ... The extent of the calamity is measured by the drop in total personal income in the state—from $270,000,000 in 1929 to $143,000,000 in 1932; and it did not again reach the 1929 figure until the beginning of World War II. Farm income ... dropped by more than half ... In 1932, 36 percent of the state's labor force was unemployed (Arrington 1961:17).

From 1847 until about 1880, Utah had an autonomous economy, providing a market for its own resources and neither exporting nor importing sizable amounts of goods and materials. Between the early 1880s and 1950 Utah's economy became like those of other Rocky Mountain and Southwestern states, including Arizona, Colorado, Idaho, Montana, Nevada, New Mexico, and Wyoming: it lacked markets able to consume what it produced, relied on imports, and had a specialized but undiversified economy. Utah followed a pattern that would prevail throughout much of the Mountain West for several decades:

> This is the highly specialized, exploitative economy involved in extracting from the earth a product which was transported in bulk to the East or Europe for milling, processing, refining, pack-

ing and/or fabrication into useful goods ... machinery, equipment, and ... consumer goods came back in exchange.

This sector, which made the West's most noticeable contribution to the emerging industrial capitalism of the nation, featured the colonialistic, absentee-financed, one-crop economy which was repeated in a somewhat different context internationally. Thus, in 1860, Colorado had 82 percent of its work force in mining, and Nevada 51 percent ... in 1870 Idaho had more than 60 percent ... This pattern of skimming off the cream from nature's reservoir of resources characterized the extensive agriculture [including cattle and sheep raising] of the area as well as the mining, and prevailed for several decades (Arrington 1963:20–21).

Such exploitation made Utah a colony and, together with its marginal agriculture and a disincorporated, escheated church, gave the state a very fragile economy, completely beyond the control of its own population and institutions.

Even so, neither the government, public opinion, nor Eastern capitalism could have successfully colonized Utah: the church might have been destroyed and the population subjugated, but the area would never have been made productive and certainly would never have been turned into a business-oriented, Republican stronghold. These results came about because the Mormon church and its population cosponsored the process of colonization. For example, in the case of sugar manufacturing in Utah the church adjusted to control by external circumstances. First the church founded the industry as a cooperative enterprise; then church ownership was supported with private, often non-Mormon capital; and finally the church lost ownership to non-Mormons, with Mormons continuing to influence managerial policies.

Mormons had attempted to set up a sugar beet industry in the 1850s to conserve the money sent East for the product, estimated by the 1880s at a million dollars a year (Arrington 1958:386, 391, 407–408; 1966:95–120). The industry, though a failure in the 1850s, was underwritten by the church again in the late 1880s, this time successfully. The project was undertaken to help achieve economic self-sufficiency for Utah and simultaneously provide employment for part of the Mormon population. The Presidency and the Twelve threw their full support behind sugar manufacturing:

After the cornerstone for the factory had been laid, the first Presidency issued a formal call to the leading financial men in the various wards and stakes to subscribe for stock in the concern and thus raise money for the company's notes and the construction costs as they came due. In support of the circular, members of the Council of Twelve Apostles visited conferences and priesthood meetings in the various wards and stakes and urged the faithful to support the enterprise—at first by subscribing stock, and later by buying its sugar. In these speeches church authorities stressed the employment it would provide, the scriptural admonitions to become self-sufficient, and the unfavorable treatment which Mormons were receiving from eastern corporations being established in the territory (Arrington 1958:388).

The depression of the early 1890s forced the church to look for Eastern investors to buy its bonds which underwrote the sugar company stock. It found Joseph Banningan of Rhode Island, who invested $360,000. By 1896 the Utah Sugar Company had become a technical and financial success, laying the foundation for what has since become a vast sugar-producing industry in Utah and Idaho. Despite the financial success accompanying this and other ventures, by late in the century the church had decided to pull out of all business. President Lorenzo Snow, who succeeded Wilford Woodruff in 1898, determined to get the church out of "financial involvement . . . in business and speculative ventures" as well as out of debt (Arrington 1958:406). In 1902 the church sold its sugar holdings to Havemeyer and the American Sugar Refining Company, taking care that the many Mormons who held small amounts of stock as a religious obligation were also bought out at the same price:

> The church insisted that all smaller stockholders who wished to dispose of their stock must be given the opportunity at the same price, and about 90 percent of the 800 stockholders are said to have sold at that time. In the announcement which made the conditions of sale public, the following statement is pertinent: "The question as to who should control has cut no figure, as it is stipulated, and was in fact one of the requirements made by the eastern parties that President Joseph F. Smith should remain at the head of the company; that Mr. [Thomas R.] Cutler [a bishop in the church] should remain its manager; that a majority of the board of directors should reside in Utah (Arrington 1958:407).

The church's statement about who controlled the enterprise after Havemeyer had bought the company ignores the transfer of ownership and profits out of Utah. Instead, the retention of Mormon figurehead control is stressed, as well as the continued use of Mormon managers and employees. In one swoop Mormons had lost financial control and turned themselves into managers, binding themselves by both moves to controlling ties outside Utah. Mormons who had once been owners were transformed into laborers and managers keenly responsive to those very external pressures that the church had so long fought to exclude.

With minor variations, this scenario characterized the building of the salt, hydroelectric, gas, streetcar, woolen, cotton, and a dozen other industries, including mining and smelting, cattle-raising, and timbering. In all these cases, the church ultimately lost control over industries that governed the lives of its people. By 1907 the church had sold its Utah Light and Railway Company, its Beach Company, its Salt Lake and Los Angeles Railroad, its interests in the Inland Crystal Salt Company, its iron and coal claims, and a lot more (Arrington 1958:408–409).

These moves by the church placed its population in an economically subordinate position. But they did more than that for they separated the church as an institution from the welfare of its people. None of these moves meant bankruptcy for the church, for after a period of loss and disorganization the institution emerged prosperous: "In 1957 the Utah-Idaho Sugar Company had a net worth approximately $20,000,000. At that time the church owned 80 percent of the preferred stock and about 50 percent of the common" (Arrington 1958:408). The church retrieved and extended its wealth by acquiescing to capitalist methods, including the search for profit, and by allowing the growth of disparities in wealth within its population. As a result, individualism, speculation, and inequality became the expectable consequences of Mormon life. These moves show that within Mormonism faith had become separate from church policy, and social welfare from religion.

The transformation of the church in the 1880s, 1890s, and early twentieth century in Utah was also true of the Mormon areas in Arizona. With several church leaders in jail in the 1880s and leadership decapitated, the economy of the Mormon communities fell into disarray. Mormons then stopped voting as a bloc for the Democrats and divided themselves between Republicans and Democrats. Only escheatment was avoided, since the church was not a corporation in Arizona.

Subsequently, the major industries to be established and controlled by outsiders in the Little Colorado region were cattle-raising, lumber or pulp-paper production, and tourism. The first was established in the 1880s, the second and third in the early decades of this century. Although avoided as investments by the agrarian-oriented Mormon population, these major enterprises now employ a significant percentage of the population, including Mormons. Service industries, insurance companies, retail stores, and machinery suppliers have also become important employers in the twentieth century. National companies, such as motor companies, insurance companies, food chains, and banks, have dealerships or outlets in the Mormon and non-Mormon towns to serve the local population, including the Indians, federal employees, and summer tourists. These businesses help support the local economy, but because they are merely branches of large corporations headquartered elsewhere, profits are removed rather than being reinvested in the local area, so their contribution is limited. Consequently, the Little Colorado has an undiversified industrial base largely oriented to exports. Its income is beyond its own control, and its population is reliant on jobs controlled outside the area.

By 1930 the predictability of nineteenth century employment had completely disappeared. It was replaced with a pattern common to marginal industrial societies, in which a person holds many kinds of jobs and frequently switches among them. The fundamental distinction between the nineteenth and twentieth centuries lies not in the relative amount of income or the opportunity for employment, but in the rapid changes that an individual had to make to earn a living. Whereas the nineteenth century required versatility on the part of all family members, who were exposed to the variety of tasks associated with agrarian life, rarely was a person faced with becoming a miner, ironmonger, or banker in addition to being a farmer. The situation at present is very different, with a person often going from cutting timber to selling used cars, from herding cattle to serving as county assessor.

Flexibility was essential during the last hundred years. But while the farmer of yesterday did dozens of tasks per year, they were tied to predictable seasonal changes; his descendants, on the contrary, have to perform a variety of tasks whose nature cannot be predicted in advance. The more recent employment patterns in Joseph City, Arizona, on the Little Colorado River show the diversification of job types since 1920 (table 13). Most noteworthy is the decline of agriculture, virtually the only nineteenth century occupation among Mormons in Arizona, which dropped as low as 45 percent by the 1920s and 18 percent in the 1960s.

The dependence on national markets, constriction of local capital, and absentee-controlled profits placed the local populations outside employment security. This was a complete reversal from the era when the region was governed and cap-

Table 13. *Occupation Distribution in Joseph City, Arizona, 1920–1965 (percentage).*

Occupation	1920–1929	1930–1939	1940–1949	1950–1959	1960–1965
Professional, technical	7.35	10.48	14.89	16.50	18.29
Farming	45.48	32.14	23.40	24.27	18.29
Managerial, pro-prietorial (ex. farming)	4.41	11.90	13.82	15.53	14.63
Clerical	2.94	3.57	3.19	5.83	7.31
Sales	1.47	2.38	2.12	2.91	7.31
Craftsmen	13.24	10.48	14.89	15.53	14.63
Operatives (mining, etc.)	14.70	21.42	22.34	14.56	15.85
Domestic	0.0	0.0	0.0	0.97	1.22
Services (ex. private household)	8.82	10.48	4.25	2.91	1.22
Farm labor	1.47	0.0	1.06	0.97	1.22

Source: Westover and Richards 1967; Leone 1974: 748–749.

italized by the church. Before the church was disincorporated, no one in the leadership would have been crass enough to overlook the effects of circulating a person through so many different kinds of jobs; awareness of those effects, in fact, lay behind the policy of economic self-sufficiency. Such independence and the security it provided existed because, to a degree undreamed of by modern employers, the church underwrote an individual's existence. No similar guarantor of stability exists today.

The subordination of the Mormon colonies like those along the Little Colorado in Arizona is the result of the church's own development. On the one hand, the logic of sanctity demanded consensus and egalitarianism. This produced a cooperative society with little economic difference between people. On the other, the drive for earthly success generated capital, class, and the small-scale profit-making and economic rationality personified in Lot Smith's business ventures, Jesse Smith's bank, and the High Council's businesslike decisions. The conflict between the two rationalities, sanctity and success, basic to Mormon history, negated many of the more conscious plans brought to the Salt Lake valley in 1847. The church sponsored innovation just as it tried to avoid the worst aspects of industrial capitalism. The men who lived out the conflict between socialism and progressive success were the same generation who had converted in order to escape the social and spiritual destruction brought about by the Industrial Revolution in the American northeast and western Europe. Nonetheless, the internal structure of Mormonism began to dominate its surface content, and the worst effects of capitalism returned. When the federal government destroyed the Mormon state and subordinated and colonized the Mormon population, the conflict between communalism and capitalism within Mormonism combined with external events to produce a changed religion, one which kept pragmatic rituals, sponsorship of technological improvement, and flexible, rational-looking decisions. But these became masks hiding changeable conditions, random employment, and the memorylessness needed to live with both.

7

Creating Mormonism:
Talks, Testimony, and
Sunday School

By the early 1900s Mormonism had changed. Independence was lost, in one sense because the kingdom had been occupied and in another because the institutions upon which Mormonism based its differences had been forsaken. By the 1870s private wealth had produced class and secular thought within the church; by 1890 these characterized the hierarchy itself. Gone were communal property, egalitarianism, and plural marriage. But more than social practices had been lost; the program that produced them had also dissolved. The severing of church and state killed the economic commonwealth represented by common property; the collapse of the church's political party killed the hope for social renovation; and the Republican ties of the hierarchy silenced the criticism of American capitalism. Without a consistent set of oppositions or a critique of society, free access to renovation dovetailed with economic and political subordination to produce a service population that did not know what it stood for.

Under force, the church was compelled to disassemble the programs that had operationalized its differences, so these differences were dying, but not in the sense of becoming part of Mormon history or precedent. Rather, the Mormons' assumption and promotion of change, coupled with the absence of a coherent program of opposition, produced people who remained convinced that they were different but who ceased to know why and also ceased to have a history, despite their elaborate record-keeping, that would tell them how. Having disassembled what it was, Mormonism began to operate in new ways.

Mormonism handles the material world with an immediateness, skill, and effectiveness that are crucial to the success its people enjoy. The strength of Mormonism is that it distinguishes, divides, subdivides, classifies, segments, and reorders the world for its believers; the world brings to Mormons, especially to them as economic subordinates, a host of facts, processes, concerns, demands, and problems which shape Mormonism because Mormonism is committed to shaping them. Mormonism is composed of a panoply of words, thoughts, maxims, elaborated principles, clichés, explicit beliefs, sacred texts, traditions, and values which are the symbolic inheritance of its members. These overlapping notions lack either precision or specificity, taking on usable and precise meaning only in context, and only in application by an individual Mormon to a given situation. Mormonism has meaning only in use.

In general, meaning is bestowed by people using symbols in contexts before an audience. In this respect Mormons contrast with most other Americans and certainly most other Christians, who create meaning in an enormously varied set of contexts which have little to do with institutional religion either as a source of values or as an audience before which to work out specific meanings and applications. Mormons, however, bestow most of the meaning in their lives within the institutional framework of Mormonism. Whereas the audience in other Christian churches receives, more or less passively, meaning declared from the pulpit, Sunday school teacher, or other authoritative religious source, every Mormon is the preacher, teacher, exegete, and definer of meaning before an audience of peers, who a moment or a month later may switch positions with him.

Mormons create their own theology and philosophy in the literal sense, and in the context of the church they work out for themselves most of the problems faced in life. They do their own thinking, which is to say that they create their own meanings, in the talks that they give in Sacrament

Meetings, in the testimony that they give on Fast and Testimony Sunday, in Sunday Schools and Family Home Evenings, and in at least a dozen other church contexts. These contexts give meaning to the values and other ideas with which a Mormon confronts the everyday problems of life.

There is a dynamic relationship between a concept and a given situation. They form each other. The situation is presumably resolved or clarified when illuminated by an idea or value, which in turn receives concrete meaning that has the effect of convincing believers of the efficacy of their religion. The idea also shapes the situation on which it is used, predetermining that a situation will be handled in a certain way and not in others and that in the solution all the social relationships embedded in the idea brought to it will be maintained and continued. This is particularly true of Mormonism because many of the ideas are synonymous with each other, recapitulating each other's appraisals of reality and their solutions for it.

Mormons make themselves a function of the here and now. The contexts in which religious concepts and daily life are welded together illustrate how neither concept nor life is allowed to develop any hint of inappropriateness in the face of the other. Usually the dialectic between the two is one of a group's handles on the present, because the ideal and real are often perceived to be in conflict, thereby pointing up the inappropriateness of one or the other. Among Mormons the dialectic happens so fast that past experience, as codified in the ideal, and the present problem addressed never have a chance to seem in conflict. Consequently, they do not comment on each other, and as a result, Mormons serve the present.

The beginning of this process is the link between sanctity and material life. After the ability of religion to govern key variables was replaced by other sources of power, the expectation nonetheless remained that religion would address material issues directly and specifically. This surviving expectation is much more keen than it is in most Christian churches, and it was not broken when the ties between church and state and between church and economy were broken. It is not that sacred sentences remained overspecified; rather, religious experience remained defined, as in the last century, by success and failure in the material world.

The state of Mormon theology and thought, as appraised over the years by both Mormon and non-Mormon scholars, has been found to be theologically weak, underdeveloped, and amateurish. Consider the following:

> Mormon theology is young and unsophisticated and is not overencumbered with creeds and official pronouncements. Its structure has been virtually untouched by serious and competent effort to achieve internal consistency of exact definition. Yesterday it was vigorous, prophetic, and creative; today it is timid and academic and prefers scholastic rationalization to the adventure of ideas. It is in great need of a definition of the relation of reason to revelation that will preserve the intellectual integrity of the Mormon people and encourage them in an honest and courageous pursuit of truth. It needs a conception of religion in history which will conform to the profound Mormon insight into the dynamic character of all things and thereby release the Mormon religion from the tyranny of the past (McMurrin 1965:112).

Or consider a parallel sentiment on Mormon theology: "The church has, with few exceptions, no theologically qualified leaders who can guide it in its encounter with secular thought. Members of the higher councils may be educated men, but ... in terms of theology, the church is governed not only by laymen but also by amateurs" (O'Dea 1957:229–230). These two statements pinpoint aspects of Mormon theology that may weaken the religion and which might be remedied if Mormonism trained competent professional theologians, but there is also another way to interpret them:

> The assumption in most of the major Protestant denominations is that the church member can be considered responsible for himself. This trend seems likely to continue, with an increasingly

fluid type of organization in which many special purpose subgroups form and disband. Rather than interpreting these trends as significant of indifference and secularization, I see in them the increasing acceptance of the notion that each individual must work out his own ultimate solutions and that the most the church can do is provide him a favorable environment for doing so, without imposing on him a prefabricated set of answers ... it is the chief characteristic of the most recent phase [of religious evolution] that culture [beliefs, ideology] and personality themselves have come to be viewed as endlessly revisable (Bellah 1970:43–44).

The development of this kind of relativity hardly conforms to the accepted picture of Mormonism, yet the church is in fact a good institutional example of how the process works.

Mormonism is almost always characterized as hierarchical, authoritarian, and literalistic; frequently it is likened in organization and dogmatic rigidity to the Roman Catholic church. But these represent the surface, not the core, of contemporary Mormonism. At the heart of Mormonism is a continuous revision of meaning by the individual believer, a process facilitated by the immediacy and availability of revelation and the freedom to discuss all religious topics in the conviction that all can be equally well understood. All topics are subject to revelation; more to the point, all are given potentially equal weight. No difference in conceptual complexity or importance is recognized. Issues such as a beatitude and the nature of the godhead are equally comprehensible.

Mormonism as a religious system is indeed full of unresolved difficulties, which are cause enough to sound the call to professional theologians, who traditionally organize and harmonize the discrepancies inevitably arising in a religion after the initial period of revelation. And given the logic of history as seen in the development of Christianity, such a call would be reasonable. But Mormonism is not a part of traditional Christianity; it is a whole new version. It lacks professional theologians and philosophers, not as the result of accident or poor education, but for the same reason that it has few professional historians: Mormonism has evolved a do-it-yourself theology which makes the growth of professional theologians impossible as well as unnecessary. A group of professional theologians would be a disadvantage to Mormonism: they would clash with a population of the faithful charged with the same tasks. Even more fundamental, a formal theology would centralize the creed and rigidify the doctrinal base of faith. Ironically, contemporary Mormons believe that their doctrine is already centralized, clearly defined, and easily identified. The very enormity of this illusion is what allows Mormons their diffuseness and variation in belief, which has produced their adaptability to the present.

Mormonism publicly proclaims the duty of every member of the church to flesh out the bones of the faith for himself. To this end, the church established a set of institutions whereby Mormons can talk to each other on a local level about matters crucial to existence. In themselves, such institutions are not unique to Mormonism; they are common to most of the religions founded around radical theological critiques in America during the nineteenth and twentieth centuries. But with the absence of professional theologians to contradict, counterbalance, or stop doctrinal error, the Mormon institutions take on added importance. When joined to the freedom of access of all Mormons to revelation and the visionary gifts of the Holy Spirit, this constellation of institutions forms the basis for doctrinal diffuseness.

A dual process is at work in Mormon theology. First, symbols such as the Holy Ghost, meekness, and the millennium are filled with meaning. Second, while the symbols are vague, they contain a view of the world with latent and implicit assumptions about the individual and his relationship to the community, the existence and nature of the supernatural, and the point of life. These symbols predispose those using them to construct the world in a particular way. When the symbols are used, they automatically propagate and reproduce the general world view and social reality encoded in them, while reciprocally, the contexts that they are helping to sort out give the symbols specific meaning.

The first occasion on which meaning and context are defined is the Sunday Sacrament Meeting talk, which is analogous to sermons in mainline churches. These talks, occurring weekly and lasting about twenty minutes, are personalized statements made by the ordinary Mormon members of a congregation to a few hundred peers. The talks are full of detail and, at their best, quite gripping.

Every Sunday, usually in the late morning or during the afternoon, Mormons hold their chief and most formal worship service. It is centered around the communion service, referred to as the Sacrament Service, which differs little even in the prayers of consecration over the bread and water (formerly wine) from most Protestant and Catholic churches and, like them, is surrounded by hymn-singing and other predictable events. After the sacrament has been administered, two sermons are given, called talks, which vary in length and sometimes in number. Since the bishop of the ward is by tradition not supposed to do much formal talking to his own congregation, talks are given by a wide variety of people who come mainly from two groups: adult members of the ward and visiting Mormons, usually church functionaries, from other areas.

All the material on oral presentations used in this book was gathered by attending meetings and then taking notes as soon as practical after the meeting ended. Nothing was tape recorded, and consequently little is verbatim. Tape recording would have been an intrusion into a religious service, highlighting my own presence. In my notes, however, I attempted to be as literal and exact as possible, while also noting contexts, like audience reaction, which depended on a point of view. The conclusions can be checked against the practices in almost any ward in America.

Mormons are generally agreed on what composes a good talk regardless of the context in which it is delivered. It must be technically skillful: loud enough, logical, and not too long. It must be authentic, involving genuine emotions and real-life situations, and not rely on borrowed vignettes or be ridden with scripture. Above all, it must not be a sermon: it must avoid righteousness or excessive piety and not remove the self from the message. For the successful message is the self and its exigencies.

Mormons are also in agreement about who gives the best talks: their own neighbors. Because functionaries are not keyed into local problems, their talks do not have that naive, authentic, unpracticed quality that comes from members of the ward. Mormons enjoy talks by visiting or returned missionaries, who often give emotional witness to the truthfulness and efficacy of the faith. They also enjoy visiting bishops, church leaders, and lesser functionaries. But when speeches become generalized or hackneyed, as they tend to be when delivered by a professional talker on a circuit, Mormons do not rate them high.

Mormons tend not to compare or pass judgment on the substance of performances within the area of religion, doctrine, and theology, although they do in almost every other domain. They do not discuss talks afterward or rate them against each other or against previous experience. If asked, they offer opinions, against which there is no taboo, but do not offer them spontaneously either to outsiders or to each other. The difficulty is trying to rank the quality of an expression that emanates from the Holy Ghost. Ranking anything beyond the quality of delivery would imply that the Spirit speaks uniformly from person to person, which would be nonsense.

It is a bishop's duty to plan the format of each Sacrament Meeting. The major element subject to change is the speaker or speakers. A bishop lines up speakers in advance, often taking advantage of the advance notice he has received from visiting functionaries. He may also approach a ward member to give the talk. His requests are not frequently turned down. The speakers chosen usually have some special quality to recommend them. The best audiences are obtained when the speakers are trying to solve a problem that touches on the daily lives of the congregation.

One Arizona couple, just returned from living several years on the Navajo Reservation, addressed a talk in August 1969 at Holbrook Ward, Arizona, on the subject of how to live with Indians, how to do business with them, how they relate to Mormon families, and how to treat them as equals. Eastern Arizona Mormons live on the southern edge of the Navajo Reservation, which also contains the Hopi Reservation. They are also on the eastern edge of both Western Apache Reservations. Indians are in fact the base of much of the Mormon economy, so old-fashioned Indian hating does not put bread on the table or money in the bank. It therefore behooved this audience to hear from a couple who had solved some major problems during their long practical experience of living and working among an Indian population whom everyone knew to be crucial to the local economy.

The husband, who talked on business matters, was a representative for one of the town's car and truck dealerships, a substantial and critical local business since the pickup truck is the chief vehicle on the reservation. He had experience in handling successfully a dozen different issues faced directly by a major fraction of his audience. His talk, consisting mostly of concrete examples, showed how most Navajo, few of whom have been converted, were just as likeable and trustworthy as anybody else. They were responsible, handled money well, repaid loans, made time payments, and were helpful to his family. The speaker implicitly condemned the older but still current Mormon attitude that Indians are barely capable of taking care of themselves and need to be looked after like children. From close personal experience, the Mormons were assured that Navajo were worthy of receiving equal treatment with everyone else. The wife told how friendly Navajo families had been to them, how well their children had gotten along together, how comfortable the Navajo had made them feel as newcomers to the reservation, and a host of similar vignettes which made the Indians into neighbors who could be treated as equals because they shared the same problems of everyday life.

When this couple had gone out to the reservation, they had taken along a series of abstract Mormon principles as well as some poorly articulated ideas about modern Indians.

The mixture of theology and values was subsequently turned into a way of life. When they came back, they could therefore show their peers, who were struggling with many of the same problems, how Mormon principles were linked with practical, everyday behavior and, as the Mormons say, how they lived Mormonism.

Mormons, in addition to being involved economically with Indians, have a formal ideology about them. The *Book of Mormon*, which is a history of the New World before the coming of the Europeans, gives Mormons a special historic mandate to missionize among the Indians, all of whom are New World descendants of people ultimately derived from Palestine. But of the two great peoples inhabiting the New World in the *Book of Mormon*, American Indians are derived wholly from the Lamanites, a people who disobeyed and prostituted God's word and who wiped out the Nephites, a people who had kept God's word. Further, like blacks, Indians are promised that they too will eventually become "white and delightsome." In addition, the Mormon church has a traditional hostility to Indians, stemming from nineteenth-century land claims, not a little racism, and a paternal and patronizing attitude. Yet Mormon theology also holds Indians to be human, having rights and, if converted, entitled to full membership in the church, a privilege long denied to blacks. In sum, the average Mormon faces a theology which is ambivalent on Indians and which has never been coherently articulated or consistently applied. Transitional ideas and programs now exist, but the contradictions and cosmological inconsistencies inherent in the notion that Indians are theoretical equals but actual inferiors are nowhere resolved. That task is the job of all Mormons who deal with Indians, and the only help they get is from others in their ward in exactly the same position.

This is just what the couple from the reservation did. They told their fellow Mormons how to harmonize their attitudes to Indians so as to produce behavior that was workable, effective, and profitable. Official Mormon theology on Indians may remain vague and confusing, but for the Mormon speakers and their fellow ward members the theology was put together, articulated, and made to work. American Indians, Lamanites, obligations to missionize, notions of individual equality, ideas about good business relations and the nature of other cultures—all took on a degree of precision and definition they did not ordinarily have. Inductively and with emphasis on empiricism, this couple welded belief to action.

Once the labels had been applied, the social relations inherent in them—such as business profit and loss, and the superiority of the believer to the inferiority of the unconverted—were automatically evoked and reproduced. Profit-making and missionary work are social relations of dominance and subordination, and actions taken in the name of "good business" and obligations to reconvert the fallen served to elevate these deeds as selfless and honorable.

Truth was recognized in the vignettes, although it certainly was not there inherently. Since the truth was a Mormon creation, its function was to extend the social world in which all Mormons lived. The meaning was formulated by ordinary believers, was never examined for possible conflict with other Mormon ideas, and was regarded as just as legitimate as any other Mormon view on the same subject. The situation illustrates the decentralized creation of meaning, as well as the fact that decentralization has a second dimension: meaning is continually recreated and reimposed. The individual who creates meaning may also change it over time to fit changed circumstances. Both the decentralization and the changeability would remain largely hidden. Further, this manner of creating meaning quickly dissolves the specificity given to symbols. Meaning, brought into being with a problem, dissolves from memory when the problem is solved. There is no institutional way or desire to perpetuate specific applications as one would preserve precedents in formalized theology and exegesis.

Another typical Sacrament Meeting talk occurred on August 15, 1971, in the Eighteenth Ward in the center of Salt Lake City. The ward's core population is retired elderly people, often widows or widowers living on fixed incomes. Compared with the rest of America, Mormonism is unusually successful in maintaining the ties that bind older people to family and church life. Mormon society does not suffer from the "old age" problem as much as the rest of the country does. Given that family life is considered the heart of successful church membership, there is a built-in place for grandparents and great-grandparents. The large extended families of most Mormons provide ample room and affection for the family's oldest living generation. Crucial church duties are also fulfilled mainly by older people. Women do genealogical work; both men and women do temple work. Women whose families are grown may trace the family's ancestors and then take past relatives vicariously through the temple rites. Retired people play a leading role in the performance of these rites both as proxies for the dead and as ritual functionaries in the ceremonies.

The talk in this ward was given by a man who had been a bishop when younger and was now a sealer in the temple, a ritual performer of consequence. He spoke before a congregation at least 60 percent of whom were elderly people, many of whom also worked in the temple or at various church tasks. He addressed the problem of avoiding a rut in temple work, just as in any other routine, and of learning to keep the repetition and potentially dulling activities from destroying the meaning of the work itself and hence the meaning of daily life. His solution was to get inspiration from the people who came before him filled with spirituality. He borrowed his own spirituality vicariously from them. He talked of the pleasure that he and his wife derived from temple work and recommended such volunteer work as a method of avoiding the dispiriting routine of retirement. Ironically, however, he lamented the new retirement policy of the church, which also applied to volunteer workers, which would cast him on his own spiritual resources. His ultimate solution, as is the case with many elderly Mormons, was to count on the afterlife.

The solution offered was as complex as it was incompletely satisfying. Temple work and genealogies are exclusively church tasks. They are religious pursuits in a religion where daily routines are sacred, and the purely sacred has been disestablished; they are priestly duties in a religion with no sanction for priests. However, because the work is only partly satisfying, it results in the need for extensive problem-solving discussion among those affected, which occurs in the local ward meeting before the people most concerned.

Because of changes in the larger society, the conditions of family life, especially extended family life, are starting to break down. The traditional extended family still exists only in rural areas, and as a result, Mormon elderly are displaced, like the elderly everywhere. Mandatory retirement is hitting the church too. Hope for celestial glory is all that remains in a religion which says that any religion unable to save people temporally cannot save them spiritually. Therein lies the conflict: doctrinal emphasis on the family and on fruitful, productive work all one's life, in sharp disharmony with the social reality and even with some current church practices.

How is the conflict resolved? The church has already recognized that elderly and retired people require special efforts at fellowship in the ward, and efforts are made to integrate them into these activities. But recognition of the problem, like its solution, is an inductive process for Mormonism: both must come from those who are experiencing it. The problem is articulated by those involved in playing church traditions and scriptural invocations against the social reality. Such localized discussion does not mean that the problem will be solved, merely that it will be aired. When ordinary people think in this way, the result is that abstract contradictions are not as likely to be seen. The practical contrasts are drawn with great precision and specificity, but such a system allows for much conceptual fuzziness at more general levels of meaning. As a result, Mormonism can go for long periods without seeing that its doctrinal house may be in disorder—without seeing, for example, that its retirement policies abandon its own elderly, just as its ambivalent attitudes to American Indians are perpetuated by invoking long-falsified nineteenth-century justifications, or that its programmatic incoherence generally casts its believers as servants to society. In this kind of setting, the conflicts may not be conceptually resolved, but their emotional impact on individuals is discharged.

To some degree, people try to show each other how to solve specific problems, and the models can be picked up or not. But what is being modeled is a method; the highly idiosyncratic application of commonly held symbols to everyday reality guarantees that the truth seen in meaning will shift as the units composing it do. Mormonism has discovered a way of keeping meaning dynamic and therefore fresh; it produces a continually revised world which nonetheless has the appearance of always staying the same.

Distinct from such joint problem-solving is the individual's use of an audience as a foil to reflect the truth of his own reasoning. This is the role of testimony. The first Sunday of every month is Fast and Testimony Sunday. Mormons fast from Saturday supper to Sunday supper on this occasion, and instead of the usual talks during church, the "stand" or pulpit is open to anyone in the congregation. During this three-quarters of an hour, anyone may go to the lectern and bear testimony to the truth and efficacy of the faith.

A testimony, like a talk, is offered to the congregation. However, testimonies are more spontaneous, more personal, and only secondarily meant to instruct. An audience is necessary to receive testimony, although it is not assumed that the audience learns anything concrete from it other than the depth of the witness' belief. Nonetheless, testimony, like a talk, links abstract Mormonism to daily reality and creates Mormonism for the individual in a way that highlights the idiosyncratic nature of meaning as well as the institutional containment of that idiosyncracy.

Testimony Sunday usually begins with a brief time set aside for children, from age five, to give their testimonies. They usually tell briefly of their love for their parents, brothers, or sisters and recite the formula: "I am thankful for this church and I know it is true and for the Prophet Joseph Smith. And I say these things in the name of Jesus Christ." Children say little that is spontaneous, but by the time they reach high school, they know how to talk to an audience. The average high schooler knows good rhetoric and carries such skill around for life regardless of context, including secular contexts. But in the context of testimony, the ability at public speaking, coupled with the freedom to discuss emotion-laden crises, produces a first-class drama.

A typical example of such a testimony took place on September 5, 1971, in the Holbrook Ward, Arizona. A high school girl appeared before her ward and told that the night before she had gone to a movie with some friends. Afterward she left them and went home feeling depressed. She "felt like dying." Then she read her "Patriarchical Blessing," a personalized, semiprophetic statement about the course and purpose of her life. The blessing said she had a mission to fulfill in life: there was something of significance in her future that was not yet known. Concluding that it must not be time to die, she felt comforted. Now she was sharing the solace derived from the church's truth with her fellow ward members.

This testimony is important for its source and content. The teenager was received with readiness by her fellow Mormons as one of them. The problem she told them about was also far more complex, sophisticated, and personally authentic than would ordinarily be discussed or even admitted by most denominations. Depression is not caused by movies, although it can be triggered by them, and she wisely did not becloud her testimony with any reference to the movie's content. The movie was not cause, merely context. There was public acceptance that teenagers can have such complex and difficult-to-deal-with feelings. The ward was full of her age mates who, through her, were being assured that something exists inside the church which is designed to give them comfort in crises. The church does not provide them with psychologists and psychiatrists, but it provides at least half the solution these professionals provide: a frank admission that psychological difficulties exist for nearly everybody; that they can be discussed, not hidden; and that they can be relieved by ordinary, sympathetic human attention.

In a theological sense, this testimony addressed a paradox

of critical importance: a personal sense of loss despite a loving God. The testimony of the girl touches on the most complex problem in all Mormon theology. For the Mormon, God did not create evil in any of its manifest forms, including depression, which can be interpreted as an expression of loss. Evil, like good, is a force inherent in a universe which, like God, always was. These forces are uncreated, as is God; they have always been. The same is true of "intelligences," or the spirit beings from whom humans come and from whom they derive their free agency. God himself overcame evil but is not independent of it. He has provided the tools to overcome it, of which his church and its institutions, including partriarchical blessings, are examples.

But Mormonism also says that God is perfect, supreme, almighty, and all-knowing. These, among the standard Christian attributes for deity, are also a part of Mormonism's view. They coexist with the more radical and limiting characteristics of God, both of which have roots in early Mormonism. Sterling McMurrin argued that the more radical aspects of Mormon theology have tended to give way in contemporary Mormonism to a fellow-traveling neo-orthodoxy which highlights the existence of an old-fashioned Protestant God with omnipotent characteristics (1965:106–107). But it is probably better to say that the material for such a recent tendency has always been in Mormonism, and has only been put to new and more intense use now. As a result, any Mormon knows both ideas: God is a God with problems, yet he is also an omnipotent and classically Protestant God. Such as open assertion in church would be unacceptable, for Mormonism could not tolerate a public debate on an inconsistency at so general a level. Moreover, the faithful could not handle such an abstraction. But for a teenager to get up and say that in the face of evil she asked God for help and got it is a standard and unexceptional piece of Christianity.

But even this is not what really happened. She did not pray; she read her blessing and figured out for herself that she need not be depressed. She helped herself and knew it; God never entered the telling of her story as a person or a name. She, with her blessing, solved the problem. In some real way, she did not take her problem to a God who has problems of his own. She shouldered her own burden. This is classical Mormonism. But the whole was attributed to a God so powerful that he knew every creature's future and, for those who were fortunate enough, would reveal its salient features to them. She said that God is contingent and so she had to solve her own problem; she also said that God is omniscient and knew the solution to all problems and had provided her with a document which would help her through them all. God is limited and omnipotent at the same time. The young woman's testimony was a common-sense presentation of that which lived harmoniously with a logical impossibility.

In an attempt to harmonize these two different views of God, Mormonism has specified some areas where God is omnicompetent, while refusing to specify others. God, for example, knows all but cannot control all. He cannot control all because man has free agency which is itself not a gift from God but exists apart from God. The concept of God is changing, being specified as conditions change. This creates discrepancies, which are dealt with practically and forcefully by people drawing upon their own needs and experiences. Out of such tension the meaning of Mormonism continues to evolve.

Mormon theology as such is never regarded by Mormons as a sufficiently problem-ridden area to deserve much attention. It is an area of givens, not disputes. As a consequence, the girl's testimony was an attempt to make sense out of the various ways one can look at God, but it was not basically a theological discussion. Rather, it was a way of creating "objective" reality out of symbols, of giving the symbols of depression, partriarchical blessing, Joseph Smith, the church, Jesus Christ, and truth a tangible reality which made them more concrete, objective, and sensible to herself. She made the faith live by making these items objectively true.

This testimony also challenges the separate existence of a dual world. While the young woman thanked the omnipotent God of orthodox Christianity, who as part of his omnipotence was all-caring and all-predicting about her and her future, she placed her primary reliance on herself and on the Mormon vision of a contingent God who expects us to help ourselves. Since she was on a par with God in many ways, she might truly expect to help herself successfully. As a Mormon, she had the right to place herself just slightly in back of God's own self-development and expected to reach it with the inevitable movement of time. She did not wish for a strength granted in the future; she used a present strength, true both for her and for God. As a result, the characteristics of a heavenly existence must not differ profoundly or contrast with this life. When Mormonism gave a person the strength that God has, it delimited even further the comparative frame of reference that a Mormon can bring to immediate problems. Mormonism allows believers to suppose that they can compare themselves favorably with the deity, and in doing so, it virtually eliminates any way Mormons might see how they are situated in the world. This situation is similar to the absence of precedents in the nineteenth century trials in that they systematically eliminated the past's relationship to the present. In the testimony the separateness of future heavenly states is compromised by making them extensions of earthly life. Just as the past was not turned into historical precedent by using it systematically to comprehend modern conditions, heaven also does not provide any contrast because both God and his environment are just continuations of well-known earthly processes and are therefore not much different from current life.

Another case of testimony on September 5, 1971, in the Holbrook Ward, Arizona, illustrates many of these points more forcefully. Early in a testimony meeting, the ward bishop announced a new president of the Relief Society, which is the most important post for a woman in the ward. After several other announcements, the testimonies began. Part way through, the newly appointed president walked to the stand to bear her testimony. She began by crying and then related how a short time before she had had a dream in which she was cleaning the area in the chapel behind the stand where the choir sits and had come across a man huddled in a corner weeping. She went over and tried to comfort him. As she did so, a pair of big eyes looked up at her and said, "You've let me down." This made her feel wretched. Then the tone of her voice became wry as she said that a week after the dream the bishop had called her into his office and "told me about authority," which is the right of men to rule in the church. "Then I saw that same pair of big blue eyes as he asked me to be Relief Society president." The punch line was delivered directly to the bishop with the implication that he had predetermined her decision to accept his offer by enlisting the help of the Holy Ghost, who had spoken through her dream.

One of the themes in this testimony is authority: authority to interpret personal statements from the Holy Ghost, as well as obedience to higher authority, represented by the bishop. Analytically, however, there is a broader issue, the construction of a safe and creative outlet for unconscious expressions. Faced with dreams, fantasies, and other unconscious phenomena, all of which seem episodic, unpredictable, and obscure, every Mormon has to deal with, classify, order, and label them. A lively tradition of personal dream interpretation was expressed in the journals of the nineteenth century, and a lively interest in them remains today. By and large, Mormons make no use of psychiatric insights, although the church itself is not opposed to psychiatry.

There is no rule of exclusion or inclusion to tell whether or not a dream is the voice of God. "You just know when a dream comes from the Holy Ghost," one informant said. This harks back to the issue of authority because it raises the problem of direct access to God, the question of who speaks, who is spoken to, and who interprets. Any member of the church may have inspiration or revelation, and there is great latitude for personal interpretation; in fact, the only check is the public presentation, which puts some limit on the meaning given to a dream by an individual.

In modeling dream interpretation, the new president also modeled authority. She did it in a context that preserved the dream's emotions, thereby admitting how crucial they are to the understanding of dreams. She gave herself the right to interpret the dream, but in explicitly recognizing the bishop's "authority," she also recognized his ultimate control over the verification of its meaning. She all but said he had caused the dream in the first place. Even if the church had an explicit theological position about dreams that matched their complexity, constant exemplification would be required to make such a set of canons coincide with the reality of dreaming and dream interpretation. Instead, Mormonism has used a benevolent attitude toward dreams in the past and a benign inattention to them in the present, to allow for their diversity and to provide a tolerant medium for the discussion of the meaning of that diversity without central interference.

To have a member of a congregation demonstrate the meaning of a dream that is plausible and emotionally satisfying would in itself be exceptional in any other church. However, in Mormonism, it is not unusual. Fuller and more complex discussions of dreams have occurred among other groups in other contexts within the church, like Family Home Evenings. Despite such sophistication, the major steps taken in this testimony were externalizing or objectifying an event, the dream, then holding it up as representative of a general category, authority, and finally recognizing the personal truth or meaning in it. In order to do so, at least two standard terms or symbols were used, the Holy Ghost and authority, and by virtue of these two ideas a novel event, the dream, was defined in such a way that its interpretation reproduced the existing hierarchy of authority: women subject to men, ward members to bishop, organization presidents to higher authority, and all to the supernatural. The symbols, when combined with an event, were used to reproduce part of the social order, but in use were also given specificity and concreteness. They take on meaning as well as provide it.

According to the psychoanalytic version of what was going on, the woman was telling herself in the dream that she felt guilty: "You have let me down." The exact nature of the guilt is not known, except that it centered on a male authority figure. In reporting the dream, she directed some anger to the bishop, the very man who had just honored and subordinated her. Now, had she chosen to use symbols or labels like the unconscious, guilt, and anger, the meaning of the dream would have been different; it would have been seen as her own creation, not that of the Holy Ghost speaking about authority.

Either a theological or a psychoanalytic perspective imposes standardized labels on events before an audience to create meaning. While there is no difference between the two perspectives in this respect, ultimately there is a level of self-conscious awareness of the process that distinguishes the two. Both Mormonism and psychiatry are centered with unusual force on the self, but the former has the effect, not of freeing, but of creating an uncritical attitude that hides much of reality, especially the role of the individual in creating meaning.

Notions like the Holy Ghost and authority direct attention outward away from the self and the present toward the world of unempirical beings. When that world is seen as real, all the social relationships latent in the terms are also reproduced. Whereas the unconscious is a construct like the Holy Ghost, it at least admits that dreams are the dreamers' alone and speak principally to private and present concerns. Psychoanalysis asks its followers to accept the reality of the unconscious just as Mormonism asks its believers to accept the reality of the Holy Ghost. The psychoanalytic method, however, allows the possibility of seeing the inherent arbitrariness of all these creations and of finding that they are not objectively true but contain truths only if people can penetrate their own creations. This comparison between dream interpretation as theology and as psychoanalysis is not meant to suggest the superiority of either but merely shows how profoundly relative the new president's interpretation was, as well as how deeply any interpretation buries dreamers in the society in which they dreamed.

Mormonism emphasizes a process best described as do-it-yourself theology. Whenever Mormons get together, they are invited to talk about all aspects of their faith and church, and they do so without a structure which actively prescribes the right answer to any question. Mormonism is thus a way of helping its members think out the solutions to problems with each other's help and in such a way that, when the problems change, the way to think about them does too. It allows for dynamic problem-solving by local, homogeneous groups.

Sunday School, as opposed to talks and testimony, is a vital aspect of Mormon thought for another reason. All Mormons attend Sunday School throughout their lives. It is not just for children. Classes are held on Sunday morning, are organized by age-grade, and in the case of adults are led by a member of the class who is appointed by the bishop. Sunday School for children corresponds to the divisions of grade school, with the teacher trying to elicit spontaneous, extemporaneous responses that nonetheless coincide with what the manuals indicate is an appropriate way of answering. Above high school, the categories include young married couples, the middle-aged, and those past middle age. The last two distinctions are not particularly important and tend to merge into one class. All Sunday School groups are provided with manuals, and full participation in the class is not supposed to be possible unless an individual has read the lesson beforehand, but in fact this is almost never the case. Full participation is independent of formal preparedness, and usually only the most pedantic stick to the manual, which contains enough lessons to take a class through a year. Manuals are conceived as a means to promote discussion; they are not catechisms functioning as guides to absolute truth. Their format is: puzzle, exemplary vignette, scripture verifying the example, and an invitation to discussion. The puzzles or problems range over several traditional areas with which adult Mormons are already intimately familiar. The theological areas include the nature of God, the Savior, the Holy Ghost, and eternity. Other areas are the nature of interpersonal relations with parents, children, and neighbors. The philosophical issues include the nature of authority, repentance, obedience, commitment, morals, and freedom.

If, for example, the lesson for a given week is "Blessed are the meek," the manual provides several pages of exemplary material on the general principle. The initial declaratory material attempts, usually in semicolloquial fashion, to state what meekness is. With the aid of words from church leaders and "wise men from all ages," meekness is defined. Then comes a story of how someone who had a problem solved it by using the principle of meekness. There may then be questions designed to provoke discussion. The time spent in class on the manual itself is insignificant. All participants consciously value free discussion, and roughly three-quarters of the hour-long class is actually extemporaneous. To start off, the class leader may ask a member what meekness means and how the person attempts to apply the principle, or what the prophet Joseph Smith said about meekness. The discussion is certain to have two characteristics. First, regardless of the topic of the lesson, participants attempt to relate some aspect of their life to the idea behind the lesson. Whether it is meekness, the nature of the millennium, or the role of authority in the church, individuals tell how they used the idea to solve specific problems. The discussion is completely personalized and autobiographical; the participants are pragmatic and commonsensical. Sometimes they give the impression that the whole corpus of Western theology and philosophy is unnecessary obscurantism, which the Mormon people, in their wisdom, have disestablished in favor of their own straightforward rationality.

The second characteristic of Sunday School discussions, and indeed of all similar affairs within the church, is that the leader or instructor does not sit in judgment on individual comments made. Nobody is contradicted. There may be sixteen different opinions on when the millennium is going to occur, but no one calls particular guesses unsound or doctrinally adventuresome. Church members may say something outrageous about politics and authority or describe meekness in a way that is not meek, but usually they are just ignored. Whatever is said, it is almost never contradicted, called wrong, or labeled as being opposed to church doctrine or policy. Not that this can be called intellectual freedom within the church; the opposite may in fact be true. But by design, on matters labeled "spiritual," considerable flexibility is permitted and even sponsored in a way that is at best only dimly recognized by anyone in the church.

People in Sunday School speak in turn, but they often speak past each other. To call this "discussion" is probably to confuse communal participation with private monologues delivered before an audience long used to personal, idiosyncratic turns of logic. Personal statements often, however, elicit sympathetic reactions which affirm the previous option and then extend it to a new area of personal experience. This parade of personal opinions goes on virtually unchecked. Individuals who are better educated, better read in church literature, or more intelligent could be in a position to point out nonsequiturs, bad history, contradictory precedents, or even faulty doctrine. Such persons could easily lead or even dominate a class. But if they tried to do so without an appointment from the bishop, their peers would feel not so much threatened as denied democratic access to that body of ideas all Mormons may discuss equally. They are guided by feeling, experience, and intuition, sometimes also by personal revelation. Nonsequiturs, nonexistent historical examples, and confused thinking are not appropriate critical categories when dealing in information whose source and inner logic are beyond the merely rational and historic. This basis of intellectual democracy exists when Mormons talk to each other about their beliefs, and this reasoning prevents any really effective hierarchy from emerging in intellectual matters.

The nature of Mormon Sunday School is mysterious only to those who listen uncritically to what Mormons profess about their church and its doctrines. The ordinary Mormon is capable of matching the ordinary American Catholic when it comes to proclaiming doctrinal orthodoxy. For most Mormons, the church has an answer for all questions and is secure in a seamless fabric of theology that is fast against all man-made logic. Mormons know exactly what they are supposed to believe, or so they feel. In fact, however, Mormonism is all but creedless and stands completely without exegesis. Mormons point to the Thirteen Articles of Faith as a statement of what they believe, but these do not compose a creed. No Mormon is quizzed on belief in them, and little attention is paid to them in the usual course of church life.

What must a Mormon believe to be a Mormon? The answer is found in a common set of verifications. All Mormons believe that Joseph Smith was a prophet of God and that the church he founded is the true church. These are the two critical points that Mormons do not share with any other Christians and which they uniformly share with each other. There is a great deal more, like the Plan of Salvation and Articles of Faith, but these do not form part of the irreducible statement of belief. The point is that, if a group of Mormons were asked what they are required to believe, there would be no unanimity beyond the first two points. The diversity does not spring from poor religious education but from the essentially creedless nature of the religion. Its effect dominates modern Mormon thought.

The concepts discussed individually each week in Sunday School are applied to particular problems which show considerable variability. Thus, the theology is tied to specific instead of abstract levels. The first consequence is that over the years the enormous variety of meaning tends to expand each category and to duplicate the ground each covers. Second, the theology is segmented. It is no longer a pyramid of interrelated concepts about God, man, and nature and their joint relationship which can be used to deduce an idea of what reality ought to be. Rather, Mormons have a set of autonomous and disarticulated concepts which, while strong enough to mask economic, political, and psychological reality, have nevertheless lost the ability to comment on them, an ability that they conspicuously possessed in the nineteenth century.

The positive side of Mormon theology—its flexibility—and the negative side—its loss of transcendence—stem from Mormons having a synthetic world view. They lump together many general ideas and daily problems and rarely isolate a particular issue by calling it inharmonious, fundamentally different, or paradoxical. Thus, cycling the theology before the religious public keeps it full of meaning while it also masks large amounts of diversity and contradiction. Despite the economic and social diversity, unpredictability, and incoherence that Arizona Mormons have been living with since the turn of the century, enormous change has been synthesized. By lumping changes under a relatively small number of theological categories, their full diversity has not been noticed nor their full disruptive impact been felt. Since the local Mormon population has attuned itself to change, making an ever more successful living from it, it must be assumed that the Mormon way of synthesizing makes use of change without experiencing the disruption inherent to it. But the inescapable conclusion is that in the way they are now used, Mormon ideas cannot be arranged to create a negative commentary on the events which they classify. Through overlap, on the one hand, and isolation, on the other, the relation between the pieces of the system have disintegrated; the internal logic that the system once had has been functionally destroyed. Thus, like the past, it has ceased to exist.

Perhaps the most curious feature about Sunday School classes among adult Mormons is that they tend to comprise independent monologues, not real discussions. People present themselves and their views: they come to a conclusion, articulate it publicly, and have it confirmed. This process is the core of modern Mormon thought; it turns the call for systematizing theology and philosophy into a false issue, which fails to see that on at least one point—free access to theology—Mormon doctrine is vitally and brilliantly alive among the people, having emerged just where everybody officially proclaims it ought to be, but where no one is prepared to find it. Safe in the hands of the people, it can take whatever turns are required; unimpeded by higher authority or formal logic, Mormons do not see what they are doing, which is keeping a vital faith vital, creating and recreating Mormonism just as Joseph Smith wanted. What Smith and modern Mormons seem to have discovered is that truth is dynamic.

Here is the essence of Mormon theology, whether it appears in talks, testimony, or Sunday School: it is centered on the individual. Mormons actively create their own private understanding of it, and its meaning is not challenged. This highly idiosyncratic interpretation meshes completely with the personal flexibility adults need to exploit the changeable environment in which they must live and survive. Personal thought and personal buffeting coincide. As a result of this extreme decentralization, the monologues in Sunday School are a guarantee of reproducing existing social reality, which is itself epitomized by change. Given the absence of theologians, the rapid revolution of theological concepts in lay hands, and the frank expectation of using them on practical problems, Mormon theological concepts are a function entirely of the present. And since the concepts contain no means for developing critical self-awareness of what is going on, Mormons, on an individual basis, subject themselves to change while being convinced that their lives are stable.

8

The Uses of History

Mormons have developed a vigorous tradition of lay history, producing thousands of personal journals and family histories. This is amateur history, basically chronicle and vignette, not interpretation; its skeleton is kinship, not politics or economics, and it is unreservedly uncritical. Since for religious reasons every family in Mormonism must concern itself with its own past in one form or another, the tradition of lay participation permeates the church. It is grounded in the obligation that living Mormons have to the dead. Deceased relatives, no matter how far removed, who lived before the advent of Mormonism, are eligible for the temple rites and hence for elevation to the higher levels of the afterlife which would otherwise be closed to them. No one who has died can be taken through the temple rites until his family ties with the living have been secured.

Family ties are established through genealogies, which are constructed exactly like those done by professional genealogical researchers and professional anthropologists interested in kinship. This large-scale pursuit involves gathering primary data from around the world and often yields family trees going back hundreds of years, occasionally to the Middle Ages. The process nets an evolving skeleton of names, which are provided in abundance by the church's central genealogical service, along with kinship charts and short courses in do-it-yourself genealogy. The church has been microfilming genealogical records, parish registers, courthouse and town hall records all over the English-speaking and Scandinavian worlds. It has now begun on the Spanish-speaking world because many converts are from Latin America. Millions of pieces of raw genealogical data have been computerized for rapid retrieval.

When the individual has traced a new link in his ancestry, it has to be verified by church experts in Salt Lake before the newly found relative can be taken through the temple and officially entered on the family's chart. This requirement keeps the recreation of the past intellectually responsible. In establishing and running a complex and sophisticated genealogical organization, the church explicitly attempts to make the use of the past accurate.

The strictly religious obligation concentrates on names and genealogical ties; it does not concern itself with material which would turn a kinsman into a comprehensible historical figure. It is not concerned with context. However, the unofficial but widespread attitude is to gather as much accompanying information about one's dead as possible. Mormons actually want a rich context in order to understand who their kinsmen were.

If the family keeps narrative materials in addition to the genealogy, recent events from the family past can be fitted into the chronicle. Nineteenth century Mormons also left numberless documents which are indexed in Salt Lake at the Historian's Office. These are the source of much of the data used to build family history. Attention is paid to the dates of crucial life events, like a child's blessing and the induction of men into the various levels of the priesthood. Diaries, journals, letters, and other literary memorabilia can often be found to flesh out the skeleton of kinship.

A family with several generations of Mormons often compiles and publishes its own history for limited distribution. Some also maintain family newsletters. The family history, usually put together by an older member who has done extensive genealogical work, can be used to link several hundred living individuals to several hundred, and sometimes several thousand, individuals in the past. Such histories may contain long extracts from the journals and papers of nineteenth-century pioneering ancestors. Usually, they report colorful vignettes, events, encounters with the famous of the church, and anything else portraying a vanished way of life.

The church does not specifically sponsor family histories, but it does invest heavily in establishing genealogical links. In this activity the focus of history is on kinship, and kinship focuses on the self and its relations. This produces two results: all ties are viewed from an egocentric perspective, and the largest possible grouping is the family. In a family's terms, the most complex, ever-changing facet of its life is the addition of kinsmen in the past and present and the relations maintained with kinsmen still alive. The genealogy is in flux, continually being added to at the top and the bottom.

The history that concerns the average Mormon involves a living individual linked to a dead one; it does not involve an analysis of groups, classes, economic or political processes, institutions, or any kind of quantitative material. History is an individual matter, the personal quest of a modern person for a dead one; the emotional force of the individual is clearly fixed on specific persons instead of being diffused over vague determinisms and hard-to-locate historical processes. In this way, the past is easier to identify with and more convincing, because the process carries a conviction established through emotional satisfaction.

Once a kinsman is identified, the picture of the past he or she is associated with is given further validity in the religious experiences of the temple rites through which the dead are vicariously taken. A living relative may take a dead family member through the same range of temple endowment ceremonies he or she has been through for himself. The highly personal nature of this process allows a believer to identify with the subject. Such unconscious identification involves transferring one's thoughts onto a subject, with the result that the subject is seen as objectively containing what is actually being imposed on it. Thus, because the figures from the past seem objective, they act as a more faithful reflection of the present and situate a person more completely and comfortably in it.

The principles operating in this process were typified

during one of the History Weeks sponsored annually by Brigham Young University. In March 1975 two Mormons made presentations aimed at obtaining and working with the materials of Mormon family history. The key presentation was a discussion of quilts. People were shown a display of quilts, all of which had been made by Mormons at a variety of Western locations. The quilts, usually made from old family clothing, were sewn by women and often represented the work of three generations working together. The speaker suggested that quilts are useful aids to jog one's memory about past events. As an example, she recalled that once, when sick as a child, she had used the quilt on her bed to pass the time by remembering its pieces' original function. One piece had come from her brother's pants, another from her grandmother's dress, still another from an aunt, her mother, and so on. She amused herself by traveling back over the past with the memories called up, which were pleasant to dwell on, could be provoked at will, and covered a wide range of experiences. Thus a quilt, or any similarly varied item, was a way to recapture one's rich and forgotten past. It stimulated memory which, once unlocked, was a guide to the past.

Another Mormon gave a talk on "memory chests" which emphasized that family memorabilia could make history live. She talked about family trunks and their contents, suggesting that many of the items served as living reminders of one's personal past. These chests contain albums, jewelry, old books, letters, and other memorabilia. The memories stimulated by such objects are valuable because they help a person gain access to the past, and in this sense the memory chests and the quilts serve an identical function: recapturing an objective, personal history.

Because anyone can produce a family history in this way, anyone who has a memory to be jogged has a history, and that history is not thought of as biography, autobiography, or psychohistory, but as family history. Such a highly personal and creative effort is similar to the process taking place in talks, testimony, and Sunday School, where the personal understanding of theology and philosophy is a vehicle for constructing and reconstructing the personal view of the world. People use discourse on the future to understand the present, and they also use genealogical discourse on the past to accomplish the same ends.

These points are evident in the Mormon's story of the quilt. The musings and reflections she described when gazing at the quilt, chosen from the infinite repertoire of possible recollections, were her statements, doubtless her creations as well, that said as much about her as about the subject matter, and which carried her unconscious comments on being sick and whatever else was happening at the moment. When these memories were recalled, her condition served to replay fears and wishes established early in life which would be played out again and again to produce many similar images and symbols. From this perspective, history is idiosyncratic and changeable with the individual's momentary needs, while being permeated by the individual's long-term psychological makeup. Here, then, is a changeable image constructed in the present made up of items from the past and given an identity thought to be objectively valid.

The use of memory chests shows this process more clearly. An individual or a family coming upon a set of objects can recall pieces of family history associated with the material examined. Memory is thus a valid point of entry into the past, and kinsmen acting together can produce more memories and stimulate each other, thereby increasing the flow of information desired. This well of memories, which can be brought up with cues and hints, is regarded by Mormons as bottomless. Objects help it to function, and new objects help to retrieve other and different material. The same object can also provoke different memories at different times. Historical material is always being added, but since it is not usually written down, it is not clear what has been forgotten, what is continually rediscovered, and what is newly dredged up. This makes for a certain dynamism between the stimuli of the present and the memories from the past. Because those in authority want conclusions to be favorable and supportive of the present, little attention is paid to how memories are dredged up or to the interpretations given them.

Mormons are not in a position to ask themselves how memories are produced, or how certain memories are associated with certain artifacts, or how these associated memories change, or why, out of the range of memories tied to almost any object, some are selected and not others. Because the factors operating to stimulate memories are not examined, Mormons think that what they remember is a commentary solely on the object and not on their personal motives at the time of recollection. No matter how epistemologically questionable lay history may be among Mormons, however, they do not invent a past that did not happen. Mormons are not telling lies, nor are they creating fairy tales; they are giving meaning to the past as well as shaping it by imposing order and sense on it. This is the historical process in a nutshell, which works to create an image separate from the viewer's that appears to be natural or given. The process hides the arbitrariness of the historical interpretation itself and ensures the acceptance of the situation regarded as objectively distinct.

The full participation by Mormons in historical material has created an elaborate, sustained, do-it-yourself system. The central church provides the rationale and motivation, the framework through kinship and genealogical charting, and the data in abundance. It also provides a mechanical check on accuracy. Further, once the new pieces of the historical record have been produced, the church provides a ritual to legitimize them. With all these homogenizing tools, based on the proliferation of kinsmen in the present and future as well as in the past, the individual Mormon is able to put together a satisfying picture for himself.

Such idiosyncratic shaping of the past is taken further by means of the *Book of Remembrance* that every Mormon family possesses, in which it keeps its genealogical charts and records of important information, such as schools, business activities, church positions, places of residence, talents and interests, faith-promoting experiences, travel, and outstanding acquaintances. This looseleaf book centers around a "Pedigree of Progenitors," the record of one's ancestors as these are discovered and initiated into Mormonism through church rites. But the *Book* is so organized that it focuses on the merits and accomplishments of the individuals compiling it. With the help of a "Progress Chart" the compilers can check on their efforts to complete a pedigree chart, write their own history, join a family organization, and help others start a *Book of Remembrance*. People are urged to keep clippings and to start a chronology of their life. These items become part of the model used to construct the biographies of ancestors. While constructing an autobiography, therefore, one is also constructing the prototype for biographies of one's ancestors. As a university graduate expressed it: "One of my eighteenth century ancestors also went to a university. I was so pleased to find that the family had such interests going back so far." There is an obvious predisposition to concentrate on traits in the past most interesting to oneself.

Mormon history is clearly in the hands of the people. And the people change the pattern of the past; they are continually rewriting history, individually and at will. Of this they are unaware, as they are unaware that they change their perception of the past depending on what is called for in the present. Usually the factors in the present which govern the interpretation of the past are economic and political.

History is usually thought to be objectively true by those who research and write about it. This is true whether the historian is amateur, professional, Mormon, or gentile: history is taken to be independent of the writer and to have a life of its own. The objective independence that the past is thought to have hides both the role of the present in bringing it to life and the factors in the present that determine the shape of the past when it is resuscitated. Given that the past is used in the service of the present and that the factors determining its use are unseen or disguised, the particular innovation in the Mormons' use of this otherwise universal process is that they locate it among all their people, where it functions unfettered to allow each person to find his or her own image in the past as well as a new image whenever that becomes necessary.

One of history's functions is to mask factors that operate best unseen, but in Mormonism there is an elaboration of the masking process in which the history that each person believes to be true is the history that each manufactures. An autobiographical identification with the past, which is a normal development, thus becomes in Mormonism a validation of one's creative effort, rather than being one's creation standing in the way of that effort's validity: the more recognizable is the past, the more successful has been the effort at recovering it. In this way, Mormons lock themselves into the present more effectively than the rest of society. Consequently, Mormons never see profound change and are even prevented from seeing the causes of it because all history is an individual's reflection; and just as a mirror never tells a viewer what it saw yesterday, history never tells Mormons what they or their society looked like before. It cannot do so because the living Mormon is the image in the mirror.

Genealogical history accomplishes this masking in two ways. First, it disguises the real conditions of existence among the living by creating an imaginary idea of what the actual relations were among the dead. Second, in being told, written, and believed, in being applied or extended to any given situation, it reproduces the actual economic and social conditions of existence operating among those who do the telling, believing, and objectifying. So, not only does Mormon history disguise much of reality, but it perpetuates it as well.

Disguising past reality is exemplified by the fact that in the nineteenth century on the Little Colorado in Arizona, 80 percent of the inhabitants of any one Mormon town married someone from that same town (Leone 1972). Villages were 80 percent endogamous. Much of the 20 percent rate of exogamy was composed of the leading Arizona Mormon families marrying into each other regardless of where they lived in the territory. This statistical observation is completely hidden, however, in the family histories and journals of the Hatch and Freeman families, two moderately prominent families of the Little Colorado area. Each of their histories contains amusing, elevating, and truthful stories about the members of the family. The histories mention who married whom, and they may pick up a stray economic factor in the marriage or the fact that someone was commanded to be polygamous against his better judgment. But neither history reveals that the families of the hierarchy protected their own power and wealth through a network of intermarriage ranging over the whole Little Colorado colony, or at least that family ties were so arranged that all people with power and resources were tied together through intermarriage and could consequently provide any community or any individual with aid in an emergency. Remember Lot Smith and his connections. No matter how professional historians or social scientists looked at the same facts related in family histories, they would not find the illustrations of chance circumstances and free agency that the Mormon assumes is the explanation for events. This is the crucial difference between the faithful, who assume God's ever-present hand in any one person's life and historians who, although they may be good Mormons, do not allow the hand of God to explain what is plainly in the hands of men.

In this example, kinship ties are assumed by the faithful to proliferate haphazardly, whereas any scholar by his very training must assume that events are not random but are part of a naturalistic pattern that can be identified and explained. History based on kinship eliminates this scholarly point of view, making it unlikely that any normal set of historical causes could be identified in past events. In this way much of past reality is overlooked, and since kinship organizes data in the present as well, it excludes many relationships the scholarly world assumes to operate there. A genealogical view thus hides many factors operating in history, and because it is a habit of mind among the living, it automatically affects an understanding of the factors operating in the present.

Beyond disguising many conditions of existence in the past and present, it reproduces much of what is being disguised. Mormons on the Little Colorado in Arizona, for example, are surrounded by Indians who are directly tied to their general economic well-being. The area is strewn with the ruins of some 12,000 years of prehistoric occupation. The local Mormons regard and refer to the Indian population, both extinct and extant, as Lamanites, descendants of people who played a dishonorable role as related in the *Book of Mormon* by disobeying God's word and by annihilating those who had kept it. For Mormons, all Indians are brethren, being basically undifferentiated descendants of this *Book of Mormon* people. Most local Mormons unquestioningly accept that the origins and history of both living and prehistoric American Indians are truly portrayed in the *Book of Mormon.* When presented with the idea that the Western Apache and Navajo are part of recent, fifteenth century Athabascan migrations into the Southwest and, as a result, are totally distinct from the Hopi and unrelated to the prehistoric peoples of the area, Mormons are uninterested or uncomprehending. They do not accept the distinctions between fundamentally different cultural units, and more important, they do not believe that these societies have long and mutually exclusive histories.

Most Mormons have no idea that there is an alternative explanation outside the *Book of Mormon* for the peopling and history of the New World before the arrival of Columbus, and that it was not all Nephites and Lamanites as stated in the First and Second Nephi. They are unaware of what the rest of the world has concluded.

Categorizing Indians as descendants of those who failed to keep God's word and who were punished with red skins—whether assuming that they will one day become white and delightsome or that they are all alike and have always been an undifferentiated mass—is a way of using a supposedly objective past to perpetuate present social relations. To say that belief in the *Book of Mormon* rationalizes present attitudes and practices toward Indians misses the point; it actively reproduces and extends them. When Mormons discuss Indian relations in terms of *Book of Mormon* categories, which imply kinship as well as inferiority and subordination, they organize the data, events, problems, impressions, and inchoate sensations that they have about Indians at any one time into a coherent set of categories which allow them to make sense of the world and to act upon it. Educating hundreds of Navajo at Brigham Young University, placing thousands of them in Mormon homes while they attend boarding school outside the reservation, and sending missionaries to their reservations are programs that stem from injunctions to preach and convert the Indians. All these efforts nonetheless assume Indian inferiority, which is overtly expressed as a spiritual lapse vis-à-vis the role played by ancient Indians in the *Book of Mormon*. Mormons perpetuate this inferior relationship in their very efforts to overcome it. For in preaching inferiority, they come to believe in it; and their overtly religious programs derived from the historical mission set out in the *Book of Mormon*, draw Indians into their own economic and political orbit. Converted Indians thus automatically maintain their sense of inferiority because they see themselves in *Book of Mormon* terms and, as Mormons, remain Indian on Mormon terms. For both Mormons and believing Indians, the history in the *Book of Mormon* expresses objective truth and, in expressing it, brings it into being. In this way history duplicates and thus perpetuates current social reality.

Given how Mormons build their individual histories and how they use histories like the *Book of Mormon*, it is no wonder that the church has discouraged any intellectual tradition that would interfere with disguising historical factors or with maintaining much of the social reality through the uncritical way lay history is done. Both the church's treatment of intellectuals and Mormons' anti-intellectualism are complementary examples of how the do-it-yourself revisionism of Mormon history is sustained while hidden from view. "The intellectual is not at ease in Zion," concluded Davis Bitton, a Mormon (1966:132). Even though for most of their history Mormons have dwelt on intelligence, learning, thought, and knowledge as well as freedom of thought, authority, and intellectualism, Bitton concluded that anti-intellectualism best characterizes the Mormon attitude to disciplined thought today. The extension of this argument is that Mormons have a complex and superficially understood past. Though not long in terms of the other Christian churches, it has one distinctive feature: voluminous, coherent written records for its duration. With such a well-documented record at their disposal, it might be assumed that the church and its allied historians would have dispelled the obscurities, fictions, and falsehoods that even the scholarly world maintains about the institution and its faithful. Not so, however. Very little of the record has been interpreted and made into history. There are few active historians within the church, and until recently a Mormon historian was an apologist or outcast. Although the last decade has seen a healthier group of historians, lay and professional, in the ranks of Mormonism, the number is still small, and they are unsure of how their church regards them. The most obvious reason for this is that a corps of professional historians and intellectuals could challenge the fictional, uncritical, and adulatory aspects of lay history. When historians use kinship and genealogy as organizing tools, these are almost always combined with analysis of the accompanying social structure to produce social history and prosopography. They never produce family trees as a way of ordering the chief events of the past. Professional historians may point out that kinship and history via vignette are covers, if not fictions, for the real currents of the past. Kinship particularizes and fragments; the colorful tales that flesh it out obscure the deeper currents. Professional historians may choose an explanatory base in economics and materialism, as most prominent Mormon historians have done, or they may choose some form of idealism. They may use demography or politics to organize data; but whatever they choose, they have the means at their disposal to show why there are vignettes in family histories, what links them, and what economic and social factors lie behind kinship patterns. The widely acknowledged anti-intellectualism in the church and the minor role accorded professional historians and other intellectuals are complementary stances which allow do-it-yourself history free reign. But there is a deeper reason for eliminating the role of the professional thinker in Mormonism. For historians in the church today there is a direct relationship between the most prominent and those highly regarded in the rest of the world. Among Mormon historians, fame within the church is largely a function of fame outside it; to maintain place, one must maintain fame. This situation entails continual attention to what the external world of professional historians thinks. It ties professional Mormon historians closely to the non-Mormon world and to its opinions. They use non-Mormon canons of evidence, assumptions, and methods, and even study the same problems as other historians at any given moment. Consequently, the professional Mormon historian is in a unique position to present his people's history to his own people in outsider's terms.

History is one way of controlling what Mormons think of themselves and consequently how they behave. It is one device for controlling a whole population's self-image. Mormons seem at the moment to be the sole owners of their own past. But they certainly were not in control of what the world thought of them during the polygamy era when thousands of exposés were produced. The lesson of that era is that when a group of people is subordinate, there are two audiences to address: those doing the dominating and those being dominated. One way to dominate is to create an unflattering image or stereotype of the subordinate party. The stereotype is ultimately powerful because the subordinates accept its validity; it has some historical facts in it, among them subordination. Right now, Mormons are in control of their self-image and to some degree of the image that America has of them.

Mormonism uses three devices to maintain what the stereotyped group, in this case Mormons themselves believe. It controls many of its own media, including the medium of history, the stuff of which stereotypes are made; it controls a potentially dangerous subpopulation, the professional historians and intellectuals; and it has placed its history in the hands of its people. As a result, the meanings given to the

Mormon past are decentralized and dynamic, having been constructed in a sustained dialectic between an individual's personal life and the information from the past. In this way, a Mormon seems to create his own image, and all who could interfere with it are carefully controlled.

One side-effect of Mormonism's democratized historical endeavor is that history is measured by an infinite number of personal standards and is thus disarticulated. Kinship highlights uniqueness and thus atomizes history, which in consequence is deprived of interpretive consistency. Because professional historians are regarded with suspicion, they can not bring discipline to the way data from the past are treated, and in this process Mormonism's own past, including its critique of American society, have been disassembled. Mormonism started out as an intentional negation of America. Although by the turn of the century the program of negation had disappeared, the critique is a part of the record and could be rediscovered, but it is not because of the way historical materials are ransacked by one individual looking for one other individual. People shuffle and reshuffle the data of the past in order to bring about rapid adjustment to the continually changing conditions under which Mormons live. Thus changes are rationalized, projected elsewhere, and hidden, and the Mormon's actual condition, clearly characterized by Smith's critique of society, lies with the rest of the Mormon past, disarticulated.

In order to understand the Mormon attitude to lay history, the church's anti-intellectualism, and the small place for professional historians in the church, one might assume that if Mormon history had not been disarticulated and if all these impediments to true history were removed, Mormons would have a comparative picture made up of the contrast between what they had been and what they are which would tell them something they would find valuable. But this assumption misses the fact that this history-ridden institution never asks the question: how did the past become the present? The question violates the very way Mormons think; it virtually cannot be asked.

Mormons assume everything—past, present, and future—

is a continuum, guided by one purpose: a plan unifying the universe in such a way that nothing is excluded. Because humans now know what that plan is, there is no knowledge excluded from human comprehension. Thus no time and no culture are beyond the plan or their informed understanding. And thus nothing is or was or will be basically different from what they know.

To assume that the past could tell about the present except in a superficial way would give previous times a self-sufficient reality or independence that they are not supposed to have if one believes that the world is one, unified, and continually guided reality. Contrasts between today and other times would make something different, and nothing is supposed to be different.

The conventional historical approach would bring modern Mormonism out of its own past and would initially find Mormons wanting because they do not think this way. So, to some degree, the very structure of a book like this one violates the nature of what it describes. In using historical flashbacks as precedents for understanding living Mormonism, I risk misrepresenting what is most important about Mormonism. Mormons do not chop up time into segments; they see a continuum of unbroken movement and direction. Because Mormon theology holds that nothing is static, there are no slices of separate and therefore static time. Because these do not exist, neither does precedent, nor history in the conventional sense, nor the obligation to learn from the past or even to remember it. Because everything is judged by one standard, nothing is so different or distinct that it may be beyond understanding. This view explains why one has difficulty understanding how the events and eras of Mormon history are articulated for Mormons themselves. The problem is why the past, except for genealogy, seems to be so irrelevant to Mormons; why to them their history seems so unrelated to their present.

I have interviewed people in their nineties, who lived through much of what is described here, and yet the link between the past and present, even between 1890 and the 1920s, is elusive. Mormon history, whether from primary sources or from historical analyses, produces clear images of people operating harmoniously and successfully at another time. But the puzzle remains of how they got from there to here. People in their eighties and nineties, for example, could tell me less about the historical events they had lived through, even simple and obvious things that I later discovered easily in records, than younger people could, although these too were surprisingly uninformed about their own past—all this despite our culture's endless repetition that those who refuse to learn from the past are condemned to repeat it. Those very Mormons who conscientiously do genealogical work cannot talk coherently about the past that they themselves have lived through.

This is the historical puzzle of Mormonism. It presents the circumstance of an entire population which has written down virtually every important, and unimportant, thing, put them all in one library, and given everybody access to them. This remarkable circumstance becomes more puzzling upon discovery that, despite real use and familiarity with these data, most Mormons, especially older ones, can report virtually nothing about the past. My conversations with people did not ask interpretive or analytical questions but ones like, "Do you remember such-and-such a dam," "Can you tell me about such and such," or "What did the bishop's storehouse look like and how often did you go there?" Although Mormons knew such things existed, beyond the flat statement of fact they offered no new information. Often they repeated a tale I had already heard many times before, one originally heard in pulpits, and despite a hospitable desire to communicate about their much-valued history, Mormons were equipped to say almost nothing about it. These eighty- and ninety-year-old Mormons seemed not to have a memory and were unable to say how today had grown out of yesterday. They could not do so because the past was never segmented or divided into history, and history was never used as precedent. And it need not be because reality is, as Joseph Smith claimed, a continuum which is changing according to a plan that is known. Thus, the past is basically no different from the present or the future.

9

Empty Opposition

After Mormondom lost its independence, it achieved ecological stability but lost its economic stability. An unpredictable, uncontrolled economy accompanied the removal of the church from direct management of economic and political affairs and the imposition of subordinate status. Thus one kind of changeableness was replaced with another, both involving material conditions and the affairs of daily life. However, the conditions Mormons were subjected to starting around 1890 were essentially the same conditions under which Mormonism was founded between 1820 and 1840. In those earlier years Mormonism analyzed, reacted to, and absorbed the very conditions that its people would move back into at the turn of the century. Thus one of its primary assumptions, dynamism, which was a reflection of the world of 1830, was also an accurate assessment of the world of 1900 and continues so today. Because the world into which Mormons moved back after their period of independence was organized according to the same principle on which Joseph Smith had based his analysis, his people found what they had long been preadapted for.

A deliberate emphasis on change links the two centuries of Mormon conceptual life. But during those two eras material reality has gone through three stages. The unstable world of the early Industrial Revolution was the first social matrix in which Mormon theological conceptions were formed. Then came the politically stable era of Mormon territorial life, although phases of it were ecologically unstable. Finally around the turn of the century the unstable world of a more fully developed industrialism encompassed Mormonism. The actual world, regardless of the phase of Mormonism's development, always validated and helped to perpetuate the theological proposition that all things are subject to change. The matrix of Mormonism's historical growth is thus complementary to its theological continuity.

Complementary to Mormonism's insight into a dynamic world is its assumption that truth was changeable and that religious experience could be found directly in the successes of daily life. Each of the historical worlds in which Mormonism lived was one of considerable change, and since the material world was the touchstone for religious experience, truth had to be as flexible, or at least as additive, as Western life had become since the late eighteenth century. Thus change and the uniformly material nature of the cosmic and mundane worlds produced a religion engaged in everyday existence: a practical religion. The religion was in fact so engaged in the last century that, using sanctity as a resource, it produced ecological stability, technological progress, and wealth. The tithing system showed that religion worked. The water control system showed that working brought actual success, including deliberate self-improvement. The courts showed that success produced wealth, which was expressed socially as class differentiation and secular rationality. A practical religion generated all this material success. This practical involvement that lies at the root of the modern Mormonism was maintained by what brought government by sanctity into existence: unpredictably changeable conditions. What is common to the religion in either century is the insecurity to which its believers were subject. This insecurity is reflected in and adapted to through a theologically acute view of reality which describes these conditions as acceptable.

A further link between the nineteenth and twentieth centuries is the absence of precedent and its other side, memorylessness. The absence of law based on precedent is the same practice sponsored, although in a more complex way, in talks, testimony, and genealogy. None of these

activities refer to the past as a systematic way of comprehending the present. Elaborate minutes, records, data
sheets, accounts, and a virtual sea of minutiae were written
down and carefully husbanded. Some of this material is still
referred to by Mormons, but not as a way of learning about
the present except insofar as it may provide clues to improvements that have occurred. Mormons do not believe
that those who refuse to learn from the past are condemned
to repeat it. The past cannot be repeated because change is a
constant and progression the motive force. Since truth is additive because everything is always changing, the utility of
history is at best limited.

When Mormonism placed itself in immediate touch with
the world, thereby tying it to any given moment, it also un-
tied itself from any past moment. Sanctity cannot have a
memory, because this would compromise the flexibility
needed in the face of uncertainty. But the question is why
the absence of precedent carried over after sanctity was replaced, similar to the earlier question why practical religion
did not disappear or diminish after the theocracy was transformed. The answer is that Mormons assumed that truth is
change and change truth. The immediate and practical,
rather than what has already happened, are both the sources
of truth and the keys to its verification. In a world that always changes, success can be built upon flexibility. But such
a strategy produces a new attitude to the past, epitomized by
the popular non-Mormon saying, "Today is the first day of
the rest of your life." While the past still happened, meaning
is provided for it not through history but through projection
or even neglect.

To sum up, two important facets of Mormonism in the
nineteenth century are tied to its current success: practical
religion and memorylessness. These central facets, though
associated with the character of sanctity, survived the time
of its use. Having appeared in the last century, they stay
with the religion today because of the insecurity and unpredictability which underlay life then and do so still.

In the early decades of the twentieth century, modern
Mormonism began to crystallize, emerging as a church after

its destruction as a political entity. Even though its hierarchical form of government remained, the chief priests stopped saying priestly things, theological discourse slowed, and leaders tied to lifelong posts disappeared. People were circulated through posts, which meant that opinions changed as personnel did. By shifting people through jobs, by inviting them to think and behave according to the post they temporarily occupied, the church used its hierarchy to model the changeable world its people lived in and thus trained them for the new conditions. A side-effect of this subjected Mormon theology and history to the circulating personnel who were not in a position to maintain any consistent body of thought that would provide distance and independence from the world. Instead, the flexibility needed to make the most out of a changeable daily life had no use for the stable precedents of theology or a consistent history. People so circulated had no use for segmenting the past and thereby making history out of it, nor the conceptual apparatus to conceive a coherent theology. Consequently, the comparative view necessary to perceive change did not exist.

By the turn of the century the church no longer defined itself as being opposed to capitalism or the United States but instead as being "peculiar" or generally "opposed." The definition of what the religion meant, including its peculiarity, became one of the duties of every Mormon. The content of belief, circulated among all Mormons regardless of place in the hierarchy, made "peculiarity" in the sense of a coherent opposition to the surrounding society virtually impossible, so Mormons became peculiar without knowing what they were peculiar about. This left Mormons completely submerged in the present without any way of identifying what the present did to them or asked from them. Through various techniques Mormons collapsed a dual cosmos, keeping only the present; as a result, they were not constrained by any way of perceiving change. Transcendence collapsed.

Karl Marx predicted that those who preferred utopia to the class struggle and revolution as a way out of the Industrial Revolution would ultimately become "mere reactionary sects." To some degree, this can be interpreted to mean that the outcome of Mormonism was inevitable, given the remedy it chose. The last century was full of utopias in this country and abroad. All died out or were, like Mormonism, transformed. The members of most utopias were reabsorbed into society after having populated some frontier or performed some social experiment that society was later willing to undertake itself in an altered form.

Simultaneous with the birth of these utopian movements were various religious movements which did not reject industrial or capitalist society but worked inside it to cater to the needs of those whose lives were most disrupted. Such religions include Christian Science, Spiritualism, and slightly later, Pentacostalism, Jehovah's Witnesses, and Seventh-day Adventists. There is no essential difference in the outcome of utopian Mormonism and the operation of any of these other churches. While they took different paths emanating from different critiques of society, they all ultimately came to serve one kind of minority or another. Their service helps members accept the present by using a special mode of thought that prevents awareness of change, perception of contradiction, or consistent opposition. This mode of thought emphasizes the sect's peculiarity or uniqueness, which means that all referents for meaning are derived from the group, not from the past, the future, or the living other. The members of such sects refer only to themselves for knowledge and consequently can only recapitulate what they know, who and where they are. Such a myopic habit of thought helps to keep minorities in a subordinate position and is the result of the social programs and theologies Marx called a misanalysis of the structure of capitalism.

Mormonism underwent the very transformation that Marx feared. Spawned, along with a large number of other mostly religious movements, by the major changes in human affairs in the nineteenth century, Mormonism rejected, though not completely, its parent and then was reabsorbed by the parent as a useful, even productive, and supportive complement. The modern period of late capitalism has thus been presented with an effective set of supports which adjust themselves to absorb the most ferocious aspects of change while not seeing some of its most upsetting effects.

Modern society has produced a generally present-oriented set of populations, which are successful because of their extreme changeability. This characteristic seems to be the major benefit they give to the overall adaptability of society, while to their members their major drawback is a loss of critical ability. Their inability to harness negations and oppositions leads to both an acceptance of the established order of things and a lack of inventiveness. If social and economic conditions have no comparative context, they cannot be seen as needing to be tampered with or changed. Consequently, there is little profound analysis or experimentation regarding most areas of social life within Mormonism and its kindred movements.

Although the founders of Mormonism did not necessarily misunderstand the root causes of the social conditions against which they were reacting, the second generation of Mormon leaders from the late 1870s on certainly had little comprehension of or little chance to use whatever insights the founders of the faith had bequeathed them. No effective effort was made to halt the development of economic and social classes inside the kingdom, and no effective critique of private property and private ownership of natural resources was mounted. Earlier, throughout the 1850s and 1860s, church leaders had echoed Joseph Smith's insistence on communal ownership of resources, with individuals holding only what property they needed for their own subsistence. Through outside pressure and its own incomplete understanding of how classes arise, the church leadership allowed wealth to concentrate in one group, which soon developed a set of values peculiar to itself and inevitably came to include most of the church leaders. Upon the crisis with the federal government in the 1880s, these leaders failed to see that the external ownership of their resources that would guarantee their long-sought ecological stability would also guarantee the area's long-term economic instability. Subordination became even more marked with the church-sponsored entry of private capital and industry into the area, as these soon came to control many of the chief resources.

Even though Mormonism sponsored much of its own transformation, in no sense was the transformation engineered. Few within the church saw it happening. Mormonism evolved in response to the same dialectical processes that gave rise to nearly all nineteenth-century American utopias. Almost all were in rebellion, and most sought the isolation of frontiers. But the rebellion was meant as a vanguard action to show the rest of society the way, and the frontier was part of the society's parent: utopias as a result never became completely separate, integrated wholes. They never desired total independence from the United States; they enjoyed brief lives because they never developed the resources for genuine independence. Their inability to separate themselves was born of many factors which amounted to a misanalysis of industrial capitalism.

Mormonism, like other utopias and religious reforms, exhibits a structural weakness produced by its method of rebellion: separation but never with the intention of founding a new nation; isolation but without self-sufficiency; egalitarianism but with an incomplete critique of how that social condition is maintained. The pull between these aims and the inadequate means used to achieve them caused their transformation. The existence of spatial frontiers created a pull between utopian experiments and the industrializing world as the latter looked on frontiers as zones for potential exploitation even as the utopias composed of exploited populations looked to the same areas as zones wherein to escape further disruption. Utopias were products of industrialization and simultaneously were endowed by it with an internal structure that guaranteed their participation in the expansion of industrial capitalism rather than freeing themselves from it.

In the settlement of the American frontier, whether managed from the East Coast of North America or from Mexico City, which was also concerned with colonizing much of the same area but at a different time, religious institutions were frequently used to occupy areas when a central government was technologically and politically incapable. Methodist and Presbyterian churches on the Middle Western frontier,

Marcus Whitman in Oregon, the Oneida Community, the Shakers, and the Mormons did what the Jesuit and Franciscan missions accomplished for other governments in different parts of the same frontier West. Groups of highly disciplined people often valuing personal poverty went into a wilderness believing that they were serving God; they used sanctity to organize and govern themselves and their small communities. They scouted, settled, mapped, built, experimented with local resources, laid claims to the land, extinguished native American land claims, subordinated the former owners, and opened the territory to other settlers and to the central government and civil administration.

All these religious communities set out to be independent of the societies they hailed from; they wanted to set up the kingdom of God on earth and thus to show the rest of society the way to redemption. However internally contradictory these aims, their value in the larger colonizing process was evident. None of these communities could have supposed that theirs was the first step in a long, exploitative colonial process. Again and again, as soon as the initial colonizing job had been completed, resources discovered, and a local work force organized, the central secular government stepped in, dissolved the utopia, mission, or kingdom of God, and reabsorbed the community, calling it the colony that it was. Although each religious community had reached a different level of internal development when reabsorbed, together they exhibited all the stages of state formation, sometimes including a brief effort at independence.

The ideologies of these religious communities differed from each other, but all operated on sanctity and consequently were subject to two specific pressures. One was the potential displacement of sanctity as soon as the community had made a success locally; and the other was the displacement of sanctity once the parent state had overwhelmed its offspring with superior technology and organization.

Thus the development of Mormonism was part of a worldwide process which was accelerated, if not initiated, by the Industrial Revolution. One side of this process was the growth of colonialism through the expansion of coun-

Roots of Modern Mormonism

tries and the growth of empires adding to their territories. The other side was the growth of cures for the worst aspects of industrialization. One cure was Mormonism. The two sides, industrialization and its remedies, played themselves out on the North American frontier and included Mormonism's growth, transformation, and misanalysis of the factors responsible for its own existence.

Why did all nineteenth-century utopian analyses of industrial society miss the point? Why did successful movements like Mormonism, which fully recognized what it did not want, succumb to the society it had rejected? Attempts by early religious communities to understand industrial society were so inaccurate that their followers never saw that they were not really separate and that they had lost whatever distinctiveness they once possessed. These analyses of and remedies for capitalism, whether produced by Joseph Smith, Robert Owen, or Mary Baker Eddy, missed its expansive power and its inexorable absorption; they therefore guaranteed the existence of believing populations tied to society, producing for it, and exploited by it. Like Mormonism, many of these movements were captured; but again like Mormonism, many of them did not struggle and to some degree walked right back into the society they had earlier left. The key to producing model citizens out of former pariahs was the conscious and explicit recognition in all these analyses of society of the relativity of truth, knowledge, or meaning. Most of these religions understood that reality changes, but none succeeded in teaching their followers a method to continue the insight of many of their founders, that reality is constructed and the construction shifts.

If, as Mormonism assumes, change characterizes all reality, this thesis leads to two further conclusions: the place from which reality is viewed cannot be fixed, since it too is subject to change, and the view from each place must be different, since the places are always changing. Moreover, the difference in view from one spot to another produces discrepancies, in part because people tend to think they can grasp reality despite its assumed changeability and in part because the views themselves differ. Any certainty derived from fixity is at variance with the assumption that all is change and therefore uncertainty. Mormonism has to handle the contradiction between assuming change, on the one hand, and, on the other, placing labels that create discrete categories which by their nature misrepresent change and indivisibility and thereby recreate misunderstanding.

The difference between views of reality was dealt with by Joseph Smith and Brigham Young, who said that all people and all systems may know some truth; that knowledge may change and improve since reality changes; and that views are inevitably different, contradictory, and even at odds within themselves. Smith and Young also implied that contradictions can be used to understand one's own position. Victorian Mormonism celebrated its contradictions with the rest of the world, and by being theocratic, polygamous, and classless, it allowed everyone involved to know what it did and did not stand for.

But there were contradictions within Mormonism as well, and because Mormonism was not conscious of them, two of them negated what Mormonism was supposed to accomplish. The first contradiction arose from trying to build a commonwealth by means that regenerated capitalism. The second contradiction arose from trying to be different from the rest of society while eliminating all systematic differences. These contradictions, though different, were produced by the same underlying assumption of Mormonism: nothing is permanently separate or hidden from man; ultimately man may know everything. This basic postulate that man and nature are complementary and part of the same plan is at odds with perpetual change because it contradicts the changing relationship between knowledge and the external world. It interposes system, plan, and rationality where the assumption of change does not. It contradicts the relativism latent in the assumption of change.

Since the Renaissance the Western world has also understood change and relative knowledge and assumed that systematic knowledge of some form of "other" apart from the self is the key to self-positioning. Efforts to know forms of the "other" like the past and different cultures eventually led to the conclusion that the "other" cannot be known because the tools for such knowledge are themselves positioned within a fixed point. As a result, the Western world postulated hidden and unknowable worlds. It pursues them, to be sure, but assumes only approximations and regards the act of understanding and compartmentalizing as the very part of human nature that produces much of the discrepancy between humanity and nature, for nature is not discrete but humans think in terms that are.

Mormonism based itself on the ability to know, epitomized in the slogan "The glory of God is intelligence," which, because of the similarity of God and man, allows man to hope for all knowledge. The religion is thus built on a contradiction but does not see it explicitly. Mormonism is based on the assumption that a method is at hand which will make things known because a coherent reality exists with limits and natural processes. It also assumes this reality is changing. Mormonism has never gone beyond this assumption to explain how a fluid reality can also be coherent and understandable. It follows from the assumption of change that knowledge will be relative depending on the point of view chosen. This is so both because all points of observation are subject to change and because humans break up the continuum of reality by imposing discrete labels on it and so, far from being able to see reality for the flow that it is, often, by nature, fix reality into units and obscure it. Thus, by assuming that everything changes including understanding, Mormons in the long-run produce only relative knowledge.

Nonetheless, Mormons are certain. The assumed similarity of man, God, and the universe that is produced by their being governed by the same principles makes them mutually intelligible. Consequently, Mormons deny a world beyond human comprehension whether it is the past, other humans, God, or nature. This produces their well-known certainty.

Because Mormons came to believe in revealed truth, certain knowledge, and the God-given accuracy of their own positions, they did not see that only by admitting the changeableness of the world and the arbitrariness of their own reality could they continue to keep the world's hands off them. The trick was not in agrarianism, egalitarianism, or withdrawal; it was in understanding that these were means, not ends. As a result of this misunderstanding, the religion that was intended by its founder to be a supple method for understanding a fluid reality became, in the hands of most believers, a rigid doctrine used to hold the fluid world still.

One profound difference between the founders of the Protestant Reformation and the founders of religious and social alternatives to the Industrial Revolution is the clear understanding held by the latter of the dynamic nature of what they called truth. Joseph Smith and his peers glimpsed the createdness of truth, its capacity to change, and its ultimate locus in the individual, not the church or a class of specialists. Throughout the nineteenth century in Europe there was a growing understanding of the arbitrariness of classifications and the misleading nature of surface meanings.

Darwin, Marx, Freud, Einstein, Heisenberg, and later Wittgenstein articulated the dynamic nature of reality, the arbitrariness of perceptions and the impossibility of overcoming that arbitrariness. All these analytical systems were produced in a maturing industrial society and were both products of its changeability and attempts to describe it. In other words, they embodied precise articulations of or important insights into the world that was their matrix, but they were preceded by people like Joseph Smith and Mary Baker Eddy who used religious referents and ecclesiastical organization to couch similar, though usually less precise, insights. The religious innovators were produced by the same culture that produced the scientists, and the religious analyses and programs contain the same basic insights about what is known and how it is known: knowledge is often intuitive, grows and changes with personal understanding, and contains contradictions.

This set of understandings was encoded in Mormonism in various ways: truth was to be revealed as people appeared ready to receive and comprehend it; all people were entitled to and could expect personal revelation; Mormons were to stand in opposition in all things; God was a man and was contingent, while humans were divine and would become more so. Thus Mormonism began with the idea that truth is relative in the sense that it is the product of the situation in which it is defined. But that insight was misplaced in the course of the late nineteenth century in favor of techniques and social programs that Mormon leaders thought were the key to maintaining their original goals. Gradually Mormonism was transformed from a religion whose central truth was a method for perceiving a changing world based on maintaining contradictions, to a religion whose truth became fixed and isolated items like the authority of its priesthood, its authenticity as Christ's church, the truth of its prophet, and the importance of tithing, the temple, and the family. These replaced the expansive and continuing commentary that Joseph Smith and his fellow leaders had offered against the accepted ways of looking at the world and which was to be a way of glimpsing the operations of reality. Isolated items of difference replaced a way of achieving systematic self-positioning.

When the reality of Mormons' life changed beyond their control, their set of insights, dimmed by partial understandings as well as misunderstandings, failed to free them from a now dominant society; rather, it made them completely its subjects. For while Mormonism possessed a modern and sophisticated understanding of the world, namely the changing nature of truth, it failed to perpetuate the insight. Later generations of Mormons did not retain Joseph Smith's understanding of change. They passed up Darwin for Linnaeus, Marx for Jefferson, and Freud for the Holy Ghost. They passed up the best insights of the nineteenth century, including those of their own founder, and wedded themselves to things from which the insights were supposed to provide freedom. The self-awareness of their own position, which was to provide the security needed when assuming a fluid world, was denied to Mormons in this century when their theology, history, and virtually every other coherent difference were vulgarized. When Mormons accepted a changing world but maintained no differences with it, they

lost the freedom their founder intended them to have. Instead of producing a population which knows what it stands
for and thus knows how to use modern society's characteristics for its own special ends, Mormonism has produced a
population which directs itself according to society's ends
while hiding that fact from itself. Joseph Smith wanted to
maintain opposition and uniqueness. These traits would
have continually produced the contradictions and negations
any group needs in order to identify its position vis-à-vis all
others. But instead of a bold and daring population sure in
its stance, Mormonism has produced a population with a superficial certainty. Despite a vast and largely successful effort to live in the world, Mormons nonetheless know they
are possessed, controlled, and owned. Their knowing is not
overt but felt. Although they are vocal about disliking outside control and struggle for greater freedom and awareness
under such political banners as states' rights and opposition
to big government and federal interference, Mormons have a
deep feeling that politics, economics, and society in general
have slipped out of local control and are ruled by seditious
outsiders whose interests are opposed to their own.
Grassroots conservatism harnesses the unease felt by some
of the Mormon population in the intermountain West, an
unease that stems from too little facing of the real conditions
of life, too little understanding of how life has to be led in
order to be even moderately productive, and too little explicit recognition of how much has to be ignored in order to
maintain a warm openness to the world.

Nonetheless, Mormonism invites its faithful to face some
central contradictions head on, and thus makes an effort to
maintain the independence and critical stance that it once
had to the world. The outstanding Mormon peculiarity in
the nineteenth century was plural marriage, which today is
inconsequential, though still found in out-of-the-way places.
It was replaced as a symbol of Mormon peculiarity in both
the public and the Mormon mind by the church's denial of
the priesthood to blacks. The church had always effectively
excluded blacks, but it chose to reiterate its position during
the 1950s and 1960s when its policy looked like a major con-

tradition in American society. In this one respect Mormons, who in the course of the twentieth century had
become consummately American, allowed themselves a
distinctness, uniqueness, and peculiarity. Here the church
stood alone among all churches, making a negation, creating
an opposition, which set it apart.

Since there never has been an appreciable black population in areas where most Mormons live, such exclusion made
little sense. The historical explanation of the doctrine as a
holdover from the days when the church in Missouri had to
compromise on the slave issue for survival is also inadequate.
It does not explain why the church took such pains to eluci-
date its position in the 1950s and 1960s, when such an act
made it look especially peculiar.

Mormonism's most noticeable negation served a hidden
function. On the surface, it convinced all believers that they
belonged to a strong, self-assured, principled, and weighty
institution, willing to gainsay the world on a matter of importance. But this emphasis on a relatively unimportant
matter in terms of the church's own doctrine prevented
Mormons from seeing how completely they capitulated on
all the rest. So the great negation was ultimately empty. It
established Mormonism's peculiarity in the eyes of both believers and observers, but it did not give Mormons a place to
stand on any matter of principle or practice that would allow
them a clearer view of where they are in relation to the rest
of the world. While such a negation did not provide transcendence, it did provide for domination: it turned the
church into a pariah in its own country and also managed to
make many Mormons secretly suspicious of themselves for
having to condone such a socially unacceptable doctrine.

By its position, the church had not so much given its
faithful a handle on the modern world as it had given that
world a handle on its faithful. The key symbol of Mormon
contradistinction to the world was one for which its people
neither were respected nor respected themselves. In fact, the
symbol that they had chosen to demonstrate their own superiority was the tool that furthered their own subordination.

Mormonism's most recent negation placed a tool in the

hands of any other powerful group which could use it to keep Mormons separate and also subordinate. The dominant world used the label of racism to attack a religious group and keep the subordinates in their place. Any minority's particular beliefs or practices can be ridiculed and turned into a weapon of subordination. Mormonism nonetheless chose not only to emphasize its stand on blacks but to do so at a particular time when polygamy exposures among modern Mormons shocked no one and thus Mormons were faced with the loss of their most convincing symbol of uniqueness. At that point they began publicly to celebrate their position on blacks, recreating a negation and placing it squarely in the hands of the parent society, whose response was predictable. Consequently, Mormonism remained unable to alter its own position: it invited and retained pariah status; it welcomed domination; it continued to allow the United States to criticize, persecute, and even legislate against it.

Then in 1978 the leaders of the church announced they had received a revelation that blacks should be admitted to the priesthood, and the most recent symbol of Mormon peculiarity disappeared. With this event the question is whether Mormonism will replace this contradistinction with some other or will allow itself to be seen as less and less different from any other church and Mormons as less and less different from other Americans. The church could let its opposition to the Equal Rights Amendment, abortion legislation, the spread of birth control information, the entry of women into professional life, and gay rights become a vocal policy opposing the redefinition of traditional family life and sex roles that has been taking place in the United States for ten years. Mormons' activities on these issues do not make them unique, although the effectiveness of their organized opposition makes them leaders. With such opposition, Mormons may be in the process of recreating a peculiarity, focusing on an attitude to women and the family that would provide a strong sense of uniqueness.

Because Mormonism has become a colonial religion and has eliminated the normal ways people become aware of their position in the world, like a consistent theology, a coherent history, or a critique of society, it is probable that some symbol of opposition to the world will take the place of the exclusion of blacks. Such a symbol would preserve a sense of uniqueness and maintain peculiarity, contradiction, and the resultant conflicts. A symbol of difference would provide a place to stand and therefore a measure of reality. The purpose of all effective opposition is to change the individual's perceptions of life, to transcend everyday existence. But the revelation of 1978 compromised that sense of transcendence by removing Mormonism's chief difference.

Peculiarity allows Mormons to see themselves as separate and superior, provides spiritual strength, and thus produces the dedicated, honest individuals much of America associates with Mormonism. But as colonials, Mormons ultimately have no place to stand to gauge society. They have lost all substantial differences and become society's servants since the turn of the century. They have used one or another outstanding contradiction to hide their lack of difference and their colonial status from themselves. Neither their considerable institutional wealth nor their growing international success have been used to eliminate this status nor to retrieve any of the differences the church once maintained against industrial capitalism. Current reserves of money and power, larger than anything in the Mormon past, could be used to sponsor substantial change in almost any direction. Yet Mormonism's most successful adaptation is its present ability to produce colonials: changeable people without memories. In order to alter this situation, Mormonism would have to overcome its own internal weakness and dominate itself.

Appendix

Works Cited

Index

Appendix

Tithing Receipts in Little Colorado Towns, 1887–1898

The source of receipt figures is "Record of Stake Funds, Snow-flake Stake," 1882–1901:89–250. Tithing disbursements are not shown. Amounts of less than one dollar are rounded off. "Building material" is usually lumber. "Liquid" is usually molasses. Combined categories, such as "Grain & hay," appear that way in the record.

ST. JOSEPH (JOSEPH CITY)

Tithing by town (ward)	1887		1888		1889	
	$	%	$	%	$	%
Cash	77.0	12	83.0	11	15.0	2
Labor	—	—	26	3	55	6
Grain	157	25	217	29	268	31
Meat	9	1	12	2	—	—
Vegetable	22	4	41	5	—	—
Dairy	22	4	47	6	—	—
Liquid	24	4	14	2	—	—
Merchandise	—	—	9	1	29	3
Stock	229	37	228	30	339	39
Building material	—	—	22	3	—	—
Hay	26	4	54	7	156	18
Miscellaneous	1	.16	—	—	—	—
Dairy & vegetable	—	—	—	—	—	—
Grain & hay	—	—	—	—	—	—
Poultry	—	—	3	.4	—	—
No category	57	9	—	—	—	—
Total	611		772		984	

St. Joseph (*continued*)

Tithing by town (ward)	1890		1891		1892	
	$	%	$	%	$	%
Cash	215.0	18	147.0	25	127.0	19
Labor	83	7	—	—	5	.7
Grain	—	—	—	—	183	27
Meat	—	—	—	—	—	—
Vegetable	—	—	—	—	—	—
Dairy	192	16	—	—	111	16
Liquid	—	—	—	—	—	—
Merchandise	65	5	34	6	14	2
Stock	243	20	199	34	161	24
Building material	—	—	—	—	—	—
Hay	—	—	—	—	81	12
Miscellaneous	28	2	—	—	—	—
Dairy & vegetable	—	—	111	19	—	—
Grain & hay	376	31	97	16	—	—
Poultry	—	—	—	—	—	—
No category	—	—	—	—	—	—
Total	1204		590		684	

Tithing by town (ward)	1893		1894		1895	
	$	%	$	%	$	%
Cash	191.0	26	105.0	17	339.0	44
Labor	—	—	1	.16	—	—
Grain	171	23	100	16	76	10
Meat	—	—	—	—	—	—
Vegetable	—	—	—	—	—	—
Dairy	—	—	—	—	—	—
Liquid	—	—	—	—	—	—
Merchandise	72	10	48	10	89	12
Stock	41	6	26	6	64	8
Building material	—	—	—	—	—	—
Hay	95	13	150	25	45	6
Miscellaneous	20	3	—	—	—	—
Dairy & vegetable	141	19	153	25	158	20
Grain & hay	—	—	—	—	—	—
Poultry	—	—	—	—	—	—
No category	—	—	—	—	—	—
Total	734		635		772	

ST. JOSEPH (*continued*)

Tithing by town (ward)	1896		1897		1898	
	$	%	$	%	$	%
Cash	199.0	27	396.0	41	640.0	54
Labor	—	—	—	—	—	—
Grain	117	16	119	13	103	9
Meat	—	—	—	—	—	—
Vegetable	—	—	—	—	—	—
Dairy	—	—	—	—	—	—
Liquid	—	—	—	—	—	—
Merchandise	44	6	19	2	69	6
Stock	60	8	122	13	112	9
Building material	—	—	—	—	—	—
Hay	137	18	149	16	159	13
Miscellaneous	—	—	—	—	—	—
Dairy & vegetable	189	25	143	15	104	9
Grain & hay	—	—	—	—	—	—
Poultry	—	—	—	—	—	—
No category	—	—	—	—	—	—
Total	748		952		1190	

WOODRUFF

Tithing by town (ward)	1887		1888		1889	
	$	%	$	%	$	%
Cash	36.0	6	32.0	8	83.0	14
Labor	33	6	6	1	10	2
Grain	148	25	131	32	219	36
Meat	22	5	3	.7	—	—
Vegetable	12	4	—	—	—	—
Dairy	7	1	20	5	49	8
Liquid	20	3	—	—	—	—
Merchandise	209	35	5	1	157	26
Stock	63	11	84	21	78	13
Building material	—	—	35	9	2	.3
Hay	20	5	43	11	—	—
Miscellaneous	—	—	—	—	16	3
Dairy & vegetable	—	—	—	—	—	—
Grain & hay	—	—	—	—	—	—
Fruit	—	—	48	12	—	—
Total	621		410		602	

WOODRUFF (*continued*)

Tithing by town (ward)	1890 $	1890 %	1891 $	1891 %	1892 $	1892 %
Cash	118.0	15	71.0	10	25.0	3
Labor	57	7	1	.15	85	9
Grain	—	—	—	—	139	15
Meat	—	—	—	—	—	—
Vegetable	—	—	—	—	—	—
Dairy	—	—	—	—	—	—
Liquid	—	—	—	—	—	—
Merchandise	397	50	318	48	147	16
Stock	—	—	227	34	259	30
Building material	31	4	—	—	—	—
Hay	—	—	—	—	100	11
Miscellaneous	10	1	—	—	105	11
Dairy & vegetable	32	4	34	5	48	6
Grain & hay	149	19	26	4	—	—
Fruit	—	—	—	—	—	—
Total	797		681		917	

Tithing by town (ward)	1893 $	1893 %	1894 $	1894 %	1895 $	1895 %
Cash	79.0	14	142.0	25	167.0	26
Labor	24	4	28	5	17	3
Grain	52	9	64	11	115	18
Meat	—	—	—	—	—	—
Vegetable	—	—	—	—	—	—
Dairy	—	—	—	—	—	—
Liquid	—	—	—	—	—	—
Merchandise	104	18	73	13	60	9
Stock	136	24	2	.3	4	.6
Building material	—	—	—	—	—	—
Hay	79	14	90	16	122	19
Miscellaneous	48	8	38	7	60	9
Dairy & vegetable	57	10	140	24	107	16
Grain & hay	—	—	—	—	—	—
Fruit	—	—	—	—	—	—
Total	581		581		655	

WOODRUFF (*continued*)

Tithing by town (ward)	1896		1897		1898	
	$	%	$	%	$	%
Cash	140.0	22	214.0	28	456.0	51
Labor	14	2	30	4	19	2
Grain	110	18	75	10	97	11
Meat	—	—	—	—	—	—
Vegetable	—	—	—	—	—	—
Dairy	—	—	—	—	—	—
Liquid	—	—	—	—	—	—
Merchandise	42	7	89	12	103	12
Stock	2	.3	—	—	22	2
Building material	—	—	—	—	—	—
Hay	198	32	196	25	65	7
Miscellaneous	16	3	43	6	20	2
Dairy & vegetable	106	17	125	16	107	12
Grain & hay	—	—	—	—	—	—
Fruit	—	—	—	—	—	—
Total	629		774		894	

TAYLOR

Tithing by town (ward)	1887		1888		1889	
	$	%	$	%	$	%
Cash	122.0	12	66.0	6	315.0	20
Labor	29	3	51	4	75	5
Grain	295	30	375	29	617	40
Meat	31	3	49	4	—	—
Vegetable	65	7	182	14	—	—
Dairy	20	2	28	2	224	14
Liquid	32	3	—	—	—	—
Merchandise	69	7	51	4	111	7
Stock	29	3	115	9	74	5
Building material	11	1	56	4	60	4
Hay	295	30	312	24	—	—
Miscellaneous	—	—	8	.7	91	6
Dairy & vegetable	—	—	—	—	—	—
Grain & hay	—	—	—	—	—	—
Fruit	1	.1	—	—	—	—
Total	1004		1299		1573	

TAYLOR (*continued*)

Tithing by town (ward)	1890		1891		1892	
	$	%	$	%	$	%
Cash	209.0	13	141.0	10	139.0	9
Labor	58	3	46	3	57	4
Grain	—	—	—	—	283	18
Meat	—	—	—	—	—	—
Vegetable	—	—	—	—	—	—
Dairy	—	—	—	—	—	—
Liquid	—	—	—	—	—	—
Merchandise	292	17	118	8	124	8
Stock	221	13	105	7	165	11
Building material	42	2	—	—	—	—
Hay	—	—	—	—	470	30
Miscellaneous	151	9	18	.3	43	3
Dairy & vegetable	240	14	330	23	272	18
Grain & hay	493	29	658	48	—	—
Fruit	—	—	—	—	—	—
Total	1706		1414		1557	

Tithing by town (ward)	1893		1894		1895	
	$	%	$	%	$	%
Cash	73.0	7	144.0	12	114.0	11
Labor	82	7	159	13	23	2
Grain	190	17	165	13	187	19
Meat	—	—	—	—	—	—
Vegetable	—	—	—	—	—	—
Dairy	—	—	—	—	—	—
Liquid	—	—	—	—	—	—
Merchandise	70	6	29	2	37	4
Stock	105	10	63	5	37	4
Building material	—	—	—	—	—	—
Hay	325	29	439	35	318	32
Miscellaneous	6	.5	29	2	88	9
Dairy & vegetable	255	23	228	18	188	19
Grain & hay	—	—	—	—	—	—
Fruit	—	—	—	—	—	—
Total	1130		1259		995	

TAYLOR (*continued*)

Tithing by town (ward)	1896 $	1896 %	1897 $	1897 %	1898 $	1898 %
Cash	144.0	12	175.0	15	280.0	23
Labor	18	2	3	.3	3	.2
Grain	194	16	361	32	491	40
Meat	—	—	—	—	—	—
Vegetable	—	—	—	—	—	—
Dairy	—	—	—	—	—	—
Liquid	—	—	—	—	—	—
Merchandise	55	5	34	3	38	3
Stock	2	.17	5	.4	6	.5
Building material	—	—	—	—	—	—
Hay	461	40	270	24	280	23
Miscellaneous	49	2	14	2	3	.2
Dairy & vegetable	268	22	278	24	125	10
Grain & hay	—	—	—	—	—	—
Fruit	—	—	—	—	—	—
Total	1192		1147		1229	

SNOWFLAKE

Tithing by town (ward)	1887 $	1887 %	1888 $	1888 %	1889 $	1889 %
Cash	265.0	11	240.0	8	292.0	10
Labor	65	3	115	4	112	4
Grain	400	17	537	18	989	35
Meat	28	1	65	2	—	—
Vegetable	46	2	235	8	—	—
Dairy	571	3	41	1	187	7
Liquid	61	3	—	—	—	—
Merchandise	259	11	463	16	540	19
Stock	494	19	652	22	593	21
Building material	10	.4	56	2	64	2
Hay	476	20	556	19	—	—
Miscellaneous	185	8	5	.2	80	3
Dairy & vegetable	—	—	—	—	—	—
Grain & hay	—	—	—	—	—	—
Fruit	20	1	—	—	—	—
Total	2334		2969		2855	

SNOWFLAKE (*continued*)

Tithing by town (ward)	1890		1891		1892	
	$	%	$	%	$	%
Cash	257.0	8	252.0	9	356.0	11
Labor	10	.3	52	2	359	11
Grain	—	—	—	—	503	15
Meat	—	—	—	—	—	—
Vegetable	—	—	—	—	—	—
Dairy	—	—	—	—	—	—
Liquid	—	—	—	—	—	—
Merchandise	533	16	570	20	483	15
Stock	1037	30	730	26	739	22
Building material	96	3	—	—	—	—
Hay	—	—	—	—	374	11
Miscellaneous	47	1	62	2	178	5
Dairy & vegetable	188	6	287	10	323	10
Grain & hay	1240	36	896	31	—	—
Fruit	—	—	—	—	—	—
Total	3411		2851		3319	

Tithing by town (ward)	1893		1894		1895	
	$	%	$	%	$	%
Cash	259.0	9	268.0	11	371.0	16
Labor	270	9	141	6	42	2
Grain	427	15	560	23	438	19
Meat	—	—	—	—	—	—
Vegetable	—	—	—	—	—	—
Dairy	—	—	—	—	—	—
Liquid	—	—	—	—	—	—
Merchandise	493	17	409	16	454	20
Stock	459	16	336	14	230	10
Building material	—	—	—	—	—	—
Hay	528	19	396	16	413	18
Miscellaneous	148	5	111	5	113	5
Dairy & vegetable	281	10	253	10	277	11
Grain & hay	—	—	—	—	—	—
Fruit	—	—	—	—	—	—
Total	2867		2498		2341	

SNOWFLAKE (*continued*)

Tithing by town (ward)	1896		1897		1898	
	$	%	$	%	$	%
Cash	384.0	16	469.0	18	463.0	21
Labor	45	2	12	.5	171	8
Grain	414	18	588	23	498	22
Meat	—	—	—	—	—	—
Vegetable	—	—	—	—	—	—
Dairy	—	—	—	—	—	—
Liquid	—	—	—	—	—	—
Merchandise	484	21	558	22	557	25
Stock	170	7	195	8	65	3
Building material	—	—	—	—	—	—
Hay	677	29	440	17	379	17
Miscellaneous	12	5	32	2	20	1
Dairy & vegetable	172	7	291	11	97	4
Grain & hay	—	—	—	—	—	—
Fruit	—	—	—	—	—	—
Total	2362		2585		2182	

SHOWLOW

Tithing by town (ward)	1887		1888		1889	
	$	%	$	%	$	%
Cash	18.0	5	7.0	3	74.0	17
Labor	61	17	42	15	10	2
Grain	88	24	67	24	148	36
Meat	41	11	20	7	—	—
Vegetable	20	6	—	—	—	—
Dairy	9	2	11	4	126	30
Liquid	1	.27	—	—	—	—
Merchandise	58	16	54	20	16	4
Stock	65	18	33	12	18	4
Building material	—	—	18	6	7	2
Fuel	—	—	7	3	—	—
Hay	—	—	2	.7	—	—
Vegetable & liquid	—	—	16	6	17	4
Miscellaneous	—	—	—	—	—	—
Dairy & vegetable	—	—	—	—	—	—
Grain & hay	—	—	—	—	—	—
Total	364		283		418	

SHOWLOW (*continued*)

Tithing by town (ward)	1890 $	1890 %	1891 $	1891 %	1892 $	1892 %
Cash	18.0	3	3.0	.6	19.0	4
Labor	—	—	22	5	—	—
Grain	—	—	—	—	139	27
Meat	—	—	—	—	—	—
Vegetable	—	—	—	—	—	—
Dairy	—	—	—	—	—	—
Liquid	—	—	—	—	—	—
Merchandise	47	7	62	13	70	13
Stock	127	20	81	17	139	27
Building material	—	—	—	—	—	—
Fuel	—	—	—	—	—	—
Hay	—	—	—	—	—	—
Vegetable & liquid	—	—	—	—	—	—
Miscellaneous	58	9	90	19	85	16
Dairy & vegetable	132	20	137	28	69	13
Grain & hay	267	41	92	19	—	—
Total	651		489		522	

Tithing by town (ward)	1893 $	1893 %	1894 $	1894 %	1895 $	1895 %
Cash	10.0	4	95.0	17	15.0	5
Labor	—	—	9	2	10	3
Grain	75	29	92	16	89	27
Meat	—	—	—	—	—	—
Vegetable	—	—	—	—	—	—
Dairy	—	—	—	—	—	—
Liquid	—	—	—	—	—	—
Merchandise	20	8	3	.5	.19	—
Stock	98	37	151	26	83	25
Building material	—	—	—	—	—	—
Fuel	—	—	—	—	—	—
Hay	1	.4	5	.9	—	—
Vegetable & liquid	—	—	—	—	—	—
Miscellaneous	—	—	89	16	23	7
Dairy & vegetable	58	22	128	22	109	33
Grain & hay	—	—	—	—	—	—
Total	263		549		330	

SHOWLOW (*continued*)

Tithing by town (ward)	1896 $	1896 %	1897 $	1897 %	1898 $	1898 %
Cash	36.0	11	58.0	15	65.0	29
Labor	2	.6	3	.8	3	1
Grain	122	38	218	56	86	38
Meat	—	—	—	—	—	—
Vegetable	—	—	—	—	—	—
Dairy	—	—	—	—	—	—
Liquid	—	—	—	—	—	—
Merchandise	35	11	.20	—	35	16
Stock	33	10	—	—	2	1
Building material	—	—	—	—	—	—
Fuel	—	—	—	—	—	—
Hay	19	6	23	6	—	—
Vegetable & liquid	—	—	—	—	—	—
Miscellaneous	—	—	—	—	15	7
Dairy & vegetable	78	24	84	22	19	8
Grain & hay	—	—	—	—	—	—
Total	347		389		226	

PINEDALE

Tithing by town (ward)	1888 $	1888 %	1889 $	1889 %	1890 $	1890 %
Cash	31.0	17	112.0	33	2.0	.5
Grain	21	11	69	21	—	—
Meat	16	9	—	—	—	—
Vegetable	1	.5	—	—	—	—
Dairy	19	10	35	11	—	—
Merchandise	45	24	—	—	111	27
Stock	44	24	75	23	17	4
Building material	7	4	19	6	—	—
Miscellaneous	—	—	22	7	22	5
Dairy & vegetable	—	—	—	—	41	10
Grain & hay	—	—	—	—	214	53
Total	187		337		410	

PINEDALE (*continued*)

Tithing	1891		1892		1893	
by town (ward)	$	%	$	%	$	%
Cash	9.0	3	32.0	13	35.0	21
Grain	—	—	143	60	78	47
Meat	—	—	—	—	—	—
Vegetable	—	—	—	—	—	—
Dairy	—	—	—	—	—	—
Merchandise	35	14	10	4	.18	—
Stock	35	14	27	11	15	9
Building material	—	—	—	—	—	—
Miscellaneous	—	—	—	—	6	4
Dairy & vegetable	43	17	28	12	33	20
Grain & hay	137	53	—	—	—	—
Total	260		241		169	

Tithing	1894		1895		1896	
by town (ward)	$	%	$	%	$	%
Cash	24	19	54.0	41	79.0	36
Grain	132	59	39	30	68	32
Meat	—	—	—	—	—	—
Vegetable	—	—	—	—	—	—
Dairy	—	—	—	—	—	—
Merchandise	.32	—	20	15	40	19
Stock	—	—	13	10	—	—
Building material	—	—	—	—	—	—
Miscellaneous	17	8	—	—	—	—
Dairy & vegetable	33	15	5	4	29	13
Grain & hay	—	—	—	—	—	—
Total	241		132		218	

PINEDALE (*continued*)

Tithing by town (ward)	1897		1898	
	$	%	$	%
Cash	102.0	37	93.0	29
Grain	121	43	91	28
Meat	—	—	—	—
Vegetable	—	—	—	—
Dairy	—	—	—	—
Merchandise	1	.4	52	16
Stock	12	4	58	18
Building material	—	—	—	—
Miscellaneous	—	—	—	—
Dairy & vegetable	43	15	31	10
Grain & hay	—	—	—	—
Total	281		327	

Works Cited

ADAMS, ROBERT McC. 1966. *The Evolution of Urban Society*. Chicago: Aldine.

ALTHUSSER, LOUIS. 1971. "Ideology and Ideological State Apparatuses." In *Lenin and Philosophy*. New York: Monthly Review Press.

ARRINGTON, LEONARD J. 1958. *Great Basin Kingdom*. Cambridge: Harvard University Press.

———. 1961. *From Wilderness to Empire: The Role of Utah in Western Economic History*. Institute of American Studies, Monograph no. 1. Salt Lake City: University of Utah Press.

———. 1963. *The Changing Economic Structure of the Mountain West, 1850–1950*. Monograph Series, vol. 10, no. 3. Logan: Utah State University Press.

BELLAH, ROBERT N. 1970. "Religious Evolution." In *Beyond Belief*. New York: Harper and Row.

BITTEN, DAVIS. 1966. "Anti-Intellectualism in Mormon History." *Dialogue* 1:3:111–134.

BRODIE, FAWN M. 1963. *No Man Knows My History*. New York: Alfred A. Knopf.

CORBETT, MICHAEL R. 1973. "The Coming of Age of an Ohio Community, 1811–1851, As Reflected Through the Trial Records of the White Oak Presbyterian Church." Senior thesis, Princeton University.

DOLGIN, JANET, DAVID KEMNITZER, and DAVID SCHNEIDER. 1977. "Introduction: As People Express Their Lives, So They Are." In *Symbolic Anthropology*, ed. Dolgin, Kemnitzer, and Schneider. New York: Columbia University Press.

"High Council Minutes, Eastern Arizona Stake and Snowflake Stake." 1880–1898. Minutebook. Salt Lake City: Church Historian's Office.

"High Council Minutes, Snowflake Stake." 1898–1907. Minute-book. Salt Lake City: Church Historian's Office.

"High Priest's Quorum Minute Book, Snowflake Stake." 1866–1892. Minutebook. Salt Lake City: Church Historian's Office.

"Historical Record, Snowflake Stake." 1890–1892. Minutebook. Salt Lake City: Church Historian's Office.

"History and Settlement of the Snowflake Area." 1870–1912. Recorded by Joseph Fish until 1893 and thereafter by Levi M. Savage. Minutebook. Salt Lake City: Church Historian's Office.

LARSON, GUSTAVE O. 1971. *The "Americanization" of Utah for Statehood.* San Marino, Cal.: Huntington Library.

LEONE, MARK P. 1972. "The Evolution of Mormon Culture in Eastern Arizona." *Utah Historical Quarterly* 40:122–41.

———. 1974. "The Economic Basis for the Evolution of Mormon Religion." In *Religious Movements in Contemporary America,* ed. Irving I. Zaretsky and Mark P. Leone, Princeton: Princeton University Press.

LUCKMAN, THOMAS. 1967. *The Invisible Religion.* New York: Macmillan.

MCCONKIE, BRUCE R. 1966. *Mormon Doctrine.* Salt Lake City: Deseret Press.

MCMURRIN, STERLING. 1965. *The Theological Foundations of the Mormon Religion.* Salt Lake City: University of Utah Press.

MARTIN, PAUL S., and FRED T. PLOG. 1973. *The Archaeology of Arizona.* Garden City, N.Y.: Doubleday/Natural History Press.

MURPHY, ROBERT F. 1971. *The Dialectics of Social Life.* New York: Basic Books.

MURRA, JOHN V. 1962. Cloth and Its Functions in the Inca State. *American Anthropologist* 64:710–728.

O'DEA, THOMAS F. 1957. *The Mormons.* Chicago: University of Chicago Press.

PETERSON, CHARLES S. 1973. *Take Up Your Mission: Mormon Colonizing along the Little Colorado River, 1870–1900.* Tucson: University of Arizona Press.

PLOG, FRED T., and CHERYL K. GARRETT. 1972. "Explaining Variability in Prehistoric Southwestern Water Control Systems." In *Contemporary Archaeology,* Mark P. Leone, ed. Carbondale: Southern Illinois University Press.

RAPPAPORT, ROY A. 1968. *Pigs for the Ancestors.* New Haven: Yale University Press.

———. 1971. "The Sacred in Human Evolution." *Annual Review of Ecology and Systematics* 2:23–44.

"Record of Stake Funds, Snowflake Stake." 1882–1901. Minutebook. Salt Lake City: Church Historian's Office.

"St. Johns Stake Historical Record." 1887–1915. Minutebook. Salt Lake City: Church Historian's Office.

SMITH, JOSEPH. 1968. *The Doctrine and Covenants of the Church of Jesus Christ of Latter-day Saints.* Salt Lake City: Church of Jesus Christ of Latter-day Saints.

SMITH, LOT. 1879. Letter to President John Taylor, July 12. Lot Smith Letter File. Salt Lake City: Church Historian's Office.

———, and WILFORD WOODRUFF. 1879. Letter to Bishops Hunter and Hardy, October 29. Lot Smith Letter File. Salt Lake City: Church Historian's Office.

"Snowflake Stake Historical Record." 1886–1889. Minutebook. Salt Lake City: Church Historian's Office.

TAYLOR, JOHN. 1879. Letter to Lot Smith, August 14. John Taylor Letter File. Salt Lake City: Church Historian's Office.

WESTOVER, ADELE B., and J. MORRIS RICHARDS. 1967. *Unflinching Courage.* N. p.

WOODRUFF, WILFORD. 1880. Letter to Lot Smith, April 12. Wilford Woodruff Letter File. Salt Lake City: Church Historian's Office.

———. 1882. Letter to Lot Smith, January 31. Wilford Woodruff Letter File. Salt Lake City: Church Historian's Office.

Index